DOWN AND DIRTY

DOWN AND DIRTY

THE LIFE & CRIMES OF OKLAHOMA FOOTBALL

CHARLES THOMPSON & ALLAN SONNENSCHEIN

Carroll & Graf Publishers, Inc.
New York

Copyright © 1990 by Charles Thompson and Allan Sonnenschein

First Carroll & Graf edition 1990

Carroll & Graf Publishers, Inc.
260 Fifth Avenue
New York, NY 10001

Library of Congress Cataloging-in-Publication Data

Thompson, Charles.
    Down and dirty: the life and crimes of Oklahoma football /
Charles Thompson, Allan Sonnenschein. — 1st Carroll & Graf ed.
        p.   cm.
    ISBN 0-88184-623-6 : $18.95
    1. Thompson, Charles.   2. Football players—United States—
Biography.   3. Oklahoma Sooners (Football team)   I. Sonnenschein,
Allan.   II. Title.
GV939.T445A3   1990
796.332'092—dc20
    [B]   90-43552
                                                                              CIP

Manufactured in the United States of America

I dedicate this book to my mother, Willie Jean Yarbrough. You have been a dependable crutch for me throughout my life. I thank you for the loving support you have given me during my crisis. Hopefully, you will find a way in your heart to forgive me. Mostly, remember that your son loves you with all his heart. Thank you for being a great mom.

Charles Thompson

To Teri with love for turning it all around and making life fun again.

Allan Sonnenschein

ACKNOWLEDGMENTS

In deciding to write this book there were several obstacles standing in the way that made its completion a risky proposition, and that is why we would like to extend our appreciation to Kent Carroll, publisher of Carroll & Graf, for going against the odds. Thanks to Nancy and Ken Brown for suggesting the idea for the project and bringing it to the attention of our agent, Jay Acton.

We extend our gratitude to several people who were involved in one degree or another in the events described in the book and offered their time to talk to us about them: Former Sooner players Jamelle Holieway, Glen Bell, and Jerry Parks; Lawton (Oklahoma) High School coaches and teachers Carl Ryker and Derald Ahlschlager; former University of Oklahoma assistant coach and present head coach at Marshall University, Jim Donnan; Oklahoma football boosters and fans Frank Vale, Jr. and Sr., and Marshall Brackin, Jr. and Sr.; family and friends: Willie Jean Yarbrough, Anthony Harris, Kori Kaubin and her parents, Sharon and Norman Kaubin.

On short notice, Brett Sonnenschein accepted the tedious task of researcher for the book, and we thank him for what was a thankless task.

Allan Sonnenschein offers special thanks to Bob Guccione, publisher of *Penthouse* magazine, for his faith and trust; Peter Bloch, Executive Editor of *Penthouse* magazine, for his blessings, support, guidance, and friendship throughout the months working on this book; Betty Sonnenschein for her love and encouragement.

CONTENTS

END OF THE GAME

I stood leaning against my crutches and watched the dancers slam their feet to the pavement in perfect rhythm to the rap music blasting from the radio's speakers. Stomp! Stomp! Stomp! Once classes started you could always catch a "stomp show" outside the entrance to Dale Hall on the Norman campus. It was the place where you could find the black students hanging out—gossiping, "stomping," and watching women coming to and from classes.

It was a breezy and sunny day in early January 1989, and the second semester had started only a few days earlier. I had broken my leg during the last game of the season, a losing cause against Nebraska, and had been in a cast for almost three months. Ever since they carried me off the field after the last play of that game, I had been in a lousy mood and knew that going to class was not going to make me feel any better. Tired of watching the dancers, I was getting ready to leave when Tiger Harris from the track team and John Green, my teammate on the football team, walked over to talk to me.

I didn't know Tiger very well, but John and I had gotten friendly over the previous summer when we had stayed in Norman. I had no choice about staying in Norman because Coach Barry Switzer was having me tested for drugs every week, but many of the players decided to stay when school ended in May. Why should they go home? If you were a Sooner football player, you had a good life in Oklahoma. You were wined and dined, got the best-looking women, and rarely had to put your hands in your pocket to pay for anything. The football team was the pride of the state, and just about everyone in Oklahoma wanted

11

to keep their players happy. Everyone, it seemed, wanted to go to the games, and there were never enough tickets to go around. The players had plenty of tickets, and that was the only currency we needed. At home for the summer, there was no way you'd get the same attention and treatment.

John and I had a lot of fun that summer and became drinking and partying buddies. John, Curtis Williams, and a few other players on the team had come up with the idea of starting a fraternity for the guys on the football team. There were plenty of fraternities at the University of Oklahoma, but—and I had agreed with John and Curtis—we were *The Sooners* and deserved our own club. Our plan was to make it the wildest on campus.

We didn't have letters from the Greek alphabet to distinguish our club, but identified ourselves with "W-O," which stood for "Winos." If you took your ring finger and bent it to meet your thumb, the other fingers spread out, forming the letters *wo*. "Winos" was appropriate because all we seemed to do was go out every night and get pissfaced drunk. However, in the spirit of college fraternities, we did have some tradition: whomever pledged for the fraternity had to go through a tortuous initiation rite. We would mix up gallons of a potent brew, 151-proof rum, Thunderbird, Ripple, anything a real wino would drink, and pour the gook into large iced containers. The pledge would begin drinking the slop in the early evening until he puked up his guts and passed out. It was pointless, but, looking back, everything we did that summer was stupid.

Of all the dumb things we'd done, only one had gotten me into real trouble. In addition to the drinking, I had played around with cocaine—using and dealing. Coach Switzer learned about it from his friends in the police, and had I not been his quarterback I wouldn't have gotten away with it. I was forced to attend a drug rehabilitation center for two weeks and to spend the next several months pissing into a bottle to make sure I was clean. I had been staying clean when John, who knew about what had happened during the summer, approached me that day in January:

"CT, you know Tiger, he wants to talk to you about a deal." Tiger smiled and began his rap: "Look, I got this homeboy back in Oklahoma City who can score me some coke, but me and John don't know any buyers. Can you help out?"

"Well, I'm not really sure, Tiger," I answered. I wasn't sure because when I'd been involved I wasn't doing the selling, at least not directly. Otha Armstrong, "Big O," an ex-football player who had tried out briefly with the Washington Redskins and whom I had met after my senior year in high school, did all the selling. Otha and I both knew "Snowman," a big time drug dealer in Dallas, but he never trusted Otha and Otha had promised me that if I would score the coke in Dallas, he would do the selling in Oklahoma. That was the way it went on until Switzer called me into his office and I quit going to Dallas.

Otha had introduced me to a few of his customers, one of them a strange dude named Tony. When I had asked Otha what Tony did for a living, he replied: "Well, look at it this way: when you need somebody to collect money for you, Tony is your man. He's a legbreaker."

Otha always talked too much, and one of the things he had talked to Tony about was my "man in Dallas." He led Tony to believe that I had a cocaine windfall there. When I told Otha that I wasn't going to Dallas any longer, Tony began to call me on the phone to see if I was still in touch with my contact. Starting in September Tony called me almost every day to score cocaine for him. I would tell him no, but he wouldn't quit calling me. Tony had become a pain in the ass, but because of what Otha had told me about him, I never had the nerve to tell him to stop calling. Tony frightened me, but I also didn't want him to think I was a wimp. There was a part of me that enjoyed playing a wiseguy. I wanted Tony to think I was cool.

Tony came into my mind when John and Tiger asked me to help them find a buyer for cocaine. I didn't want to be involved with drugs a second time, so I told them I would think about it and went back to the dorm. Back home, sure enough, there was a message from Tony on the answering machine. I sighed and dialed his number, knowing that if I didn't return his call the fucker would keep after me. Tony got on the phone and we bullshitted for a few minutes. Then, for what felt like the millionth time: "So, Charles, have you heard from your man in Dallas?" This time, however, after saying no, I told him: "But there's a possibility I can score some from somebody else. Let me check on it."

That is when I made the decision to talk to Tiger and John. Earlier, they had told me that their contact in Oklahoma City would be able to supply them with as much cocaine as they could get rid of. I reasoned that this was my opportunity to get Tony off my back and out of my life. It was simple, I thought; I would introduce Tiger and John to Tony, and whatever they did would be of no concern to me. That evening I went to Tiger and John's apartment.

"Look," I told them, "there's a white dude I know who is looking to score an ounce or two of coke. If it's good shit, he'll probably want more. But," I warned, "don't fuck with him. I'll put you all together and then I'm out of here. I want nothing more to do with it."

Tiger and John asked me more about Tony, and the more I told them about why they shouldn't fuck with him, the more they got nervous. One of them came up with the idea of bringing Bernard Hall with them when they went to meet with Tony. Hall was one of the tight ends on the team and a big, mean fucker. They thought that he would act as a bodyguard should

14

anything go wrong. I warned them not to bring Bernard with them. He was a damned good football player, but Bernard Hall was also an all-pro fuckup.

When Bernard was at OU he was caught stealing from other players and thrown off the team for a period of time, but as soon as he was back on he was off again when he was ruled academically ineligible. He was a loudmouth braggart who thought he was hot shit because he came from the big city of Detroit. Bernard came to Norman as a highly touted high-school quarterback, but once Switzer saw him at practice he decided the Motown star didn't have the proper skills and switched him to tight end.

Another problem Bernard had was the way he treated women. Like most of the guys on the team he enjoyed the attention he received from women on campus. Bernard's problem was that when he didn't receive the attention he expected, he demanded sexual favors from women. At the time, however, I couldn't talk Tiger and John out of having Bernard around when we were to meet Tony. I was pissed off and returned to my room. I called Tony and scheduled a time to meet. I began to worry about what could go wrong.

The day we were scheduled to meet with Tony, Tiger and John came to my dorm. Tiger did all the talking: "We've been thinking, CT, you were right about Bernard. He's bad fucking news and we don't need him."

I told them that I agreed and said it was time to go see Tony. Tiger gave me a shit-eating grin and said: "Well, there's a small problem. My homeboy got jammed up with something and couldn't get the coke for us today. You gotta cancel the meeting."

I exploded. "What the fuck are you doing to me? I told you that you don't fuck with this guy. The dude is busting my balls

15

for that shit. You better get it soon." Both of them swore up and down they would have it in a week.

They didn't have it in a week, nor did they have it the week after that. Tony kept calling me and I would repeatedly promise him everything would be worked out soon. It was getting to me. Things had been bad enough before this shit. My leg still pained me. I was angry to be caught in the middle of this bullshit with Tiger, John, and Tony. Tiger and John kept promising me that they would have the coke one day and the next day tell me about some problems they were having in Oklahoma City. I knew that Tony didn't give a shit about John and Tiger's problems so I spent my time thinking up excuses for when he called.

By the time Tiger and John did come to me on the day they were able to get the cocaine I had made a decision. I didn't want any more fucking up by the two of them and said: "Here's the way it's going to go down. You bring the coke back from Oklahoma City and meet me. You give me the stuff and I'll give it to Tony and get the money." They nodded their heads and said nothing, like in the huddle when the quarterback calls the play. They left for Oklahoma City with instructions to call me as soon as they had the cocaine and were on their way back to Norman.

To get off my aching leg I lay down on the bed and put on the television. It was January 26, 1989, at about five-thirty in the afternoon. I was watching a press conference held by the University of Oklahoma when the phone rang. Tiger was on the other end of the line informing me that John had met with "Feets," their coke connection. "Be cool, CT, he said, "we got it." I reminded him to meet me at Eighth Street and Norman, at eight o'clock, across the street from the Border Crossing restaurant.

I returned to the television press conference. Three members of the University of Oklahoma football team had been arrested for raping a twenty-year-old woman in the dorm. I saw the faces of my teammates—Nigel Clay, Glen Bell (who was later acquitted), and Bernard Hall—staring back at me from the screen. I couldn't help thinking what a glorious day this was for the Oklahoma football team: three of its players arrested for gang rape; a few days earlier, my roommate Jerry Parks arrested for shooting Zarak Peters; and in a few hours another couple of players were going to sell cocaine.

Tony met me across the street from the dorms and followed me in his black Volvo to the meeting place. When we got there, I left my car and walked over to where Tony had parked. He opened the passenger door and I got in. "Well?" he asked me. I told him that they would be there soon, but I had something I wanted to discuss with him.

"Tony, these guys don't know who you are, and I think it would be a good idea to give me seven hundred dollars, you know, half the money, before I take the coke from them."

He glared at me. "Hey, Charles," he said, putting his face about an inch from mine, "don't fuck with me."

"Wait—" I wanted to explain, but he cut me short:

"Charles, you don't ever want to fuck with me."

I tried to calm him. "Look, Tony, it's nothing more than a show of good faith. You know me, would I try to fuck you?"

"No fucking way, Charles."

After a few minutes of arguing, Tony leaned across my body and opened the glove compartment. He took out a brown manila envelope. Inside was a wad of bills. He took out seven hundred dollars and handed it to me. He told me to count it: "You can't trust anybody these days, Charles," he said, smiling.

I put the money inside my jacket pocket and went back to my car to wait for Tiger and John. Five minutes later their car and another one behind them pulled up. John got out of the car and walked over to where I was parked. As soon as he saw me he started wailing about "Feets." "Feets" had refused to wait in Oklahoma City for the money, and had followed Tiger and John to Norman. John was insulted because "Feets" didn't trust them. He was going to kick his ass as soon as this was over. While John was pissing and moaning about "Feets," Tiger came over to the car with the coke. I was getting tired of John's rantings and asked for the coke. Tiger handed over the package.

I played with the package in my hand, thinking it sure as hell didn't feel like it weighed an ounce. I turned to Tiger: "Man, are you sure this is an ounce?" It had been six months since I had been around cocaine and even back then I'd never handled too much of it. Still, what I had in my hand did not feel like it weighed an ounce.

Tiger smiled at me. "Be cool, CT, it's an ounce."

I wasn't convinced, but, on the other hand, I couldn't be certain. I thought about it and said, "Fuck it, I'll take it over to him." I walked back across the street to Tony's car and opened the door. He took the package and opened it without saying a word. I asked him what he thought about it.

He paused for a moment, then put his finger inside the package, took out some coke, and rubbed it on his gums. "Hey, this is good shit, Charles." He reopened the glove compartment and took out the manila envelope. Then he counted out another seven hundred and gave it to me.

I was so relieved to have it all over with that I put the money in my pocket without counting it. I walked over to Tiger and John and handed it to them. Tiger counted it and handed me a hundred. I didn't protest and put the money in my pocket. I walked back to my car to drive home.

I couldn't get Tony off my mind as I drove back to my apartment. There was something wrong about him. He scared me. I played football with the toughest players in the country and through the years had never backed out of a fight with anybody, so I wasn't exactly a pussy. But Tony made me feel like one. He was a white guy who wasn't very big. In fact, nothing was physically very impressive about him. He had a moustache and beard and was going bald on top. He had a round face with a nose that always reminded me of Bozo the Clown. I never got a good look at his eyes because he wore tinted glasses that he never took off. He dressed kind of casual and I never saw him without cowboy boots. He was your typical Oklahoma cowboy. Maybe it was his voice that troubled me. It was deep, gravelly, and cocksure. You believed him when he said: "Don't fuck with me!"

Tony was a big Sooners football fan, and like a lot of other guys would ask me a million questions about the team. But he was also different from other guys I met in that he was always asking me about "my man in Dallas." At first I thought he was interested because Otha had made such a big deal about the man in Dallas. It puzzled me why it was so important to know so much about a stranger, but it wasn't going to be long before I solved the mystery.

I was exhausted by the time I hobbled into the dorm. The Bud Wilkinson House, "Bud Hall," for the University of Oklahoma "student/athlete," is one of the best in the country. No other college dorm can compare to it. More than a room to sleep and study in, we were given large, modern two-room apartments with balconies overlooking the campus. Few of the guys on the team lived as well at home as they lived in the dorm. In the bedroom, Kori, my girlfriend, was sprawled on the bed studying. I kissed her and we talked for a few minutes. Kori didn't know what was going on, but she knew I had been upset and irritable about whatever it was I wasn't telling her about. She had an exam the next morning so I left her alone and went back to the other room.

I didn't want to think about anything in my life—no cocaine, no Tony, no football. With my leg in the cast I wasn't able to play basketball with the rest of the team in the off-season and to amuse myself I played Nintendo. It was perfect for my frame of mind, day or night, if I was in the apartment, I played it. I turned on the television and began the game. I had been playing for about an hour when the phone rang. It was Tony.

"Hey, what's going on, Charles?" he asked.

"I'm just sitting here messing around," I answered. "Kori is in the other room studying and I'm playing Nintendo."

There was a pause and then Tony said: "I'm a little short, my man."

"Is that right?" Although I'd heard what he said, I was so lost in the game it really didn't register.

"Charles, listen to me. I said I'm short; like eleven grams short. We got a problem."

Now I was listening. I took my eyes away from the images on the screen and sat up. "What? Eleven grams short! Shit, that's almost half." My mind began to race. Maybe Tony had made a mistake. Maybe he's lying. Hell, he could have taken it himself. He never said anything when I gave it to him. I kept thinking that way, but in my heart I knew Tony was right. I cursed Tiger and John.

Tony explained to me what had happened: "When I got home I weighed it. It was seventeen grams exactly. So I weighed it again because I figured there had to be a mistake. But no way, amigo, I've been fucked. I am eleven grams short."

I felt nervous and frightened, but I tried to be cool with him. All the time I'd been around Tony I had tried to act older than a twenty-year-old college student. I wanted him to think that I'd been around and knew more about the world than most kids my age. I wanted to let him know that I could handle this problem:

"Look, man," I tried to reassure him, "I will get you what you're owed. Hey, you know that I would never fuck you like that. I'll get you the eleven grams or your money back. You and I know that this business is too risky to fuck anybody over. I'll get right back to you."

I called Tiger and John's room and said that I was coming over in a few minutes. Tiger asked me what the big deal was all about, and after I told him he didn't say a word. "Just be in the apartment when I get there," I told him.

I didn't make any small talk when I got to their apartment: "Listen, both of you, you better get the rest of that shit for me. If you don't, fuckers, it's not you but me who has to answer to Tony. I'm the one who hooked him up to you assholes.

"You go find this fucker 'Feets' and tell him you want money or coke." I warned them to start working on it now because I had to answer to Tony.

As soon as I got back to my room I telephoned Tony. I told him about my conversation with John and Tiger, and assured him that they would straighten out the mess. But a few days passed and nothing happened. I called Tony, told him that I'd been wrong, that Tiger and John seemed to be taking the matter lightly.

"Look," Tony threatened. "I'll go and see your buddies myself. They won't take it so lightly when I show up at their door."

I said, "Well, if that's what you want to do, I'll even tell you where they live, but I think it's better if we all get together and settle this shit right away."

We agreed that the four of us would meet the following evening. It wasn't a good idea to meet at the dorm, so Tony suggested we get together at the Sooners Mall at eight o'clock. I called Tiger and John and told them the plans. They promised that they would drive to the mall with me.

It was a short drive from the dorm to the mall, and most of

the trip was spent listening to John bitch about "Feets." John wanted me to know that "Feets" was totally responsible for the missing cocaine. We left the car in the parking lot and went inside the mall to find Tony. I spotted him standing outside a fast food restaurant. I nodded my head when he motioned us to follow him back outside to the parking lot. We got to the Volvo and he unlocked the doors, motioning John and Tiger to sit in the back. I sat next to Tony in the front. He turned his head around to face Tiger and John:

"Okay, I've talked to Charles about it and we've come to an understanding. I think either you guys or your friend in Oklahoma City fucked up."

Tiger and John were scared shitless, and blamed everything on "Feets." Meanwhile—and I never thought about it at the time, probably because I was nervous—Tony was writing down everything John and Tiger told him about "Feets." At one point, John was talking so fast that Tony asked him to slow down so he could get it all on the pad. John had worked himself up to the point where he told Tony that he was going to kill "Feets" with his .45 semi-automatic. Tony took it all down on the pad. The meeting ended with John and Tiger promising to have the missing cocaine in a few days.

February 11, 1989, was the day that marked the beginning of the end. It was my turn to pay the piper. I was twenty years old and in a few days I would feel that my life was finished. Yet when I woke up that Saturday morning, the horror show I was facing could not have been further from my mind.

It was the morning after a typical long Friday night of hitting every club in Norman, drinking like a wino. I had a headache that wouldn't quit, and keeping a steady beat with the drumroll in my head was a loud knocking at the door. It couldn't be Kori, or any of my other friends. They would know better than to be visiting me so early on a Saturday. I decided not to answer.

22

Saturday was my day, I thought to myself: sleep late, play a little Nintendo, listen to the stereo, and maybe then get up for the day. I put my head under the covers, but the damn knocking didn't stop.

I couldn't stand the noise any longer so I eased my leg in the cast off the bed and slowly got up to go to the door. By the time I got there whoever had done the knocking was gone. I cursed and hobbled over to the balcony to see if I could catch the person outside. I got there in time to see Coach Switzer heading toward his car. "Oh shit," I said aloud, knowing I must be in some kind of trouble. It had to be something bad because Switzer never came to the dorm, except maybe when there were some hot recruits he wanted to impress who were visiting the players. There was no way he was making a social call.

"Hey, Coach," I called out, "was that you knocking at my door?"

He turned around to look up at me. "Oh yeah, Charles, it was me. I wanted to talk to you about something."

My heart started to beat faster. I knew Barry Switzer's moods, and I could tell from the look on his face that he was not very happy. All the players knew that look, and it said: "We got a problem and you are in deep shit!" That morning he didn't have to say a word to me. I didn't know exactly what it was, but I was sure I had fucked up somehow.

I asked him if he'd like to come back up to my room to talk to me. "No, no," he answered. "See me Monday morning at nine in my office." Before I could say anything more, he got in his car and closed the door. Oh great, I thought, now I had the whole weekend to figure out what I'd done wrong. Funny, it could have been a million things, but not for one second did I think it had anything to do with drugs. I started to think about which one of his rules for the team I had broken. God knows, there were plenty in that category.

Switzer's attitude toward the team had changed since the rapes became public knowledge and after my roommate Jerry Parks was thrown out of school for shooting and almost killing Zarak Peters. There was lots of pressure on the coach from the school and the media to tighten up the loose ship he was running. He had become stricter, but no matter how hard Switzer and the other coaches tried to crack down on us, we continued to break the rules. For example, we were not allowed to have girls or alcohol in our rooms, but a visit to the dorm any night of the week would reveal we never obeyed those rules.

For the next two days I could not get Switzer out of my mind. I knew that one of the things he was pissed off at was my refusal to get up every morning to have breakfast at seven with the rest of the team. It didn't make any sense to me to get up so early only to eat. Another infraction that he was angry with me about was my not showing up regularly at the weight room. I'd broken several other rules, but none seemed to justify a personal visit by Switzer.

By Sunday night I was scrambling, wanting to be prepared for whatever it was he was going to talk to me about the next morning. My game plan was to operate as I had done in the past when he had called me into his office to chew me out. The way it always worked was that you quickly admitted to what he was accusing you of having done, and then you turned the conversation around to something positive. Such meetings had always ended with Switzer saying something like, "Well, I understand what you're saying, but be careful in the future."

Once, Jamelle Holieway and I were summoned together to Switzer's office. He'd heard rumors that we had been seen in the company of known bookmakers. Of course, although Jamelle and I didn't remind Switzer, it was the coach himself who had introduced us to the bookies. We sat there quietly in his office while he and Donnie Duncan, the OU athletic direc-

24

tor, lectured us about the dangers of being seen having dinner with known gamblers. When the screaming died down, we swore that it would never happen again. Then, Jamelle began talking about next week's game and how we were going to kick ass. It took only a few minutes of Jamelle's rap, but Switzer calmed down and everything was cool once more in Soonertown.

Monday morning came around and I made sure to get my ass out of bed bright and early. It couldn't have been later than five-thirty, but I was going to be ready to face the coach. I went to the team breakfast, and as soon as we finished I walked over to the weight room in the athletic office building. I worked out for about an hour, and a few minutes before nine I started climbing the steps to Switzer's office, thinking all the time how much I wished I was someplace else.

As soon as I entered the office I knew that I was in trouble. Kay, Switzer's secretary, who always had a few nice words for me when I came to the office, didn't look up when I came in. "You can go in, Charles. They're waiting for you," she said, pointing to Switzer's office with her pen, never taking her eyes off the papers on her desk.

Inside his office Switzer was reading a newspaper. When I said hello he took off his glasses and just glared at me. I took a chair and sat down. Although it was February, he had the air conditioning going full blast and I started to shiver. Without saying a word, he picked up the newspaper he had been reading and handed it to me. On the front page was a story about the rapes and shooting on campus. When he saw that I had finished reading it he took it back and put it on his desk. Finally, he spoke. "Charles," he said, pointing to the newspaper, "what could be worse for the program than this?"

He picked up the newspaper from the desk and looked again at the front page. "Well?"

"Gee, Coach," I stammered, "I really don't know."

Switzer flung the newspaper down and screamed at me: "You know goddamned well what I mean."

"I guess me," I said.

"Yeah, you, Charles," he continued screaming. "Do you know that this will be all over national television and your family is going to get hurt? Charles, I've heard rumors about you being around drugs again. And you know what else?"

I looked at him without saying a word.

"Charles, the FBI also knows about it."

I panicked. "Coach, what are you talking about?"

"Charles, they've got you."

I sat there trembling, my arms wrapped around my body. I had never felt so cold in my life with the air conditioner blowing, listening to Switzer's words.

"Look, I want to help you," he said, "but you've got to tell me everything."

I was in a daze, but somehow I was able to tell Switzer the whole story. I thought that if I did tell him everything, he would help me get out of the mess, but what he said next rocked me.

"Charles, I have no choice but to dismiss you from the University of Oklahoma's football team. You are to move out of the athletic dorm, immediately!"

I couldn't believe what he'd said. "But, Coach, why dismissal? Can't you place me on probation until it's all straightened out?"

Switzer shook his head. "Charles, I can't do that because they're coming to get you. Not today, but sometime in about two weeks. There are no ifs, ands, or buts—you are going to be arrested. I want you off the campus. See if you can find a place to stay in town. We'll get you a check to pay your rent until we can get this thing worked out." He said that he would talk to the school lawyers to see if he could change my dismissal from

26

the team to a suspension. I was warned that the school was going to make an announcement at noon about my removal from the team, but was promised that no reason for the action would be given to the media.

Switzer left his office to see one of the school's lawyers and another official. I sat there alone thinking that somehow he would take care of everything. Switzer had always done it in the past, why not now? Soon after I'd been recruited and had agreed to play for Oklahoma, I had gotten into trouble for shoplifting a pair of gloves. Once he learned about it, he used his influence to have the authorities go easy with me. Like everyone else who played for the University of Oklahoma, I believed that Barry Switzer was the most important and powerful person in the state. He could do anything. That fantasy was interrupted when they buzzed me to go to one of the other offices, where Switzer, Jim Donnan, and one of the school attorneys wanted to see me.

I walked into the office expecting to hear my reprieve; instead, the attorney said: "Charles, I want to say that we cannot help you. What you say to us may eventually come out in court to hurt you. I am going to give you some good advice. You need a private attorney."

Switzer then asked if I knew any lawyers. I mentioned Ken Brown, an attorney and the father of a friend. When I told Switzer that Ken practiced in Oklahoma City, he said it wouldn't work out. I was told that I needed an attorney in Norman, someone closer to the school, whom they could work with. Coach Donnan suggested I retain Robert Pendarvis. Switzer agreed with the idea and the matter was closed. "I'll make the arrangements," he promised.

Back in his office, Switzer told me he would call Pendarvis. I was naïve enough to believe at the time that Barry Switzer had an attorney who was interested in Charles Thompson. I was a twenty-year-old student who did not understand what the real problem was for Switzer and the University of Oklahoma. After the rapes and the shooting the school was in turmoil. Now they had a drug scandal on their hands. They had to minimize the fallout from my situation. Though the players involved in the rapes, shooting, and drugs were responsible for their actions, Switzer was the man who had promised their parents to watch over their athletic teenagers away from home for the first time. Robert Pendarvis, I later realized, was as concerned about the public image of the University of Oklahoma as he was for my well-being.

I left the athletic offices and got into my flashy 300ZX—the car I'd wanted so badly the previous summer that I got involved with cocaine to afford the down payment—and drove to the office of Robert Pendarvis. He was waiting for me when I arrived, and let me know that he knew everything I had told Switzer an hour earlier. I wondered who else Switzer had told my story to. Pendarvis didn't have too much advice for me, but wanted to know where I would get the money for his fee. He suggested that I call my mother in Texas for a thousand dollars. That really shook me, but I felt I had no alternative. My mother cried, but told me that she would take care of it.

Pendarvis said he planned to talk to the FBI later that day and I was to make sure to check in with his office at about three in the afternoon. On my way out of the office he warned me: "I haven't worked too often with the feds, but I do know that they don't move on anything unless they've got a good case."

I drove around aimlessly, killing time until it was three o'clock. I called Pendarvis. He told me that he had spoken to the FBI and that I would be arrested, but not for at least three to five days. He didn't tell me why but said that I was to be at his office at six that evening.

Now, for the first time that day, I felt I could breathe a little easier. I realized that I'd been set up, and the only person who could have put me in that position was "Big O"—Otha Armstrong. I decided to pay him a visit. I got into my car again and drove like a wild man, growing angrier and angrier and breaking speed limits all the way to Otha's house. When I got there I began blowing my horn.

Otha came out on the balcony. "Hey, is that you, CT?"

"You're fucking right it is," I yelled back. "Get your ass down here."

He came downstairs and walked to my car, looking at me as though what in the world could be wrong. I told him to get in the car because we had to talk. As soon as he was inside I peeled away from the street and drove like a kamikazi pilot. Otha looked at me in terror. I knew that he knew what was wrong.

But he decided to play dumb. "Hey, CT," he said, "take it easy. What's wrong, man?"

"Otha"—I pointed my finger at his face—"I really don't know what's going on, but Switzer just told me that I'm off the team. Can you guess why?"

Suddenly Otha sat up and got that dumb look off his face. He knew that whatever it was I was going to tell him it had to be heavy for Switzer to throw me off the team. Otha always believed that Switzer would take care of me because his quarterbacks were too valuable to lose. I believe that one reason Otha agreed to set me up was that if I did get caught, Switzer would be able to cover up for me, and if I didn't get in trouble nothing would happen to Otha. The buck would stop at Charles Thompson. Now, Otha was smart enough to understand the buck had not stopped and he was next. He looked like he was going to cry.

"Right, Otha," I said. "You better start worrying. Believe me, I'm off the team, and now they're going to be coming for you.

Your friend Tony is a narc. You set me up with him." (Actually, Otha had introduced me to another friend named Al. Al, I later learned, was an undercover officer for the Oklahoma State Police.)

I turned the car around to drive Otha back to his house. After he denied knowing Tony was a cop, I said, "Otha, if you're telling me the truth, then your ass is going to be as green as mine. Unless you're a snitch, and working for the police, you're going down with me."

Otha Armstrong is a big man; six foot four and two-hundred fifty pounds, but he looked like an oversized baby in the car that day. "CT, you gotta believe me," he pleaded, tears rolling down his cheeks, "I would never hurt you. You gotta help me. I ain't got nobody out there. Please, man, don't let me go down. Don't leave me out in the cold. Man, I'm gonna run."

I gave up talking to him and let him out of the car. That was the last time I saw Otha until I turned on my television one day in August. There on the news was a handcuffed Otha Armstrong, arrested for breaking into Barry Switzer's home and stealing his trophies and championship rings. The arresting officer was the last in a long line of undercover officers Otha was snitching for. Obviously, even the authorities couldn't control Otha.

At about six o'clock I returned to Pendarvis's office where I was told the attorney was out and that I should wait for him. I was also told Pendarvis was at FBI headquarters with another lawyer from the firm. I hoped he was working out a deal for me. I sat in the empty office watching television and waiting.

After about three hours had passed, I began to get upset. Why did he want me in the office when he wasn't going to return for several hours? Then suddenly I heard a lot of noise outside and got up to take a look. Shit! There it was—the media show. Somebody had tipped them off about what was going on.

THE LIFE AND CRIMES OF OKLAHOMA FOOTBALL

It could have been somebody in the law office, but I really doubted it. It had to have been Switzer or someone in the athletic office. Switzer knew when I was supposed to be there, and these days it didn't hurt him to be nice to the media. I closed the curtains and sat down.

It was close to ten at night when I heard Pendarvis come in the back door to the office. He yelled out: "Charles, it's us. Are you still here?"

"Yeah," I answered, "right where you left me about three hours ago. What's going on?"

He walked into the office looking grim. "Well, it looks like they have some pretty good stuff on you." He hesitated and then asked, "Is there anyone you would like to call?"

"What are you talking about?" I asked.

"I'm sorry, Charles, but the FBI is here to arrest you."

"What!" I screamed. "You told me I had about a week. What happened?"

Pendarvis looked at me and said: "It just didn't work out that way."

Two FBI agents, John Hershley and Phil Shockey, entered the room. They handcuffed me and led me out the door to their car. As we pulled away from the curb I knew my life was going down the drain.

GROWING UP

I was born on May 28, 1968, to Jean Willie Yarbrough and Leacy Thompson. They didn't have a very long relationship and never married, but spent enough time together to conceive me. Between my mother and father's various relationships and marriages I have eight brothers and three sisters. I was born in Lawton, Oklahoma, but when I was three years old my mother moved my brothers—Anthony, ten, Dwight, five, and Harold, two—and my sisters—Kim, seven and Yolanda, one—to Fort Smith, Arkansas, where she could be closer to her family.

My mother has always made a living working as a seamstress. She still sews incredibly well, and can make anything—slacks, dresses, shirts, jackets. Throughout her life she has been involved in church activities. My first memories of church date from when I was six and we had moved back to Lawton. All the children had to attend services and participate in the choir at David's Chapel, an African Episcopal Church. When I was young I really got into singing. I was told that I had a sweet voice and often led the choir. This was the first time in my life I was the center of attention, and I loved the older women telling my mother how good looking and sweet I was. This attention from my mother's friends is probably what spoiled me later on. Back then they would tell me that when I grew up all the girls would be knocking down my door to get to me. By the time I was a teenager, I fancied myself a ladies' man.

In Fort Smith I was happy; it was the time I had the most fun in my childhood. We lived in the projects which were all black, and most of my friends were my cousins. I know that we were poor, but I never felt that way in Fort Smith. We were outdoors

33

most of the time and did what most kids do—played cowboys and Indians, swam in the creek, played house. I liked playing house the best, especially when I was the daddy and the mommy was Datchra.

Datchra was the cutie of the projects. My cousin Chris and my brother Harold loved to chase after her. She and I were both five and she was the love of my life. Once, Datchra kissed Chris and a few days later his tooth fell out. Not too long after that I kissed Datchra and lost a baby tooth. Harold, being the baby brother, thought he should kiss Datchra and, believe it or not, lost one of his teeth, too. This inspired us to make up a song about wicked Datchra. I don't remember all the words but it ended: "Stay away from Datchra." Of course, as I was always stubborn and in trouble, I couldn't keep away from Datchra and chased her whenever I saw her. I wound up spraining my arm trying to impress her.

In Fort Smith I didn't know any white people. The whole world was black. In "Head Start" and kindergarten all the children and teachers were black. Later, when we moved back to Lawton, it was a shock to live among and go to school with whites. We'd felt safe in the projects, and never felt intimidated by anyone there. I remember what happened the first time I wandered away.

It was the Fourth of July, and my cousin, Keith Wilson, and I were returning home after having gone to watch Fred Perkins, another cousin, box. We were looking at the fireworks in the distance and decided to get a little closer. We wandered into a white neighborhood and when they spotted us they began shooting pop bottle rockets at us. They also started to scream: "Hey, you niggers, what are you doing here?" It wasn't the first time I had heard the word, but it was the first time a white person had said it to me.

A few whites began to chase us. I was five and Keith was

eight. We were frightened and started to run away, but I kept looking back, wondering why these people were chasing me. Keith was older and wiser and didn't waste any time wondering, he was out of there. One white guy was close on my heels, but I knew that once I got to the main road where the projects were I would be safe. I turned it on, racing across the road without looking to see if any cars were coming. I had reached the edge of the projects, the white guy a few feet behind me, when a black guy standing next to a public telephone noticed what was happening. He pulled out a gun and the white guy stopped cold in his tracks. I thought it was over when he turned to go back to his neighborhood, but the guy with the gun fired off two shots. Nobody got hurt that night, but I did learn two lessons: first, there is a black world and a white world, and second, how fast I could run. Keith, by the way, wasn't too slow himself. He later became a starter for the University of Arkansas basketball team.

Living in Fort Smith was too good to last, and when I was six years old my mother met and married Joe Yarbrough, a soldier stationed at Fort Smith. When he was reassigned to Fort Sill, Oklahoma, we moved back to Lawton. I remember being unhappy about this, but it was only one of many moves my mother would make. Once in Lawton, it seemed we moved to another neighborhood every year. Times became hard for my mother. Joe Yarbrough, whom I loved very much and who was good to me, died, and bills began to pile up. My mother was restless, and seemed to find different reasons to want to move.

My mother worked hard and supported us, but it was tough being a single parent. She was strict, but she wasn't home all the time and my older brother Anthony became the disciplinarian around the house. He was both a brother and a father to me. I began to feel my family was different than others in the neighborhoods we lived in. They all seemed to have a mother, father, sisters and brothers, clothes and toys. Because there was so little money, we never looked forward to getting new things except on a birthday or at Christmas. For the first time in my life I felt poor.

Everything was different back in Lawton, and I had a difficult time adjusting to integrated areas, and felt strange being with white people. As young as I was, I realized that they were different and had strange customs. Life in the projects with my cousins and friends had felt open and free. I never noticed or cared about what I was wearing or what I said, I never thought twice about the way I acted. It was more than being young and moving to a new neighborhood with strangers. I felt I had lost something when we moved back to Oklahoma.

I went to school with children I didn't know. I hadn't grown up with them. Because of busing I never saw the other black kids before or after school. I was uncomfortable with the teachers as well as the students. The people at Swinney Elementary School in Lawton did things differently than those at Lincoln Elementary School in Fort Smith. It took me a long time to adjust and make friends.

Nobody was more important to me back then than Anthony. And nothing was more important to Anthony than sports. It was Anthony who was responsible for developing me as an athlete. Back in Arkansas I had played some football with my cousins but basketball was the sport that was king. For a time I wanted nothing more than to be a basketball player. I was in the third grade at Westwood Elementary School when an announcement was made one day that anyone interested in playing in the Peewee Football League should sign up at Bicycle Park. I didn't live far from the park so I decided to go over there to sign up that afternoon.

Once I passed the physical they handed out the equipment. I couldn't believe it! Real helmets, shoulder pads, pants, shirts. It was the first time I had any sporting equipment, and I put it all on and walked around the house looking at myself in the mirror. I knew nothing about football except "score a touchdown." It made no difference. I was going to be a football hero. They made me a tight end but for almost the whole year I never got a ball thrown in my direction. I think it was the third to last game of the season when I finally caught a pass and took off down the field, outrunning everyone. The coach came over to me and said, "Son, you are now a running back."

I couldn't wait for fourth grade to start so I could play again. Now I wanted to learn how to play the game and that's when Anthony took over. Anthony taught me everything. He would set up obstacles in the front yard, have me run drills, and time me while I ran them. He would move the trash can to one spot, a few feet from the mailbox, a few yards from the bushes, and a few more yards from a tree. I would have to run the course from the backyard to the front of the house, First, he would run the course and show how fast he did it, then it was my turn. He made me do this every day, whether or not I was in the mood, and would say, "Listen to me, Charles, and I'll make you better than O.J. Simpson." Anthony was a good athlete and I watched him closely when he played ball. The guys in the neighborhood would talk about his athletic exploits. When I got older I realized that some of them were exaggerated. There was a story about Anthony, in the sixth grade at Hoover Elementary School, jumping over a seven-foot fence without touching it. I was told that was how he got the nickname "Bird."

Anthony Harris

In elementary school we first started getting into the basics of football. I would come home from school and teach Charles some basic plays like the bootleg. I figured if he was able to grasp these concepts in elementary school, imagine

37

how good he'd be in high school. With that in mind, I kept going over the same basic plays with him. When we lived on Twenty-fifth Street, there were two brothers about our ages, and we used to play them two on two and beat them all the time.

I knew Charles was going to be a great athlete when he was about nine or ten and played in the Peewee League. None of the other kids had the abilities he had. In one game he ran for twenty-one touchdowns. By that time, besides teaching him the basic plays, I was showing him how to throw moves. I taught him how to watch the head and eyes of the defender, to know when and where to go, that if the defender flinched this way, or moved his head that way, you run the other way. He couldn't get it immediately, so to build up his confidence I wouldn't tackle him when he tried to get by me. But he never stopped working to get it right.

Anthony was tough on me when he was not developing my football abilities. There were times I came to despise him for how he treated me. He was bigger, and quick to spank me when he thought I did something wrong. It did no good to tell my mother because as soon as she was gone he made me pay for snitching. I knew he loved me, but he could be very cruel, ridiculing me and calling me names like pussy or woosy. Still it must have been very difficult for him, to be so young and responsible for his brothers and sisters.

We lived in one neighborhood where Anthony and I played against other brothers. It wasn't regular football but two on two, and we called it "P for P"—passing for punting. Anthony would drive me crazy the nights before we were to play a game. For hours, he would make up plays on paper and have me memorize them. Other brothers would go out and draw plays in the dirt, but we would be like the Dallas Cowboys: "Okay,

Charles, Number 5," Anthony would shout, and I would run a pass pattern he had written down the previous night.

Unlike the other older brothers, Anthony would give me some time at quarterback, telling me that I had a nice, soft touch and could be a great quarterback. He inspired confidence in me, and when I got to the fourth grade at Swinney, I began to show it on the football field.

Anthony saw early that I had another quality besides talent— that I was willing to learn. My brother Harold had talent, and Anthony worked as hard with him to develop it, but Harold didn't care. It wasn't only football with me, I wanted to be as good as I could be in baseball and basketball. I grew up never wanting to do or be anything but a great athlete. I never stopped wanting to learn from Anthony.

I've often wondered why he devoted so much of his time and love to me. He dealt with Harold and me as though we were his sons, and like most fathers he wanted us to be better than himself. He wanted to show us what life was all about, and to learn from his experiences. He was feeding back to us so many things, warning us what to avoid. Anthony gave up much in his own life by investing so much in me, and when he saw me on the football field at Lawton High, or OU, demonstrating the moves he had taught me, he felt repaid. It was a terrible disappointment for him to learn about my problem with drugs. It made me feel bad when I heard that he blamed himself because it was one of the lessons in life he'd failed to teach me. I know I have let him down.

On the first day of the fourth grade I couldn't wait to get to school. I was now a member of the Swinney Jets. When they gave me the team's red, white, and blue uniform I felt like a god. I also believed I was better than anyone else on the field. Back then my idols were Billy Sims and Thomas Lott and that's who I imagined myself to be when I went out to play. This was during the seventies when they were playing for OU, and, man, did I love the Sooners. Every night before going to sleep I prayed to play one day for the University of Oklahoma.

Beginning that fourth year I turned into a damned good running back, and throughout elementary school I had the reputation of being one of the best running backs in Lawton. I started to get the respect football players traditionally get in Oklahoma. Strangers came to Swinney games and screamed out my name: "Go, Charles, go." Even at such a young age there would be great rivalries between players from different schools, and people would argue who was best.

When I was in the sixth grade, Swinney had a game against Pecan Grove. The game was a big deal because Pecan Grove had a player by the name of Gino Spear. Gino was also considered one of the best athletes in Lawton and a crowd came out to see us go head to head. It may have been elementary school, but to people in Lawton it was like Charles White going against Billy Sims. I had a great day, scoring five touchdowns and throwing three more on halfback option plays.

I remember the game against Pecan Grove because it was a turning point in my football career. In Oklahoma, playing football is not something you do after school and then go home to other things, it's the first stage of what is supposed to end in the NFL. By the time you get to college you take being treated differently for granted. It's not just sports, but a way of life. By the time I got to OU I was used to the special treatment I received, used to being *the man*. It started in elementary school and continued through junior high school—I got more attention from teachers, coaches, and especially women. By the time I reached high school, a whole city knew who I was. In fact, I couldn't get enough attention, and when I wasn't playing football at Swinney I was running track, playing baseball and basketball. And I liked it, craved the attention and respect, felt pressure to maintain my level of performance. Still, there were times I did get a lesson in humility.

Terry Gaines coached me in the fourth, fifth, and sixth grades. He knew how good I was and did everything he could to make me better. He also wanted to be a winning coach and built the teams around my talents, a situation no different than at OU, where Switzer built his teams around Jamelle Holieway and me, taking advantage of what his quarterbacks did best. Coach Gaines was also one of my biggest boosters. He had a brother who played for Lawton High School who came to our practices with some of the other players. Gaines would say he had a kid who when he got to Lawton High School would be twenty times better than anyone on the team. Some of this praise may have gone to my head, but mostly I saw it as giving me the energy to go out there and practice every day to prove that I was a great player.

However, in one particular game Coach Gaines decided to teach me a lesson. At the time I had a girlfriend named Tracey Standfield. Already at that age I liked to think of myself as a sharp guy. I had been averaging four to five touchdowns a game that year, so my mother told me if I scored five touchdowns in the game that day she would take Tracey and me out to dinner. Okay, I thought, now I would have Tracey in the palm of my hand. None of us went out to dinner too often back then and it was a big deal, especially for a sixth grader.

By the last quarter we were beating whoever's ass we were playing, and I had scored four touchdowns. I was ready to go back on the field after the next possession, when Coach Gaines said, "You're done for the day, Charles." "What!" I screamed. "You can't do that. I have to score one more time." He ignored me, and I started to cry. Coach kept ignoring me, so I carried on, screaming and swearing at him.

Finally he turned around and grabbed me. "Look, who do

41

you think you are? If you want to be a crybaby, you can sit on the sidelines every game. Don't you think you should let somebody else play and have a little glory?''

I sulked after that game. I swore that I would never play another game for the team. I couldn't accept the fact that it was a team game and not a Charles Thompson game. I have to thank Coach Gaines for his lesson. Later in the week he explained that if I truly wanted to be a great player, I would have to let myself be coached. He told me then and many times later that I should never get to the point where the coach couldn't tell me what to do. When you don't allow your coach to coach, you're no longer any good. Tracey and I didn't have dinner out that night, but I had learned something.

Throughout my football career I was to suffer a disappointment that was to haunt me. No awards, honors, or touchdowns would make up for never playing on a team that won the final big game. It started in Swinney and ended with OU's 1988 loss to Miami in the Orange Bowl. I don't think it would have bothered me so much had Coach Gaines not taught me the importance of the team concept. The first big game I lost was in my last year of elementary school.

The schools were in leagues and Swinney was in the National League. To get into the city championships you first had to win your league. That last year we were much better than any other team in the league and easily won the title. It was on to the city championship. We were going great and got to the semifinals to play a school called Carriage Hills. Earlier in the year at a city jamboree we had lost to them, but going undefeated the rest of the season made us believe it was time for revenge. Well, like a lot of teams before us, we left our game in the locker room. Carriage Hills kicked our ass that day and that was the end of my elementary school football career.

THE LIFE AND CRIMES OF OKLAHOMA FOOTBALL

Not winning the big one changed my way of thinking over the years—not in elementary school or junior high so much, but definitely by the time I graduated high school and played for OU. I've always enjoyed being a star player, but I might have accepted being just another player if my team had won a championship. Every athlete wants two things: to be the best that he can be, and to be part of a championship team. I've played in many more winning games than losing, enjoyed being the guy the team goes to when they need extra yards or a touchdown the most, but I would give up much of it to have played one championship season.

It took me a few years, but I began to adjust to living in Lawton and made new friends. When I was eight there was a big kid on the block named Kevin, the first white kid I ever played with. There was another kid in our class named Matt who was riding his new bicycle to class one day. I knew Matt, but we weren't really friends. Kevin always picked on Matt and that day pushed him off the bike. Kevin, who was a bully, told me to get on the bike and ride away with it, threatening that he would beat me up if I didn't.

I had just learned to ride a bike and wasn't too good at it, but I didn't want a beating from a much bigger Kevin so I took off. I really got into riding the bike and began wandering around Lawton. I was having a good time when I looked up and saw Matt's father heading toward me. He caught me and took me home. He waited for my mom to get home and that night I got the biggest whupping of my life. I remember this well because Matt and I are good friends right up to today. He was important in helping me overcome the strangeness and loneliness I'd felt since moving from Fort Smith.

Matt and I did the normal things kids did growing up, including the dumb ones that get them into trouble. Once, I was at the playground and discovered that the building where the equipment was stored had been left unlocked. I'd been playing basketball that day and when I looked into the room my eyes lit up. All the basketball uniforms were there, and I grabbed one and ran home with it. I guess I've never changed when it comes to doing the things I shouldn't, because the next thing I do is something stupid to get caught. The next day at school I actually wore the stolen basketball outfit to P.E. class. That night there was another whupping from my mom.

Anthony Harris

I don't know any kid who got into more trouble than Charles. Every other day he came home with scrapes and bruises on some part of his body after doing something he was warned not to do. Once we were sitting on the porch when Charles decided he was going to ride his bike. I reminded him that Mama didn't want him riding the bike when she wasn't home. Of course he didn't listen, and got on the bike to take a ride. He was down the block when he saw Mama, and wanted to get back before she saw him. The bike had no brakes, but Charles was going so fast to get to the house before Mama turned the corner that he forgot about the wall in front of the house. He couldn't stop and crashed into it, breaking his arm. He was only nine or ten, but it wasn't the first time he broke a bone doing something Mama told him not to do.

Gary Frizzell is another best friend I made in elementary school. We were like brothers and have stayed that way through the years. People used to say we even looked alike. By the time we got to junior high we did everything together. It was then that we began to look at girls differently. In elementary school there were girlfriends, but mostly it was hand-holding and

44

maybe a kiss. In junior high we began to think and talk about nothing but sex. I felt that I was more streetwise than Gary and that my job was to help him lose his virginity. I thought I knew everything about sex and was going to be his teacher. I remember telling Gary about the time I had "gotten it."

When I was about eight or nine years old we went back to Fort Smith to visit the family. I was outside by myself when a couple of girls who knew my cousins asked me to meet them at an old building. I didn't know why they wanted me to meet them in a deserted building, but I figured why not. When I got there one of them told me that she wanted to have sex. I didn't know what the hell to do, but when she told me to take off my pants and lie down I did. Then she told me to put my thing in her hole, and I kept asking, where's the hole? Finally, she did it for me. I couldn't understand why my cousins laughed when I told them what had happened.

Compared to Gary I was an expert because by the eighth grade I'd had a lot of sexual experiences. Gary was shy so I would get girls for him. After that, I became a kind of hero to him. All through high school and at OU Gary and I would share sexual partners. If I couldn't talk a girl into going to bed with Gary we had a trick that always worked. We called it the "blanket trick." I would be under a blanket with a girl when I would find an excuse to get out of bed. I would take the blanket and turn off the lights; Gary, who had been hiding in a closet, would get into bed with the blanket and have sex. It wasn't too romantic, but I don't remember that any girl ever complained.

We may have been doing some silly things, but school was important not only for football and girls. In both junior and senior high school, I was an honor student. In the eighth grade I met the person who was to make the greatest impression since Anthony on my life. Her name was Mrs. Monts and she was my eighth-grade English honors teacher.

She was the one who motivated me to be a student. She saw that I had the potential and pushed me. Mrs. Monts, who was black, wanted us to be achievers. I think it bothered her that there were only two black students in her honors class and she never let us forget our obligation to do our best. She graded us harder than the white kids, telling us that blacks had to do better to stay in the race with whites.

One day my assignment was to recite the Gettysburg Address to the class. I read it over and over until I had it memorized. I remember how quiet the class was when I recited it, emphasizing Lincoln's words for dramatic effect. I knew I should have received an A, but Mrs. Monts only smiled and gave me a B. When I asked her what I'd done wrong she told me that I'd quoted the speech perfectly, but that she wanted the words to come not from Lincoln but from Charles Thompson.

Her goal was to make the black kids proud of their race. She wanted us to know that there was nothing whites could do that blacks could not do, except that we had to work harder. When she learned that I was going out with a white girl she was disappointed in me, but not because she hated whites. Mrs. Monts told me that with all the beautiful black girls at the school I was turning my back on my race because I thought it was a cool thing to be seen with a white girl. Even if I were to get advanced degrees, I would never learn more than I did from Mrs. Monts.

She warned the black students against dropping out of school. And she was critical of blacks: she told us how much we lost by thinking it cool to associate only with other blacks. She told us how we were our own worst enemies, citing violence and family breakups. The worst person, in Mrs. Monts opinion, was the black who made it big and then turned his back on the black community. It wasn't that I understood everything she was talking about at the time, but her advice was like a seed in my head that began to grow.

What was growing faster in my mind during my last year at junior high school was my dream of becoming the quarterback at Lawton High School the following September. For the first time in my athletic career my size became an issue. At five foot eight I weighed only 132 pounds, but I never felt too small to play any sport. Over the summer I kept hearing the same thing: "Charles, don't you think you're too small to play football for Lawton High? Why don't you go out for the baseball team?" Damned right I was going to go out for baseball, but I was also going out for football. It was bad enough hearing strangers tell me I was too small for football, but when friends like Gary said so I got depressed. I went to Anthony about how I was feeling.

"Charles," he reassured me, "size is all in the mind. It's not your size that counts out there, but your heart. Concentrate on your ability. I don't care how big they are, if they can't catch you, Charles, they can't tackle you. Just go out there in September and do your thing, little brother."

As soon as I got to Lawton High School I found out that Anthony was doing more than giving me pep talks. Coach Colbert, the quarterback coach, told me that Anthony had been telling him how lucky he was to be getting his baby brother. Colbert told me that Anthony said that Lawton High School would soon have the greatest quarterback in the state of Oklahoma and his name was Charles Thompson. Well, Anthony may have been selling, but the coaches at Lawton High School weren't buying, and I soon learned that I was the number-six quarterback on the team's depth chart. I was going to have to work my ass off to become a starter.

Coach Derald Ahlschlager
Head Football Coach,
Lawton High School

I first saw Charles play when the freshman team came up to scrimmage with our junior varsity team. I noticed he had a lot of quickness, but was rather small. He ended up breaking his arm and didn't get to play very much that year. We had a summer weight program and he used to ride his bicycle up there every day. You could see he wanted to be in shape to play the next year. He only weighed something like a hundred thirty pounds but he impressed me by showing up every day.

From the outset I liked his leadership abilities, his tone of voice, his presence. He started for us after four games in his sophomore year. He was very competitive, very intense, always chewing on his mouthpiece; he'd go through I don't know how many mouthpieces a year, just chew 'em clear up. He was a fine quarterback, great quickness.

He was quite a little individual. Very personable young man, wonderful personality. He liked to please. We used to eat bananas on a certain day for potassium. I was out or busy one day so I asked him if he would drive my pickup down to the grocery store to get the bananas. He was gone I don't know how long. When he finally got back he said he'd forgotten to tell me that he didn't know how to drive a standard shift. He was so personable it was hard to be angry with him.

The one time I truly got angry with him had to do with drugs. I only suspected it. We were in a squad meeting and he kind of went to sleep. I held him back to tell him that I'd observed something that shouldn't have been there. I came down heavy on him, made some threats, but I really didn't know anything concrete.

THE LIFE AND CRIMES OF OKLAHOMA FOOTBALL

When he got into trouble at OU I was disappointed for Charles. He had such a great career in front of him, not just in athletics. As I've said, with his personality he had a chance to be successful in anything he chose. He knew how to talk to people, get them on his side, get them to like him. He would have been great in sales. Just a pretty bad situation.

I didn't know what kind of life he was leading in Norman, but I knew they were having some problems with him on a couple of occasions. A couple of OU coaches asked me to talk to him once when he was living off campus with Holieway. But I really didn't think it was any of my business. That was their responsibility.

I started to lift weights and ride the miles to and from school on my bicycle to build up my body. I busted my gut in practices, but nothing got me further in my freshman year than playing quarterback on the second team. It pissed me off to see that the starting quarterback was a senior who had sat on the bench for the previous two years. It was his last year at school so the coaches were giving him his last shot. When I complained to Head Coach Derald Ahlschlager he'd tell me to be patient. That just made me stew. Being patient is something I still haven't learned. I like things to happen immediately. If I'm expecting something I want it to happen now.

The person who helped me the most during that time was Assistant Coach Wade. When he saw me looking dejected he would encourage me about my future. He got me to realize that I was letting my impatience keep me from learning while I sat on the bench. In our seventh game during my sophomore season, our starting quarterback was messing up. Coach Ahlschlager told me to get ready to play in the second half. I came in during the third quarter and threw for a touchdown. Later I had a few long gainers and we won the game. What got me excited was that I thought I had a great chance to play in the following week's game. No game we played every year was as important as the traditional Lawton–Eisenhower contest, and ever since elementary school I'd had dreams of being the star of that game.

Eisenhower–Lawton is like the Army–Navy rivalry, or Oklahoma–Texas. Both schools spend the week before the game holding giant pep rallies and parties. The town gets keyed up, and kids go to the rival schools to put up taunting decorations and signs. We would drive around town and when we saw somebody from Eisenhower we would throw eggs at them. "Egging" was part of the tradition. The local radio stations talked about the game the whole week, and by the time Saturday rolled around there were long lines at Cameron Stadium waiting to get in. Every ticket would be sold and when you counted those standing there had to be at least fifteen to twenty thousand people watching a high-school game.

By game time I had lost a lot of my enthusiasm, having learned that I was not going to start and maybe not even get into the game. It was a tough defensive game, and by the fourth quarter we were losing 7–0. For more than three quarters we couldn't move the ball past the midfield stripe. With a few minutes left Coach Ahlschlager told me to go in. Maybe, I thought, I'll realize my dream and be the hero of the Lawton–Eisenhower game.

We were deep in our territory and I began to scramble and move us downfield. It was five yards on one play, fifteen on another, and soon we were on their twenty yard line with seconds left in the game. I felt in my bones that we were going to score, but on the next play we got hit with a penalty and were moved back. When the final gun sounded, Eisenhower had won 7–0. But I had shown something to the coaches about how I could operate under pressure in big games. After the game,

THE LIFE AND CRIMES OF OKLAHOMA FOOTBALL

Coach Ahlschlager said, "Charles, you're the starting quarterback."

For the rest of that season and the next two I started every game at quarterback for Lawton High School. It was a great accomplishment for me and helped me to believe that I could play football on any level. Playing for the Sooners became less of a dream and more like only a matter of time. It was then that I saw another side of football I'd never thought about before. There was a lot of violence in the game and it attracted some crazy types. I had seen people get hurt playing football in elementary and junior high school, but usually because of some freak accident. I had broken my arm in the ninth grade because someone fell on it after a tackle. Now I was seeing guys who actually enjoyed inflicting physical harm on others.

One of the first games my sophomore year was against Moore High School. Moore had some really big guys on the team. We had plenty of big players, too, but they've always looked bigger to me when they're on the other team. When we came out on the field for the game, Moore's team was already warming up. At the goalpost at the other end of the field was a guy who must have weighed about two hundred fifty pounds. I don't recall his name but he did eventually play for OU. He was banging his head into the goal post—bam! bam! He never stopped, and I heard the sound all the way on the other side of the field. I couldn't take my eyes off him, I'd never seen anything like it. The guy was psyching himself up for the game by banging his helmetless head against the posts.

Sure enough, I get into the game and run right at the sucker. He picked me up and slammed me to the ground five yards behind the line of scrimmage. When he came down on me I thought my neck was broken. I blacked out. I remembered nothing. Later, at the hospital, Gary told me what had happened. The whole stadium went silent; either my neck was

51

broken or I was dead. My mother—and as a teenager this embarrassed me the most—came running onto the field screaming my name. Gary said that at one point before the ambulance came I tried to get up, but one of the players held me down. I don't remember it. The first thing I do remember is waking up in the ambulance thinking, Oh God, I'm dead and in heaven. I had to wear a brace after I got out of the hospital, but the best part was all the attention I got from the girls. That game against Moore was the first time I ever thought I could get seriously hurt playing football.

I may have thought about injuries, but I never let them bother me once I went out to play. In my last two years at Lawton I got a lot of attention in the newspapers and around the city. I made all-conference, all-city, and all-state. I knew that several colleges were interested in me. In my senior year we played a game in Norman against Norman High School, and this was the first time Barry Switzer came to see me play. When I saw him on the sidelines wearing his beaver coat, I got excited. I wanted to impress him, but we were playing on a rainy, muddy field. We had a hard time moving the ball, and at the end of the first half we had about a total of five rushing yards. I felt shitty.

On my way out to play the second half, Switzer stopped me and said: "Go ahead out there and show me what you can do." My God, I thought, here was Barry Switzer, coach of the team that won the national championship, standing out in the rain watching me. I knew that if I showed him something, there would be a scholarship to OU waiting for me. Fuck the mud, I got the ball and ran for a thirty-six-yard touchdown in the third quarter. It was more than a thirty-six-yard touchdown—I put on a show for Switzer and let him see every move I had. I hit the sidelines for fifteen yards, cut inside for another five, back out for five more, and finessed two or three more moves before hitting the end zone. I wasn't done for the day. In the last quarter I kept the ball and ran seventy-six yards for another touchdown. I ran off the field looking at Switzer. He didn't say anything, but he smiled at me. When I did go to OU he told me that on that day he knew I would be a great player.

Switzer wasn't there when we played Norman High School a second time that year. It was a dry field and I ran for more than two hundred yards that day, scoring five touchdowns. I hoped Switzer read the newspapers the next day when they wrote about "Charles Thompson and the Temple of Doom" after I kicked his college town's high-school's ass.

You always remember the highlights of your career, but you never forget the lowlights. We had a great team my junior year and we were expected to compete for the state championship. We had gotten to the quarter finals where we were to play Moore High School. We had lost to them earlier in the year, but now we were playing at Lawton and were ranked number three in the state. We felt real cocky going into the game, and after three quarters were dominating them 25–9. We thought the game was history.

Coach Ahlschlager agreed with us and thought it would be nice to take out the starters and let some of the second stringers play. Things seemed to happen so fast that with only five minutes left in the game, our lead had slipped to 25–20. It was time to bring the starters back into the game to make sure things didn't get any further out of hand. Immediately, our defense got an interception and we took over. I was back at quarterback and we started to drive down the field. With eleven seconds to go, it looked like the game was won when the unexpected happened.

Randy Messervy was my center all year and there were times when we had trouble with the snap. Now, with one play left in the game, I was going to fall on the ball and let the time run out. Randy hiked the ball on the wrong count and it popped right into a linebacker's hands. With the change in possession the clock was stopped with eight seconds left to play. On Moore's first play the quarterback threw the ball out of bounds, stopping the clock with only four seconds to go. There was one play to go before we could get out of there with a lucky victory.

Moore was on our thirty-five-yard line, lined up in the shot-gun. Their quarterback dropped back to throw and got rid of the ball with one of our guys an inch away from his face. I watched the ball floating up there; like a movie it seemed to be moving in slow motion. Then I saw this big white dude jump over our defender, catch the ball, and run in for a touchdown. They beat us 26–25. I cried. A few years later at OU, Terry Pritchard, who played tight end for the Sooners, would never let me forget the day he caught the pass that won the game for Moore. But at least by then we were on the same team.

Before my senior year began I had a major family problem. My mother had remarried and she wanted me to move to Dallas with her and her new husband. I didn't want to go for several reasons, but I also knew I wouldn't be happy living with my father and his wife Rudy. I had my friends in Lawton and didn't want to have to go through another period of adjustment, but the most important reason for staying in Lawton was that my senior year was coming up and I wanted to play for Lawton High School. I knew that we had a chance at the state championship and I wanted to look good for the college recruiters. It would have been an easy decision to stay in Lawton, except for knowing that I would not be happy living in my father's house.

When I was ten I'd thought that life with him would be better than life with my mom. Whenever I visited Rudy and my father I had a great time. It seemed that they had a happier home and I wanted to live with them. My mother was unhappy about it, but she agreed to allow my father to have formal custody of me.

THE LIFE AND CRIMES OF OKLAHOMA FOOTBALL

It didn't take long to realize that I'd made a mistake. I felt uncomfortable; my brothers who had lived with my father did not seem like the brothers I had grown up with. I thought that every day at my father and stepmother's house would be like Christmas. But there weren't gifts and there were strict rules. Whatever the reasons, I told my father I wanted to move back with my mother.

My father was angry when I told him what I wanted. He told me how much money he had spent in legal fees to change custody from my mom to him. He wanted me to stay and learn to adjust. I was miserable and felt like a prisoner. I didn't know what to do but run away. On a day I was supposed to have been heading to baseball practice, I ran away to my mother's house. The next thing I remember was a knock on the door and two police officers standing there with papers in their hands. They took me to a children's shelter. My father was furious when he came to pick me up. That was the only time I remember him spanking me. It took a little more time, but my father realized I wouldn't be happy until I went back to live with my mother.

I didn't feel that my father was a bad man, but rather a stranger. He was what a lot of people call a weekend dad, rarely seeing his family except on special occasions. By my senior year he was fifty-nine years old and retired from the police department because of an automobile accident. He was into horses and owned a few. He belonged to a rodeo club called the Lawton Rough Riders and they would ride their horses in city and state parades. Although I loved him we weren't close and there was another, more selfish reason why I was unhappy about living my senior year at his home. I knew that he and Rudy would try to limit my freedom.

With my mother out of the house working and involved in her church activities, I did a lot of running around and came in at all hours of the night. I didn't think I was out of control, but I didn't want any controls either; I was having a good time with my friends, girls, drinking, and smoking weed. I knew that Rudy and my dad had rules and regulations that were going to make that type of life difficult for me to continue.

I had gotten into marijuana in my junior year. Grass was the biggest thing at Lawton High and we thought it was the cool thing to do. All the guys from the teams I hung around with were always getting high. I never thought there was any harm in it, but how many young people ever see the harm in what they're doing?

We had to be at school at eight-thirty. A friend who had a car would pick me up at seven-thirty every morning. We would ride around town and get high before classes began, then go to school wearing shades so nobody could see our eyes. Actually, because I was the cool baseball and football star, I always wore sunglasses, so nobody ever suspected. As soon as it was time for lunch break we got back in the car and got stoned again. After lunch I had English class, and I would always feel like a genius when I walked into the classroom, ready to answer every question asked and, when I was really wrecked, offering some weird philosophical thoughts along with my answers. I'm not sure what the teacher thought, but I would sit back in my chair with my arms folded thinking I was fucking amazing. Of course, there were also times I was so high I would sit in class and have the giggles, tripping off on every small thing. All someone had to do was say something funny and I'd be unable to control myself.

Not everyone at school was dumb to what I was doing. One day I fell asleep in Coach Ahlschlager's meeting and he lectured me for being high. I felt guilty, but rather than own up I got pissed off at him. I decided he was persecuting me, a typical druggie reaction, and boycotted the football team for the next three practices, but I soon realized that this was a no-win situation and quickly apologized. I felt terrible about the incident because he had become close to me, inviting me to his house and doing other nice things for me.

When my friends and I weren't smoking grass we were out drinking. We had two favorite drinks: beer or a wicked 180-proof liquor called Everclear. We would drive to Wichita Falls, Texas, for beer because Oklahoma's three-point-two beer was never strong enough for us. Every party started with a drive to Wichita Falls to pick up a few cases of the real stuff. There were some nights when we partied on grass, beer, and Everclear. It's amazing that we survived those days, especially since we were driving all the time.

When there was no party, we would cruise the "circle," which started out at one end of town at a place called Wayne's Drive-In and ended at a place called Star Castles. The loop was only a few miles, and while we drove around looking for friends and girls we would drink. If you rode the circle slow enough on a Friday night, you would meet just about everyone you knew.

One night we were supposed to be at a party around nine-thirty. My friend Tommy had a car so we decided at seven-thirty to kill some time before the party by driving around the circle. We picked up another friend named "Cool" and headed for Wichita Falls. Cool was a big guy and able to bluff his way into getting booze even though he was underage. On the way back to Lawton we smoked a little grass and started drinking out of the Everclear bottle, chasing it with 151-proof rum. Before we got home Cool had passed out. Tommy got behind the wheel and we continued heading back to Lawton. At a red light I turned to Tommy and his eyes were closed. I got out of the car, pushed him over, and began driving.

All this time Tommy was telling me he felt sick. I ignored him, and then felt something wet on my arm. I had to keep my eyes open and get home, but every time I turned a corner

Tommy would roll over toward me and throw up. I must have gotten them to the party because I remember waking up in the backyard of the house. It was hanging out like this that made me shudder whenever I thought about living in my father's house.

SENIOR YEAR

Having no other choice, I moved in with my father and Rudy in the summer of 1985. Immediately, Rudy laid down the rules and there were plenty of them. On school nights I had to be home by eleven-thirty and on weekends by one. I had to leave notes when I went somewhere, and if I went elsewhere after that I had to phone in. If I needed spending money, I would have to get a job. There wasn't anything abnormal in what Rudy was asking me to do, but at my mother's house I came and went on my own time. I suspect that my mother was the reason Rudy and I didn't get along. I was her husband's son by another woman, and whenever she looked at me she saw my mother's face. To this day there is no love lost between Rudy and my mother.

But Rudy was aware of how I was brought up, and she wanted to bring a little discipline into my life. It made me unhappy, but I knew that appealing to my father would get me nowhere. He made it clear to me that he was backing Rudy, and throughout my final year in Lawton, Rudy and I continued to bang heads. I had been dating a twenty-two-year-old girl, a sister of one of my coaches, who owned a car. Because I didn't have a car I never bothered to get a driver's license, but I knew how to drive, and she would let me borrow her car. Rudy saw me driving the car and warned me what would happen if I were stopped or had an accident. I ignored her warning, and the next time she saw me driving the car she grounded me. It made no difference that Rudy was right, I felt even more resentment toward her.

What made home tolerable was how I was treated everywhere else in Lawton. Before the end of my junior year the word was out that the University of Oklahoma was interested in recruiting me. That's a serious credential in Lawton.

Because of Rudy and my father's demands that I get a job to earn my spending money, I got my first taste of the good life provided Oklahoma football players.

Before I moved to my father's house, I thought I would impress him by getting a job. I quit the basketball team and joined my brothers Curtis and Raymond, who worked at Safeway stores. My brothers were well liked by the managers and I got work as a packer because of their recommendations, but I hated the job and fucked up. Before the summer was over I was fired and had to look for a new job.

At the time, I had a good friend named Todd Murphy. Todd's mother was divorced and going out with a man named Steve Bentley, a wealthy guy whose father owned the *Lawton Constitution,* the local newspaper. Steve was an OU graduate and a booster of the school's golf team. Golf was his passion, and it was from Steve that I learned to play the game. We became good friends and Steve spent a lot of time persuading me to forget the other colleges that were interested in me and go to OU. He made a big deal about how important it was for the city of Lawton to have me represent it as a Sooner. He also knew about my situation at home and offered me a job on the newspaper.

The job paid five dollars an hour, and I was given very little work. During the basketball season I was to sit by the telephone and wait for someone to call in the scores of the local high-school games. Sometimes I would be given statistics and a few facts to prepare brief articles.

Most of the other employees at the newspaper didn't like me very much. Often I was on the phone bullshitting with my friends or girlfriends. They knew I had the job because of my status as a football player and that OU was trying to recruit me. Most of the time I wouldn't even have to show up at the job because Steve would pick me up and we'd go out to play golf or drink: Steve also gave me one of the company cars to drive. One day we went out to the golf course, played eighteen holes, and had a few drinks. I was in no mood to return to work so Steve told me to take the company car. Later in the day there was an emergency; the car was needed for a special report. Nobody at the newspaper knew where I was, so they called Steve and told him that they had been looking for me for several hours. Steve panicked because we'd been drinking, but after chasing around town he caught up with me and bawled me out. Relieved that nothing had happened to the car or to me, he warned me about disappearing, but to avoid this happening again he had a solution: it was time for me to have my own car.

Like the boosters I would soon meet at OU, Steve told me not to worry about money. He sent me to Felton Dean, a close friend of his. Felton was a black businessman who owned a car dealership in Lawton. "You go see Felton, Charles," Steve told me, "and pick out a car. We'll work it out."

I was seventeen years old, and when Steve told me to pick out a car that meant one thing to me: a brand new car right out of the showroom. I went to Felton's office and we chatted for a few minutes, and then he said let's go look at the cars. We walked out of the office and I started walking one way, toward the new cars, while Felton was headed in the opposite direction toward the used cars. My mind was on a white Trans Am I had seen in the lot, and when I turned around to talk to Felton he was still walking the other way.

I ran back to him and asked, "Where are you going, Felton?"

"Over there, Charles, to the used cars."

"I don't understand," I said to him.

We went back to his office. "Look, Charles," he explained,

61

"don't you think your first car should be a used one? When Steve called he said I should put you in the car you like best, but he also said that I should do what's best for you. This is what's best for you. When you get a new car on your own you'll appreciate it more."

Shit, I couldn't believe what Felton was saying. What a jerk, I thought. What the fuck does he care what's good or bad for me when he's not paying for the car? Even when I told him I would appreciate it just as well if my first car was a brand new Trans Am, he kept on with the same rap. He told me how he had worked to get his dealership and how much more he thought of himself because of how hard he'd had to struggle. Well, I didn't want to hear that, and I left without a car. Later I learned that the real reason for talking me out of a new car had nothing to do with improving my character. What Steve was concerned about, and passed on to Felton, was the impression I would make arriving on the Norman campus in about six months driving a brand new Trans Am. This was the first inkling I had of how boosters and coaches were always worried about the NCAA looking over their shoulders. But that day I couldn't have cared less about the NCAA; I wanted my Trans Am.

Cars were always a big thing with me, and to keep me happy Steve started to let me drive his red Porsche. He did a lot to keep me happy and interested in OU. I wasn't planning to go to any other college, but all through my senior year I got letters and phone calls from other schools. It wasn't until February 1986 that I signed my letter of intent to attend OU, and right up to the day I signed, Steve was doing everything possible to sell me on becoming a Sooner. He invited me to his house where he had a great film library of OU football games which we would watch over a few drinks. Steve would tell me how great I could be. He enticed me by playing to my ego, a very easy thing to do. He also at times helped out my family.

THE LIFE AND CRIMES OF OKLAHOMA FOOTBALL

Steve Bentley was my window to a world of big-time football. It wasn't only a world of athletes, but of businessmen, school administrators, and politicians carried away by it all. When you're seventeen you don't ask why successful business people like Steve Bentley are your friends. I never questioned what he could possibly have in common with a black teenager. Only when you come to appreciate the football madness in Oklahoma can you understand why grown men will gladly pay to be in the company of young men who in any other circumstance they wouldn't look at twice. Steve Bentley is not a bad person; in fact, when I got into trouble he helped pay my bail. Maybe we had what I learned was called a symbiotic relationship: athletes live off people like Steve, while we make them part of a world they fantasize about.

As soon as the high-school football season ended, the recruiting game heated up. Schools like Notre Dame and Minnesota were interested in me, but they seemed a million miles away from Lawton. I was familiar with three states and my first decision was that I would go to a school in Oklahoma, Texas, or Arkansas. For a short time I considered SMU, but they were beginning to have their problems with the NCAA. The school that tried hardest to recruit me, and one that I was tempted to attend, was Oklahoma State.

According to NCAA rules, once the high-school season is completed, the colleges are allowed to invite you to several of their games and one weekend visit to the campus. Because Oklahoma State wasn't too far away, I decided to go to a few of their games and to visit the campus in Stillwater. I have no doubt that OSU wanted me because of how I was treated when I made those visits. They had the greatest recruiter in the world and her name was Teri.

Teri was a beautiful, blond, long-legged junior at Oklahoma State, who had gone to Moore High School. Every time I arrived

63

at OSU Teri was waiting for me in her white Corvette. My heart would pound as soon as I saw her. She would drive me around the area talking about how great things would be if I went to OSU the following fall. "Charles," she would coo, "think about how much fun we could have. I'll have another year to go, and we could party and do stuff. If you have any problems in class, don't worry, I can help you."

Teri, always with her arm in mine, took me around and introduced me to the big shots on campus. After a long afternoon I would tell her that I was tired and had a headache, and she would say: "Oh, Charles, let's go back to my room and let me give you a massage." We would go back to her room where she would tell me to lie down while she put on some perfume: "I know you love this perfume, Charles. I think I'll drive you crazy." She did.

That girl almost had me at OSU. I never went to bed with her, but not because she wasn't willing. I think what stopped me was that I was awed by her. She was like no girl I had ever met, what I called one destructive agent. She would sit across from me with her mini-skirt crawling up her crotch and my eyes would bulge out. God, I wanted so bad to fuck her, and she would give me a wicked smile and say: "Oh, Charles, don't look." "But Teri," I would drool, "I can't help but look." "Well, Charles, okay, but just a little peek."

Using Teri as bait to lure me to OSU almost worked. A few years later, I was asked to take out an OU recruit and show him a good time. I brought along a knockout girl I knew and she gave him the same treatment I had received from Teri. The coaches knew about it, but, what the hell, they were happy when he signed to play for OU.

But it only took one visit to the University of Oklahoma to know where I really was headed in August. They had girls to show me around, none in the same class as Teri, but what

turned my head was hanging out with the guys on the team—
people like Keith Jackson, Jamelle Holieway, and of course
Brian Bosworth, the Boz. They flashed their national championship rings won that year and said: "Hey, you come here and
you'll contend for the national championship. You come here
and you'll be playing in bowl games every year." Whether it
was Coach Proctor who recruited me or Jamelle Holieway, the
pitch was the same: "You gonna be a Sooner? Might as well. It's
the best program in the country."

I couldn't believe the attention given the players by everyone
on campus. I kept hearing, "Hey, look, there's Bosworth.
There's Holieway." I ate it up. I was overwhelmed on my visit
when I saw Keith Jackson. Keith-fucking-Jackson! And there
he was coming over to talk to me about football. It blew my
mind. I went home that night not thinking about Teri.

I never worried about what my status would be at OU.
Jamelle Holieway had become the starting quarterback that year
and led the Sooners to an undefeated season. His backup quarterback was Eric Mitchell whom people were saying was better
than Jamelle. There was even talk about two or three other
Oklahoma quarterbacks going to OU the next year, but it didn't
bother me. Hell, I wasn't even concerned when Coach Proctor
told me they might switch me to defensive back. I never worried
because by this time I had tremendous confidence in myself. I
watched Jamelle play when I was in high school and thought
there was nothing he could do that I couldn't do better. All I'd
have to do was learn the wishbone offense, and it would be only
a matter of time before I'd beat him out of the job.

And then there was Barry Switzer. If you're from Oklahoma
and play football, there's only one man you want to play for.
Barry Switzer was larger than life to a young football player like
me. Great players came and went, but Barry Switzer always
stayed to develop more. For me, that was enough. For a few

weeks in my junior year I had gone to a football camp paid for by the high school. It was a great experience, as I got to play with some of the best high-school players in Oklahoma, Texas, and Kansas. Switzer met me there and told me that he was going to be offering me a scholarship after my senior year.

"Son," he said, "you're gonna come to the University of Oklahoma. When I come down to Lawton I want you to sign."

I stared at him with my mouth open, my eyes on the rings on his fingers. "Yeah, yeah," I said, and started up some stairs.

"Hey, you come on down," he said, "I'm serious. You don't think I'm serious? We're coming down to get you. You're gonna be a Sooner, son."

At the time I knew that what he was talking about was a year off and that anything could happen. Later, I would learn that Switzer had been watching me for most of my junior year, and that what had attracted him most about me was watching my moves as a break dancer for the L.A. Breakers—L.A. as in Lawton Assassins.

The L.A. Breakers were seven of the baddest break dancers in the state of Oklahoma. All of us had been dancing for a few years, but in 1983, my sophomore year, we got together to form the group. I loved break dancing and performing with the Breakers. Maybe I never got into serious trouble because I was so busy with school, football, basketball or baseball practice, and the evening get-together with the group to work out our routines. It was serious stuff and we competed against other groups in Oklahoma and Texas. We were so good that one radio station tried to organize a contest between the L.A. Breakers and the New York Breakers, supposedly the best group in New York. We made some good money winning contests. At one event in Oklahoma City the prize was eight hundred dollars and a trophy that was almost a foot taller than I!

It was hard work and a lot of fun. We had a manager who

promoted us and a talent agency in Oklahoma City. We made two videos. One of our biggest shows was at Six Flags Park in Dallas, where we won another basketball-player-size trophy and money. Our practice sessions lasted about three or four hours every evening, and we were able to get our moves down so perfectly that you'd have thought we were trained by a professional choreographer. Our best routine was called the "L.A. Zoo."

The "L.A. Zoo" was the climax to our sixty-minute act. Each dancer had a specialty, imitating a different animal; I was a dolphin. I'd lie on my stomach and wave up and down as if I were swimming, then pop off the ground, up on my feet, spin in the air, repeat it, and then turn over. Another dancer was a spider; he'd put his legs over his shoulders and walk on his hands. We also had a crab and a frog. It was really cool when we walked out attached to one another by a string, sort of like animals on a leash. There were no ego problems, either. Each dancer had an opportunity to show his stuff and be a star for a few minutes.

In my last year as a Breaker we were invited to perform at the opening of the Ray Massey automobile dealership in Lawton. That's when Barry Switzer saw me for the first time. He described his impression of me to a reporter: "I was watching this group of break dancers who were performing. They were called the L.A. Breakers, and the leader was doing the damnedest things I'd ever seen. He'd drop to the floor, spin around, get up on his feet, fall down again and come back up again like a snake. Unbelievable stuff. I said to somebody near me, 'Who's that dude?' And the guy next to me said, 'That's Charles Thompson.' I almost died. 'Charles Thompson, the Lawton High quarterback?' I asked. 'Yeah,' the guy answered. 'Holy potatoes,' I said. And I walked right over and introduced myself. What a great athlete."

I remember how I felt when he came over to me that day. He invited the group to Norman to perform for the football team. The rest of the Breakers were able to go, but not me; I was back in Lawton practicing football. Not even for the Sooners would I have the nerve to go up to Coach Ahlschlager and say, "Sorry, Coach, but I can't make practice today because I have to break dance." Still, I felt great. I knew that Barry Switzer had his eye on me.

All through the winter of 1985–1986, Bobby Proctor called me about signing a letter of intent to go to OU. There were times I'd walk into my high school's football office and Proctor would be on the phone. I never misled him and played coy like some other players who are highly recruited, but I was in no hurry to commit myself. Teri was the biggest reason why. Proctor's rap was always the same—he would tell me about the "family." There were never any specific promises or offers of anything, but Proctor would say: "Charles, at Oklahoma we're a family, and like a family we take care of our own. If you need anything, get in trouble, we'll be there."

The rap to my father and stepmother, when he called or when he visited the house, was similar: "He ain't gonna have to worry about anything up there once he becomes part of the family. We're gonna take care of him. We're gonna see that he does everything right, make sure that he keeps his head clear. Don't worry, if he ever needs anything he can come to me. We think he can help our program out, and help himself out education-wise."

By the end of January 1986, Proctor was calling my house almost every day. He was real tight with my high-school football coaches and they sometimes called him when I'd go in there to talk to them. Proctor also let me know that I'd have to sign my letter of intent before I would be getting anything from OU: "How do you expect me to take care of you now," he'd say, when I pushed him on the benefits for a "family" member, "while you're still not a member of the family? We'll take care of you once you're here; but if I do it now you might try to go somewhere else."

In February there were reports in the newspapers and on the radio that I was definitely going to sign with OU. They were accurate, and I decided to contact Oklahoma State to cancel a visit that was scheduled for the second week in February. I don't think that I had been misleading OSU, but right through January and the first week of February Coach Campbell of the football team was calling me at home. He opened the conversation with: "Well, Teri told me to say hello." He would always have some gossip from Teri to pass on to me. But when I made the call to him to cancel the visit, he appeared to be offering more than Teri.

When I told him that I was going to sign with OU he said, "What would it take for me to convince you to become a Cowboy?" I was surprised by this and was silent. I thought he could only mean one thing: Do you want money? A car? It had to be something material, so I said: "Gee, I don't know." He ended the conversation by telling me to think about it and get back to him. I never did call him back, but after speaking to Anthony and my father I was convinced that had I asked for something to sign with OSU I would have gotten it.

With Campbell or Bobby Proctor, education was always secondary in their pitches to me. This was at a time when the biggest issue in college athletics was Proposition 48, which established minimum standards for entering freshman. I had been putting off taking the ACTs but Proctor knew my high-school grades were good enough and never discussed the test. His only concern was that the results would leave me eligible to play at OU.

On February 13, 1986, I did what everybody knew I was

going to do for months. Proctor came to Lawton and with the media present I signed my letter of intention to enroll at the University of Oklahoma. It may have been a mistake to tell people from my junior year on that I would most likely go to OU. I think that scared off the competition. I know it hurt me in the major league baseball draft that year.

Lawton High School's baseball coach Carl Ryker and others told me that fifteen baseball teams were showing interest in me. Once during the baseball season I was approached by a scout whose job was to compile computer reports on individual players in my part of the country. He told me that there was a lot of talk about my power, speed, and fielding at second base, but the word was out and teams were reluctant to draft me too high because of OU's interest in me. I know that they were impressed with me because there were scouts in the stands during several of my games.

I don't remember who we were playing against, but one game in the middle innings, I had gotten hold of a fast ball and drilled it to the fence. I was off like a rabbit, and by the time the ball was thrown back into the infield I had crossed the plate with an inside-the-park home run. Coach Ryker told me after the game that he had looked at the scouts and they were all checking their stop watches, shaking their heads. They couldn't believe that I got around the bases that quickly. Ryker was told by the scouts that I was considered to be in the same speed category as Vince Coleman, Willie McGee, and Rickey Henderson. Eventually, I was a middle-round draft choice of the Cincinnati Reds.

THE LIFE AND CRIMES OF OKLAHOMA FOOTBALL

Coach Carl Ryker
Lawton High School

Charles was as popular as any kid can be and one of the greatest break dancers. He performed in a couple of assemblies and everyone thought that he was the best.

Gosh, he was real competitive, one of those true sportsmen. I never saw him start any game that he didn't want to win. Whenever he and another ballplayer named James Byrd —very talented, probably an edge better than Charles and now in the Boston organization—would get bored taking ground balls they would have this game they called "nickels." If they missed a ball they would owe the other guys a nickel. And when they did that I enjoyed it. Of course, the kids never paid up, but they guaranteed that every ball I hit they were going to field.

Charles was the leader of all that. I don't mean the betting, but the competitiveness. He liked to better the other guy. He could pick up on anything.

I've had great success with baseball players who have played football. Charles was about the fifth kid I had drafted by the major leagues and all five were football players. And the reason for this, I think, especially for quarterbacks, you got to get down and get after them. A lot of people think baseball is a sissy sport, but it takes determination and grit.

You know, if you can make it in Oklahoma, if you can stick out the long grind, you can play baseball anywhere. We had a thirty-eight-game season and that's a long season for a high-school kid. But if you have gone through a whole football season, it's not taxing because you don't lose interest. Charles —I remember looking him in the eye and seeing that fight.

He was real good with me. When Charles was a sophomore he didn't know baseball that well. He was just a great

71

athlete because he could run so well, he had a good arm and we thought, naturally, centerfield. But he got bored with centerfield and we moved him to second base, where he could be more involved with the action, and that's where he really took off. He would come to talk to me and we'd discuss how to get the edge on the other team and things like that. Charles took to coaching real well.

I still wanted to play baseball after graduation, and part of my deal with OU was that I would be able to play both sports. What prevented me from playing baseball at OU was Jamelle Holieway getting hurt in the spring of my freshman year. I decided to pass up baseball and practice football to see if I could make up some ground on Jamelle. It turned out to be the right decision when Jamelle got hurt again and I became the starting quarterback.

After I signed the letter of intent I felt relaxed. With the decision made, all I wanted to do was finish out the school year, graduate, and spend the summer kicking back and doing a little partying before reporting to Norman in August. Unfortunately, I soon learned that OU was ready to treat me like a family member and had gotten a great job for me that summer—in construction—the last thing I wanted to do. The job paid eleven dollars an hour, but construction was for men with families who had to work, and hard labor out in the hot summer sun was not my idea of spending my last vacation before going off to college. Still, OU thought they were helping me earn money for the summer and I couldn't turn down the job.

So, miserable all the time, I started working construction jobs at Fort Sill. I'd get up at seven, go to work, come home to eat in the evening, and then feel too exhausted to do much of anything else. It was starting to look like a boring summer without too much fun when Gary and I decided to spend our Sundays at

Cross Town Park. I was to get all the excitement and money I needed on those Sundays. I was also to meet some of the people who had a great deal to do with my winding up in the federal prison camp at Big Springs, Texas.

SUMMER OF '86

Cross Town Park is located in the pits of Lawton, in the poorest black slum area. If you walk down its one long block, you'll find prostitutes, called "strawberries," bars, burnt-out stores, and the bus station. Up on one corner is a whorehouse that's been in business for decades. Running parallel to the area are the railroad tracks. The place is ugly. The people there are the types you'd expect: besides the whores there are junkies, dealers, gamblers, and every kind of hoodlum. You could go through the area any night and buy the drug of your choice—some of it real, some fake. If you were stupid enough to buy the fake, you'd have to be really crazy to go back and complain. Beatings, knifings, and shootings are nothing unusual. If you're a hustler in Lawton, that's where you do your hustling.

The summer of 1986 was not the first time I had ever visited the area. Sometimes, when we had nothing better to do on school nights, Gary and a few other guys would take a car to cruise the streets. We'd ask the strawberries about their rates. We would tease them and ask about discounts on blowjobs. They would get pissed and start screaming for their pimps. We would haul ass out of there.

Sundays were real busy at Cross Town. Sunday was the "black cruise"; people looking for fun who had to work or go to school during the week chose that day to visit. There would be all kinds of activities going on—drinking, loud music, dancing, fighting. There was a basketball court in Cross Town where only the bravest would play. It was rough. I've seen guys get their legs or arms broken playing in the park. I saw guys going to the basket with blood pouring from their heads, noses, or mouths—sometimes all three. It was ghetto basketball, and if you weren't physical, you didn't play. I've heard how tough it is up in Harlem, and although I've never been there, I'll bet it's a kindergarten compared to Cross Town.

It was nearly July when Gary and I went to Cross Town. I wasn't afraid of going there, as most of the crowd knew who I was. We were cruising the street when a guy called "Big O" stopped us. He was a big sucker, about six-four and two hundred fifty pounds. His real name was Otha Armstrong and he had tried out and was cut by the Washington Redskins after playing for a small college in Oklahoma.

He put his hand on my chest.

"Hey you, Thompson," he said. "I don't care if you're going to Oklahoma, you're still shit. You ain't fast, any pussy could beat you . . ."

He didn't stop talking, trying to get me mad enough to say something to him. Finally, I said, "Fuck off, black ass," and walked away.

He ran after me and said, "You think you hot shit? You think you fast? Fuck it, nigger, I can outrun your ass. I'll tell you what: I'll put up forty dollars to your nothing that I can beat your ass."

It was an offer I couldn't refuse. There was no way I could lose to Otha, much less lose on the bet. Big O was known around the park as a bullshit artist. He made it sound as if his weeks with the Washington Redskins were like Joe Theisman's career. I don't think he got past training camp; since then, Otha Armstrong had earned his living by hustling. When he was at the park he always had something to sell: televisions, leather jackets, watches, you name it.

Soon everyone in the park was talking about the race. I looked around and all I saw were different denominations of bills in a dozen black hands. It didn't take me long to realize that Otha wasn't going to race me. His whole rap was a hustle.

THE LIFE AND CRIMES OF OKLAHOMA FOOTBALL

When four other guys agreed to race me, Otha said that it was winner take all: "Whoever wins gets the forty."

Everyone in the park got busy. Some guy walked off what he thought was a hundred yards, someone else started screaming out odds. I had no idea I'd be in a track meet that day and was wearing loafers. I decided it would be easier to run barefoot. A voice screamed: "Ready, set, go," and we were off. About ten seconds later the race was over and I had won, smiling as I took the forty out of Otha's hand and put it in my pocket.

I didn't even have my shoes on when Otha called out, "Let 'em race again." That was fine with me, and I waited to see who was going to put up another forty. Actually, there were probably a dozen guys in the park who would have been willing; that was nothing to those who were doing the betting. These were drug dealers and thugs who had more than enough money to blow on a foot race. The forty was the runners' incentive to race the hundred yards. The gamblers were betting thousands of dollars and I was getting the tips. After five races I had two hundred dollars of Otha's money in my pocket and was ready to go home. Before I left, a stranger came up to talk to me.

They called him "Snowman," and the choice of the name had nothing to do with winter's weather. He was one of the largest cocaine dealers in Oklahoma; he has the same position today in Dallas, Texas. The man who talked to me that Sunday afternoon was in his mid-twenties, tall and thin, dark complected with dark brown eyes that were always darting back and forth. He looked and dressed cool, spoke cool, and acted as if he had icicles in his blood. If I were to make a film about a big-time drug pusher, he would play the lead. He put a hundred dollars in my hand. "Here, this is what I made betting on you, keep it," he said.

I don't know if he was being truthful about giving me all the money he made betting that afternoon, but he wanted me to know that there was more money where that came from. "Hey, Charles," he said. "I've seen you run with the football, and there ain't nobody here who's gonna beat you. Y' all come back next Sunday." I didn't see it then, but Snowman already had his hooks into me. I knew he was a badass, but not how much of a badass.

Although I had never met him before, we all had heard of Snowman. We had never seen him sell drugs, but it was just one of those things you knew. During the next week I wasn't thinking about Snowman and drugs, but Snowman the backer of my races. Word about the races spread quickly and there was a lot of talk in Lawton about different guys coming to Cross Town next Sunday to whip Charles Thompson's ass. I couldn't wait for the week to end.

The next week there were different races and new racers. Snowman was there and Otha's big mouth was as loud as the week before, and the results were the same. No matter who thought he could beat me found himself finishing second or worse. Sunday races against Charles Thompson became a ritual that summer at Cross Town. By the third weekend I started to feel as if this were my job; it was becoming a well-paying one. When I got home Sunday night I was so high from winning that I couldn't wait to take the hundreds out of my pocket to show Rudy and my father. Rudy was suspicious. She found it difficult to believe that I was making all that money and doing nothing wrong. "Boy," she screamed one night, "you ain't no way in hell getting that money there racing." She would scream to my father, "Leacy, get in here. There's something wrong going on here." And when I told my father how I won the money, he lit up and said, "Shit, boy, I'm gonna go out there next week and race with you."

It was a real high to me, making more money for five or six races on Sunday afternoon than I was making on the construction job. I hated Monday through Friday, but the summer I'd been dreading I was now praying would never end. I was making more money than most eighteen year olds ever see, and I was having fun. I was doing nothing wrong and had five, six hundred dollars in my pocket all the time. And it was in my pocket because I did what I do best: I ran faster than anyone.

Each week the crowds at the park grew. More and more people came to see somebody beat the favorite. Sunday at Cross Town took on a new meaning. It was the place to go to see the big race. At first I knew who I was racing against, but after the second week I started to see faces who weren't from Lawton.

The big event came toward the end of July. Snowman may have been betting on me for the last four weeks, but there were other wise guys who were losing and getting pissed off. They decided to bring in a ringer.

Cody Duling had been an all-American track star in the mid-eighties. He was known as the fastest human in Oklahoma, and now he was brought back to Lawton to be the one who would beat Charles Thompson. The betting stakes got high, and for the first time since I had been racing at the park I felt some pressure, a real challenge. I welcomed it. I can do a lot when challenged. Duling had been a champion, and most of the characters in the park that day probably thought that this was the end of Charles Thompson. Between Otha and Snowman there were several thousand dollars bet, Snowman for me and Otha against me.

It was Cody against me that afternoon for as many times as we could race. We lined up for the first race, and before twenty yards I was three steps ahead of him and four by the finish line. There was screaming and cursing and money changing hands. I don't think we were able to rest five minutes before we lined up again. Cody was mumbling to me about how he had got off to a bad start and now he was going to whip my ass. I said to him, "Yeah, right, asshole."

This time we got off together, neck and neck to the finish line, but it was my neck in front of Cody's when it counted the most. Again, more screaming, cursing, and exchanging money. After the second race, Cody walked over to me and said: "One mo' time?"

"You got it," I answered, but I was exhausted. The fucker was fast, and I wasn't certain that I could do it again.

We took a long break and I couldn't stop panting. The dude was getting closer each race and he looked as fresh as when he first walked into the park. Everybody knew that this was the last race of the day, and all the gamblers started to scramble, getting down for the final action. Snowman looked over to me and winked, as if he were saying: "Charles, win this race and you go home a very happy and wealthy man." Once more, we lined up.

The race may have been only ten or eleven seconds, but for all of that time I don't think there was any distance between the two of us. We were feet away from the finish line, which wasn't really a finish line but a spot someone had marked, when I gave everything left in my body to pass Cody. I didn't even see who won, but whomever had bet on me was jumping around. Cody and I lay on the ground, neither one of us giving a shit who won. I had won, but I didn't care—until they started pushing money on me. I guess I cared then.

It was the end of my "racing" career. For everybody in the park it was like the Super Bowl; anything after that would be anticlimactic. I was totally wiped out, and couldn't even count the money in my hands or my pocket. I knew there was a great deal of it, but I would count it later. On the way out, one more time, Snowman winked at me.

After my races against Cody things at the park returned to normal. I went there one or two more times, but the racing season was finished. I also saw Snowman and Otha, but there wasn't much to talk about, and I had no reason to think I would ever be involved with them again. Otha did say he might be moving to Norman and would look in on me, but I thought he was talking more jive. I had more important things on my mind than Snowman and Otha: the last Saturday in July was the Oklahoma High School all-star football game in Tulsa. It was to be a showcase for the best high-school players in the state. All the colleges that had drafted us were sending coaches to observe their recruits competing against the best in the state. It was a greater opportunity for me because I learned that I was to have several assignments. I was scheduled to receive kickoffs, field punts, and play safety on defense. Later in the game I would come in and play quarterback. This was perfect, because Bobby Proctor, who was OU's defensive backfield coach, had been telling me that Switzer was thinking of switching me from quarterback to defensive back. The Tulsa game would give me the chance to prove to OU that I could play any position they wanted. Sure, I wanted to be OU's quarterback, but there is more than one place on the field to be a star.

The players arrived early in the week to practice. There was a lot of free time during the day and many of us would drift over to the large Woodland Hills Mall to check out the stores. We were sitting around the hotel when we came up with the idea of going back to the mall the next evening to see who could steal the most stuff. I had no second thoughts about this and agreed.

The following afternoon, which was Thursday, I had a date with a girl who worked in one of the shops in the mall. I had plenty of time to kill, so I decided to cruise the place. I stopped at a store called the Foot Locker and bought some sweat socks and wristbands for the game before going into the leather shop next door. In the store I noticed a pair of black driving gloves.

My first intention was to steal them, but as I walked around the store I said to myself: "Man, do you really want to take these?"

It was weird: I wanted to steal the gloves, but for some reason I kept hesitating to walk out of the store. I can't say that my conscience was bothering me, only that I was uncertain about the whole thing. Next to the exit of the store I stopped by a "For Sale" rack to look at a few items. I was still in the store with the gloves in my hand when the electronic sensor went off. I jumped when I heard the beep—scared shitless, probably because I had larceny in my heart. But, as I was in the store, I figured somebody else had set off the alarm.

From the back of the store a middle-aged saleslady came running. "You," she shouted, "get back over here, you thief." I started to look around. When I didn't see anybody I knew she was talking to me. I said to her: "Look here, lady, I'm not trying to steal anything. I ain't going anywhere. Here, take your gloves back." Her face reddened and she pushed me against the counter, telling me not to move. Her whole body began shaking and she screamed for someone to get security.

It was getting out of hand. I said: "Ma'am, I don't know what you are talking about. I'm getting out of here."

"No, you're not," she screamed, and grabbed hold of my shirt. "You better not go anywhere, young man."

There was no way I was going to convince this woman that I did not take the gloves. I may have been planning to steal them but I hadn't, so I pushed her hands off my shirt, dropped the gloves on the counter, and walked out of the store.

I figured that was the end of it, and took the escalator to the second floor of the mall. I still had time before meeting my date and decided to visit one or two more stores. At the top of the escalator I saw about eight security guards pointing their fingers at me. One of them called out: "Yeah, that's him. It's him." Maybe I should have stayed there and tried to explain, but instinctively I knew that eight security guards, all white, were not prepared to listen to a teenager in sneakers, who was black. My head and heart said run, and I took off. It was the start of a chase scene right out of an old silent movie.

I ducked into a stairwell and ran down to the first floor and out to the parking lot. Way behind me trying to catch up were six or seven out of shape rent-a-cops. There wasn't a chance they could catch me. I got out of the parking lot and continued running in the street. I knew nothing about the neighborhood, or Tulsa, for that matter, and had no idea where I was. Meanwhile, whenever I turned around there were fewer security guards, getting farther behind me. I could see one or two of them holding their guts as they tried to keep up with me. As soon as I stopped worrying about them, a small truck marked WOODLAND HILLS SECURITY pulled up and a guy poked his head out and called to me, "Hey, man, what's the deal? Come here!" I started to jog a little faster. "Hey, c'mon, let me talk to you," he said.

"Yeah," I said, "you can talk to me, as long as you keep your distance."

This went on for a few hundred yards. The truck would sneak up at me and when the driver called out I ran a little faster. Meanwhile, behind the truck a couple of jeeps got in on the chase. When they got close the truck stopped and a guy jumped out and tried to grab me. I shook him off and turned it on, running with all my speed. The chase took us to a residential area with apartments and small houses. The jeeps were really in the race now, and they began to cut through lawns and backyards to corner me. One jeep driver must have been in Vietnam or somewhere because he didn't give a shit what he did to catch me. He wrecked one lawn and tore up some woman's garden—she was hosing her flowers when he came through. You would think they were chasing Charles Manson.

They were reliving the days of the Texas Rangers, or whatever they had in Oklahoma, and nothing was going to prevent them from getting their man.

I was getting a bit tired, and had been running from them for a couple of miles, when I spotted a large two-story apartment complex. I jumped over a fence and crawled under a set of stairs that led to the apartment's second floor. I was certain that I was clear. One security jeep stopped a few feet past the fence, the driver taking a rest and lighting a cigarette. There was a pool in the middle of the complex, and a man in a bathing suit sitting there had seen me hide under the stairs. He leaned over the fence. "Hey, are you all looking for that nigger boy?" he said to the security officer, and pointed in my direction. "Oh, fuck," I said to myself, and started running again.

I got out of the opposite end of the complex and onto a main highway. With no clue about the neighborhood I kept running in a straight line. I was thinking that they couldn't keep this up all day when I heard the screech of brakes. I turned around into the arms of a beefy-faced security guard. I was too exhausted to resist. A few other jeeps and a truck pulled up behind us.

It was a hot day, temperature over a hundred, and when they threw me up against the jeep, they put my hands on the roof and I screamed and jumped back, yelling, "Fuck, man, it's hot!" But after chasing me for four miles these guys were way past giving a shit whether the heat from the car was burning my skin. They slammed me against the truck again and I tried to get away from it. "Okay, you little nigger," one of them said, "now you're trying to resist arrest." I looked at this idiot and said: "Here, asshole, you can have my hands, only I'm not going to let you burn me to death." A deputy sheriff had arrived on the scene and a security guard was telling him that I had stolen gloves from a store, beat up a saleslady, and was resisting

84

arrest. "What?" I screamed. "The gloves are in the store, I only took the lady's hands off my shirt, and I'm not resisting arrest."

These guys weren't going to chase me for four miles without having a good reason for the police, and I knew right then I was going to be fucked. I turned to the security guard who was talking to the deputy: "Wait a minute, where's the evidence? I don't have the gloves. I threw them back down on the counter." The deputy decided that we should go back to the store. They threw me in the car while I was screaming: "You're arresting me on false pretenses."

Later I was able to figure out why they decided to return to the store. That's where the gloves were and how the cops were able to get them. Of course, the security guard claimed that he found them on me. Inside the store someone got the saleslady to identify me. "That's him," she said, pointing her finger in my face. "That's the thief." They took me to the Tulsa County Jail.

Things continued to get out of hand. At the jail I learned that I was being charged with shoplifting, assault and battery on the saleslady, and trying to punch the security guard when he caught me. I was frightened. They let me make a phone call and I reached Bobby Proctor's wife; I don't know how or who told him, but she told me Bobby knew that I had been arrested and was on his way down from Norman to meet with Dick Evan, my coach on the all-star team, to bail me out. Then they took me to a cell.

I had never been in a jail in my life. This one was a large room enclosed by bars and inside it were cells that held the prisoners. By now it was early in the evening and the prisoners were out of their cells and walking around the larger room. There were at least twenty of them, some of the weirdest, most frightening men I had ever seen, who would have scared most of the characters hanging out in Cross Town Park. They all seemed big and threatening. A few had shaved heads with broken bottle scars; others were toothless, smiling out of a black hole. And tattoos. Damn, I don't think I have seen more tattoos in my life. I noticed that the toilets were not enclosed, and one dude was sitting on the bowl as though there was nothing strange about the lack of privacy. I had to go to the bathroom, but I swore to myself that I would rather explode than relieve myself. I stared at the freak show, waiting for the deputy to open the iron barred door.

I was told which bunk was mine and I went directly to it and lay down on the hard surface. I closed my eyes, not wanting to acknowledge the asylum I was in. "Dear, God, let me sleep," I prayed, "and please don't let anybody bother me." It seemed that every five or ten minutes I would hear keys jangling, and I would open my eyes thinking that someone had come to bail me out of there. One hour went by. Two hours, then three, but nobody came for me. I opened my eyes, once, and looked up at a bald-headed dude bigger than Andre the Giant who was standing over me. "Hey, man," he said, "wanna play cards?" I tried to smile and said: "No, cuz, ain't feeling too good."

In the Richard Pryor movie *Stir Crazy,* Richard and Gene Wilder are put in a county jail and they try to act cool so no one will see how scared they are. That's how I acted. When they brought the food in for dinner one of the inmates asked me if I was going to join them: "Nah, man," I turned on my cool, "you eat my stuff. Fuck 'em, I don't need their shit." He looked at me as if I were crazy to give up a meal, shrugged his shoulders, and walked away. Four hours went by. More keys jangling, but nobody coming for Charles.

Now, I really had to go to the bathroom; but there was no way I was going to lose my dignity. I started to think about anything to get my mind off it. I thought of a thousand things, but I didn't think about how serious this could be. It never crossed my mind that there was a chance I wouldn't be allowed

86

to play in the all-star game. I believed that I was innocent; I had wanted to, but I never stole the gloves. I never pushed the saleslady to the floor of the store, as the complaint had read, and I believed that I had every right to run from the security guards in the mall. Shit, they had caused more damage and hurt than me, driving their jeeps through people's lawns and back-yards, destroying property. It'll all be over, I thought, as soon as Bobby Proctor arrived to straighten out the bullshit. Where the fuck was he?

It was more than five hours after I was put in the cell that I heard the keys and a voice booming, "Thompson, let's go." They took me back to the office I'd been in earlier and waiting for me were Proctor and Evan. The deputy told me that I could leave with them. I walked over to the coaches and Proctor's first words were: "Switzer wants to talk to you. He's pissed." I told Proctor that I would call Switzer as soon as we got back to the room I had been staying at. He shook his head and said: "No, Charles, he wants to talk to you now." We walked to a public phone and Proctor dialed Switzer's phone number.

Proctor said a few words to Switzer and put me on the phone: "Coach," I said, "I can explain. I swear I did nothing." He cut me off and said: "Charles, we're going to do everything we can to get this thing squared. But I want you to understand how bad this is for the University of Oklahoma. This is bad publicity. This is a sign, a bad sign, that you screwed up. We'll see how we can get this resolved. We'll talk about it later, but for now just listen to Bobby. You do whatever he says."

We drove back in silence to the Sheraton hotel where the coaches were staying. I went to Bobby's room with him. As soon as he slammed the door he jumped on my ass: "Do you know that Switzer is thinking of letting you go? Do you realize just how much you let him down? Switzer had heard about you; how you like to play those stupid games in stores, but he wanted to give you an opportunity to play for Oklahoma." I had to laugh at that one. If Switzer was having doubts about me, why had Proctor called my house and school every day for two months before I signed my letter of intent? If Switzer had been hearing bad stuff about me, why had he allowed Proctor to abuse his friendship with Coach Ahlschlager at Lawton High School, to get him to talk me out of considering any other school but OU? This was bullshit. The only thing Switzer was worried about was what he had told me: bad publicity for OU. But what I heard next wasn't any bullshit.

Proctor had a message from one of the team's coaches that I was to leave the team the following morning. I was off the all-star team. He told me that I had to appear before the state committee in charge of the all-star game: "If you can convince them that you're innocent," he said, throwing out some hope, "Evan will have to let you play." I felt better leaving Proctor's room, thinking that I could explain everything to the committee, and that Saturday I would be playing. I promised myself that I would tell the truth, including my initial intention of wanting to steal the gloves.

I ran into some of the other players when I returned to my room at Oral Roberts University where the players were staying. "CT," they all asked, "what the fuck is happening?" I learned that the press had been all over the university dorm when they found out I'd been arrested. Nobody knew what for and there was a lot of speculation. My friend James Byrd from Lawton High told me that it had even been on television that evening. Now I could see why Switzer was pissed off. A few of the guys wanted to party, but I was beat and went back to my room. I got out of my clothes and fell onto the bed. I was asleep in minutes.

Early next morning I was driven to the Sheraton Hotel to meet the committee. I think there were five people on the committee and four of them stared at me stone-faced when I walked

88

into the room. The only person to say good morning and smile was the black dude on the committee. When I told the members what had happened at the mall nobody but the black guy seemed interested. He said they should give me an opportunity to prove my side of the story. The rest of them weren't too pleased when he suggested that all of us return to the mall and talk to the saleslady. We got into two different cars and drove back to Woodland Hills.

I waited outside the store when we got to the mall, and the committee members went in to get the saleslady. As soon as she came to the front she saw me standing by the door. She was not going to be helpful. "If that boy sets one foot in this store, I am going to arrest him," she said. She was a total bitch, answering all the questions asked her by the committee with "I don't care what he says. He is a thief. He came in the store to steal and walked out with a pair of gloves."

Bobby Proctor had come along with us to the mall. I'd had the feeling early that morning that Proctor had believed what I had told him yesterday, especially the part about not hurting the saleslady. When he asked her about it she made it sound that I had heaved her to the floor and stomped on her. It was hopeless. The black member on the committee told me that there was nothing he could do for me. I could not play in the all-star game. I had to leave Tulsa and return to Lawton. Proctor drove me back to the room to get my clothes. He knew how depressed I was and told me that everything would be worked out for me when I appeared in court.

Packing my clothes to go home deepened my depression. I hadn't spoken to my father or mother about what had happened and I dreaded making the calls. There was no question that they had heard about the incident because it was all over Oklahoma, turning into a media circus in the state; and, I was to learn from my mother in Dallas, the Texas newspapers also played it up big. One Texas newspaper had a headline on its sports page: OU RECRUIT ARRESTED IN ASSAULT. The *Lawton Constitution,* my former employer, went into overdrive and covered the story for two weeks, mostly on its front page. But when I was packing to return to Lawton I didn't give a damn about the media. I was worried about my family.

I thought I'd call my father first and wait until I got back to Lawton to call my mother. My father was wonderful about the whole thing: "Charles, you come on home and we'll talk about it. I'm sure you have an explanation about this. We love you, and you come on home, now." His words made me feel worse. I felt that I'd let the whole family down, especially Anthony. Driving back to Lawton I thought that I should drive off a bridge and make it easier for everyone. Oh, how I hated myself for blowing the opportunity of playing in that game.

When I walked into the house they were all waiting for me, watching television in the living room. I sat down on the couch not saying a word. Curtis got up to shut off the television. I had my mind made up to tell them the truth, to own up to the fact of making a mistake, and that would be the end of it. They sat silently, my dad, Rudy, Curtis, and my sister Lorna, waiting for me to speak.

I got right to the point. "Look, I'm very sorry about what happened. I didn't do what they're saying I did, but I was stupid being in that leather store thinking about stealing the gloves. I made a mistake and there is nothing I can do about it."

My father put his arm around me: "You're right, Charles, it's over and there is nothing you can do about it. Stop worrying and let it go. You've got a lot to look forward to. You still have the University of Oklahoma ahead of you." If the conversation had ended there I would have felt better, but Rudy decided to put her two cents in: "Well, Leacy," she said, turning to my

90

dad, "he may not even have that anymore. Maybe they'll think he's more trouble than he's worth."

Rudy was my first taste of how people can turn on you when you're down. I was to see, very shortly, how people can change, how they can go in one minute from patting you on the back to pointing a finger at you. After hearing and reading so much about how I was a great high-school football player destined to star for the Sooners they were now saying things like, "Oh, I knew he would fuck up"; or "I always thought he acted like a big shot." The change started the day I returned from Tulsa.

The phone kept ringing; mostly there were female voices at the other end of the line. "Is this Charles?" a caller would ask. "How are you, thief?" Or: "Aw, you done fucked up this time, asshole." After a few days of this I refused to answer the telephone. As long as the *Constitution* continued writing about me I knew the calls would not stop. Gone were the articles about Charles Thompson the Sooner; now, it was Charles Thompson the thief. I was too young to understand why I was getting this treatment. I was too accustomed to the special treatment I had been getting for my athletic abilities. I didn't realize that they were never writing about Charles Thompson the person, but Charles Thompson the local hero. This was the same thing. They were writing about Charles Thompson the thief, only now I didn't enjoy reading about it.

Coach Breeze from Lawton High School had a field day with the incident. Breeze, an assistant to Coach Ahlschlager, was never too crazy about the black players on the team. He never enjoyed the special treatment I had received, and when the Tulsa incident was a hot topic in Lawton he went around town telling people I was no good, that he had always known I was trouble.

For others who didn't like me it was payback time. Mrs. Barker, a teacher at Lawton, told anyone who would listen that

Charles Thompson was an arrogant kid who was destined for nothing, a loser. It probably would have been a good time for me to have reappraised my behavior toward people, but I chose to see only people turning on me. It didn't occur to me that maybe I was giving them cause to dislike me, which was why, when something bad happened, rather than support me, they went the other way.

Meanwhile, OU was doing everything to get me out of the trouble I was in. I had a court date in a few weeks, and now that I was an official member of the OU family, they got me legal representation. Before I appeared in court I learned from Proctor that the shoplifting charge had been dropped, but because the saleslady was adamant in nailing my ass I had to appear on the assault and battery charge. I was learning just how wired-in OU was when I discovered that my attorney was an Oklahoma State legislator. Although I resisted, the attorney insisted that I plead "no contest" to assault and battery, promising me that the judge would not be sending me to jail. I argued with him about it, but he told me that Switzer and he had agreed that this was the way to go. There had been enough bad publicity and I was lucky they still wanted me on the team.

When we got to court and I saw the judge I was relieved. He was black, and I thought to myself that they really had fixed things. I was wrong about this judge. Judge Harris jumped on my ass as soon as I stood before him to plead "no contest." He took off his glasses and stared at me: "You are a very lucky man, Mr. Thompson. I could throw you in jail for what you did. If I ever see you again in my courtroom I won't be speaking to you as politely as I am now. You aren't going to jail, but you're not walking out of here that easily. I'm going to make it a little hard for you. I want you to perform eighty hours of community work while you're up in Norman. I want that completed by the end of your first semester. If you don't, you'll never forget who I am. Now, get out of here."

I had reported to the University of Oklahoma on August tenth, before the court date. Proctor told me then that Switzer wanted to talk to me, and told me not to argue with Switzer about pleading "no contest" to the charges. In his office Switzer reiterated everything Proctor had said; it was what Switzer told me that day that led me to believe—besides walking into the courtroom and seeing a black judge—that the fix was in for me. "Both Bobby and I believe you," Switzer told me, "but Oklahoma can't afford any more bad press than we already have. We're going to resolve this in the quickest manner possible. You'll plead 'no contest' and the judge will give you some community work to do. Just don't worry about it. We'll take care of it for you."

When I returned from court a few days later I asked Switzer about the community work. Again, he told me not to worry about it and that Shirley Vaughn would take care of it. Shirley officially was a recruitment assistant, but she was Barry Switzer's right-hand woman. She handled things like airline tickets, game tickets, spending money. (In December 1988, she was cited by the NCAA and fired by OU for recruitment violations.) Switzer told me that Shirley would be able to have the community service hours written off for me. When I reported to Shirley and asked her where I should go to begin the work, she told me that it was all being taken care of. That was one of many times during my first semester that I went to her about it, and each time her answer was the same: It was being taken care of. From August to December I assumed they had gotten somebody to take my place to earn the community hours. I was wrong, and didn't figure out why they were doing it this way until Christmas.

What I finally understood was that Switzer did not want my

community work to interfere with football. He didn't want me to miss practice. If it hadn't been for the impression Judge Harris had made when I appeared before him, I never would have been worried. Whether or not OU and the lawyer had used their clout to get me off with community service work, I was certain that the judge wanted me to fulfill it. I never failed to follow up on it, but Shirley kept smiling and promising me it was getting done. "Shirley, please," I begged, "I don't want to go to jail." And I would get the smile.

Before I left Norman to go home for Christmas 1986, I stopped by her office one more time and expressed my concern. I asked her if she thought I should do anything before leaving campus because by the time I returned my community work period would have expired. She said: "I told you not to worry. Somebody is doing it in your place. We took care of it." I have no doubt that Switzer knew of this because Shirley Vaughn never did anything without his knowledge. But while I was at my mother's house in Dallas, Shirley called me, almost hysterical. Whatever she thought had been done had never happened. I had to return to court, but not to worry. The school had come up with an explanation for why I did not perform the necessary work hours. The court was going to postpone my obligation a few months, but I had to appear there in February.

No matter what I said to her, Shirley would repeat her favorite words: "Don't worry." But I was worried, and I was pissed. Why, as soon as the football season was over, did the shit hit the fan? Now in Dallas, I thought, what am I going to tell the judge? I was lucky. It turned out that Sheriff Bill Porter was close to Switzer and he guaranteed me a job working at the Cleveland County Jail in Norman. Everything worked out, but I learned the first lesson every football player learns at OU— nothing, but nothing, is more important than the football team.

Sooner Tradition

On a typical afternoon of sharing drinks with Steve Bentley and watching films of OU football games, I had an idea about writing an article for Steve's newspaper. He looked at me as if I was asking to perform brain surgery on him and wanted to know what I could possibly write about for a newspaper. I wasn't certain about exactly what I would write, but it would have something to do with some of the great Sooner players of the past. Steve said something to humor me, and returned with his drink to watch Joe Washington score a touchdown in slow motion.

His attitude pissed me off. He was letting me know that jocks don't think. They run, kick, or throw balls; they don't write words on paper. But when anyone tells me I can't do something, I have to prove them wrong. I didn't say anything more about it to Steve, but I was determined to research the history of the University of Oklahoma's football team and write an article. When it was done I would show Steve how wrong he was. Unfortunately, Steve Bentley had no interest in looking at it, but after a few weeks in the library I was able to learn there was more to Sooner football glory than the *x'* s and *o'* s on the coaches' blackboards.

The University of Oklahoma has developed two traditions since the school began playing football in 1895: winning and controversy. At the end of my last season in 1988, Sooner football teams had a record of 616 wins, 226 losses, and 50 ties. We had 18 bowl victories in 29 appearances and were Big 8 cham-

95

pions 35 times. Sooner teams were also placed on probation by the NCAA in 1955, 1960, 1973, and 1988.

For those of us who have played for Barry Switzer, it is difficult to imagine what it was like playing for Vern Parrington, OU's first head coach. Actually, OU's first coach was Jack Harts, who supervised one game from 1895–1897, but it was Parrington who set the standard for Oklahoma coaches with a winning record of 9–2–1 from 1897–1900. Unlike Barry Switzer, or for that matter most other OU coaches, Parrington was a Harvard graduate and scholar. After leaving the OU coaching job, he went on to win a Pulitzer Prize for his work in American history.

There was no big-time football during the days of Vern Parrington; players were responsible for purchasing and cleaning their uniforms. In 1900, Parrington coached OU in its first game against the University of Texas, the start of a great rivalry. The Sooners went home unhappy that day, losing to a "more experienced" Texas team that had begun playing football two years before Oklahoma.

Bennie Owen, one of the early great Sooner coaches, was a graduate of the University of Kansas who coached at Oklahoma from 1905–1926. Under Owen OU had a record of 122–54–16. Football was growing more popular at the school; still, it was a far cry from what the game would be in the days of Wilkinson and Switzer. The players were students first; neither school administration nor Owen let them forget it.

The year before Owen became head coach, the school established a rule that only students who were academically eligible were allowed to play on the team. Owen insisted that his players act like gentlemen, and unsportsmanlike conduct on or off the field was not tolerated. This was still a time when the game was played for fun, and it was Owen who wrote the "Boomer Sooner" song sung at rallies and games. Owen was one tough dude. In 1907 he lost his right arm in a hunting accident, but he never let this handicap prevent him from coaching and teaching his players.

When I was recruited to play for OU, I was always told by my coaches that they would take care of me. All the guys I played with were told that and maybe that's why we carried on as we did—thinking that they'd take care of it, pick up after us. Bennie Owen was no Barry Switzer. His players were encouraged to learn to solve their own problems. OU players under Owen knew that they were responsible for their actions.

In 1915, an important year for the University of Oklahoma's football team, the school joined the Southwest Conference (SWC). The conference included Oklahoma A&M (later Oklahoma State), Texas, Texas A&M, Arkansas, Baylor, and, at the time, Southwestern University. It was a super year for Owen and his team; they went 10–0 and won the SWC title. It was OU's first official championship.

College football was growing more popular in this part of the country, and when OU played their rival in Texas, and won 14–13, more than eleven thousand were at the stadium to see the game. At the time it was the largest crowd ever to see a football game in Texas.

There were other changes going on under Coach Owen, who was turning a school of less than four thousand into a football giant. Both coach and school officials were trying to put the University of Oklahoma on the national football map, something that would be tried again after the Second World War, but with greater intensity and more successfully. Owen's contribution to this goal was to make OU football more exciting than other schools' teams. In 1915, OU was turned into a passing team, averaging more than thirty passes a game. No other team in the nation threw the ball that often.

In 1920, the school decided to leave the SWC and join the

97

Missouri Valley Conference, which included Missouri, Kansas, Iowa State, Drake, Washington University, Grennell, and Kansas State. It was a good move to make at the time because the 1920 OU team was a powerhouse and won the conference title in its first year against their new rivals. It was also to be the last conference title for OU until 1938.

While the University of Oklahoma was trying to get national attention, at home in Norman throughout the 1920s football was becoming king. In 1923, OU played its first game at Owen Field (also known as Memorial Stadium). Eleven thousand people showed to see the game against Missouri. In 1925, the stadium was expanded to hold fifteen thousand, but the crowds kept growing and in 1928 the stadium's capacity was expanded to thirty-two thousand. In 1926, OU made its final conference move, joining the Big 6 (later Big 7 and then Big 8) along with Nebraska, Missouri, Iowa State, Kansas, and Kansas State. It was to be Bennie Owen's last season as head coach at OU. He remained at the school as athletic director until he was dismissed in 1934 when OU officials decided to revamp the athletic department.

The Sooners went through three head coaches—Adrian Lindsey, Lewis Hardage, and Biff Jones—before hiring Tom Stridham in 1937, who turned the team into winners once again. Stridham's 1938 team were Big 6 champions, undefeated that season and ranked fourth in the nation. This was the first Sooner team in their nearly fifty-year history to be ranked nationally. Stridham also took the Sooners to their first bowl game —the Orange Bowl—where they lost 17–0 to number two ranked Tennessee. The defeat was a shocker back in Norman after the team had given up only twelve points all season. An indication of how things had changed in Sooner football since the days of Bennie Owen and his gentlemen athletes, it was a viciously played game with fights throughout, and later became known as the "Orange Brawl."

Although big-time football had arrived under Stridham, it still was nothing like my days at OU. Players back then may have had a lot of attention, but they weren't treated like today's football heroes and were still regarded as students and part of the university. As Gene Corrotto, captain of the 1938 Orange Bowl team, described it:

"We lived in boarding houses here and there. There wasn't any athletic dormitory. A scholarship consisted of room, board, books, and tuition. But you had to work for your room and board. They got you a job and when you got your check you paid your room and board with it." Players worked as night watchmen and in bookstores, and Corrotto told of his job washing dishes in a fraternity house. I don't think Jamelle Holieway and I would have lasted too long in those days.

The real turning point for Oklahoma football came in 1945. Many people in the state were unhappy about the image other people in the nation had of Oklahoma. The writings of John Steinbeck and others had reinforced the Okie stereotype, and it was a deliberate decision by state officials and the governor's appointed Board of Regents, who ran the University of Oklahoma, to emphasize the school's football team to improve state morale and self-image. The goal was for the rest of the nation to think "Sooner" and not "Okie." A great football team was the means to that end. This was the birth of the monster. It was to lead to what Dr. George Cross, president of OU from 1943 to 1968, said, soon after the conception of this plan: "I want to build a university the football team can be proud of." It may have been spoken tongue in cheek, but from that point on the university was to play second fiddle to the football team. The second Sooner tradition of controversy began then.

It started with the search to find a coach who would lead the

University of Oklahoma to football glory. The search ended with the hiring of Jim Tatum, who had coached at the Jacksonville Naval Air Station during the war. This was a smart move, as Tatum was able to bring to Norman many of his veteran players from around the country. Many of them were way past the normal college age, but they hadn't used up their eligibility.

Tatum was a tough son of a gun who drove his players hard. He brought as many players as he could to his spring and summer training camps to pick from the best of them. At the time there were no NCAA rules about the type of drills a coach could use and Tatum ran his practices like a boot camp. He was not going to waste time in building a great football team at Norman. One state legislator who was an early Sooner booster said of Tatum: "He was hired at lunch and by supper he had a backfield and half a line." Tatum was also the kind of coach who felt he was not doing his job unless everyone was mad at him.

There was another side to Tatum that made him the first modern coach at Oklahoma: he liked to take care of his players, although that often meant breaking the rules. He cultivated rich boosters and alumni and appointed them as "sugar daddies" to his players. He called them "sponsors." They were allowed to enter the team's dressing room before and after games, slipping ten and twenty dollar bills in players' hands.

Tatum wasn't cheap either, and it was after a victory over North Carolina State that he called a team meeting in the dressing room. "Which do you want," he asked, "A hundred twenty-five dollars or a gold watch?" According to Red Dinkins, an end on the team, "We all voted for the money. I'd give anything now to have the watch." But a hundred twenty-five dollars was big bucks in 1945.

Before the season was over a rumor began that Tatum was looking to go elsewhere and that the University of Maryland had offered him a great deal more money than he was making at Oklahoma. Before the rumor was confirmed, President Cross, no great fan of Tatum or his coaching methods, decided to get rid of him, and offered the head coaching job to Bud Wilkinson, Tatum's assistant. Wilkinson asked for and received a four-year contract. Tatum then made his move, denying he'd ever planned to leave OU, and with a lot of support behind him from wealthy Sooner boosters demanded a ten-year contract from Cross. He also demanded total control over the athletic department. Tatum must have believed there was no way Cross could turn him down; after all, he had taken the team to the Citrus Bowl.

The battle between Tatum and Cross became a major issue in Oklahoma. Cross, to save face, offered Tatum a six-year contract but no control over the school's athletic program. Tatum refused to compromise and Cross turned to the Board of Regents for support. After some closed-door, backroom university politics, the board voted 4–3 to support Cross's compromise offer to Tatum. Tatum refused to accept it and left for Maryland, setting the stage for the Bud Wilkinson era.

From 1947 to 1963 Bud Wilkinson delivered everything ever imagined by state and school fathers. He turned a nation's attention from *The Grapes of Wrath* to the "Boomer Sooner" fight song. Until Barry Switzer arrived on the scene Bud Wilkinson was Oklahoma's greatest football coach and a state hero. He won 145 games, over 80 percent of those played in his 17 years as head coach. During one period, 1953–57, his teams had a 47-game winning streak. From 1948–1959 he won 12 straight Big 7 titles, not losing a single conference game from 1947 to 1959. By the time he left Oklahoma in 1963 there were many in the state prepared to support him for the United States Senate. Wilkinson overshadowed his teams and even his star players. There was nobody at OU more important than Bud Wilkinson.

When his new contract in 1949 was announced to be fifteen thousand dollars, a good deal of money back then, and more than the president of the university was earning, nobody was surprised or complained.

If everyone in the nation wasn't turned on to Oklahoma football, a whole state lived and breathed the Sooners. Almost every year the Wilkinson era gave them something to boast about. In 1947 they saw their first OU game on television as the Sooners whipped Detroit. In 1949, when Wilkinson's team beat Texas for the first time in nine years, 75,347 people showed up to watch the game in the Cotton Bowl. There were so many people wanting to see OU home games that the school enlarged Owen Field to seat fifty-five thousand. Even that wasn't big enough to hold the crowds when 60,145 fans turned out to see the game against Santa Clara.

It seemed that OU couldn't lose under Wilkinson. The first winning streak of thirty-five games finally ended with a loss in the Sugar Bowl, but in the Wilkinson era OU had its first Heisman Trophy winner—Billy Vessels, in 1952, and Outland Trophy winner—J.D. Roberts in 1953. Sweet revenge came to Cross and OU in 1953 when they beat Tatum and Maryland in the Orange Bowl. The Sooners were only prevented from going to the Orange Bowl in 1954 by an NCAA regulation prohibiting a team from going to the bowl two years in a row. Still, OU was undefeated that year. After ten years the University of Oklahoma had reached its goal of 1945—the state of Oklahoma was known by its football team.

Then there was the other Sooner tradition. Oklahoma was not winning all those football games because their students just happened to be the best players in the nation. Nor was Oklahoma, like several other football powers of the period, winning games by playing by the rules. But it wasn't until the early

102

fifties, when Walter Byers became NCAA head, that someone decided to see if American universities were playing fair.

For the first half of the century, although there were rules, nobody cared too much about enforcing them. Although the NCAA existed, most regulatory matters were handled by the separate athletic conferences. One obvious problem was that the conferences had different rules; there was no central control. Even if they'd had the same rules the system could never have worked, since members who sat on rules committees for the conferences came from schools that made up the conference. There was an understanding—you take care of my school and I'll take care of yours.

In 1951 the NCAA offices were moved from Chicago to Kansas City, and Walter Byers, a reporter and sportswriter, was named executive director. Byers took his position seriously, and within the first few years of his tenure, Kentucky, Arizona State, Michigan State, Notre Dame, Texas, and others were hit with probations for various violations. It was only a matter of time until Byers got around to Wilkinson and the University of Oklahoma. What he found sounded more like the University of Oklahoma I encountered.

By the early fifties the Big 6 had become the Big 7. The conference was strict in its rules about the recruitment of high-school seniors. OU coaches and school officials thought the rules were unfair, although they applied to all seven colleges equally, and decided to ignore them. OU reasoned that the rules were enforced differently in the next door neighbor Southwest Conference so they chose to follow the SWC example.

An OU coach by the name of Bill Jennings (OU head coaches rarely get their own hands dirty) approached an Oklahoma City accountant, Arthur Wood, a school alumnus, and asked him to provide money for the recruiting of high-school seniors. A passionate Sooner fan, Wood jumped at the opportunity to help the team. He provided the money and, as the NCAA would later learn after a long investigation, covered up the matter. It was to take five years to get at the truth.

The trouble for OU began in 1954 when Cross received a letter from Walter Byers asking questions about the school's recruitment of high-school football players. The letter was more inquiring than accusing. Cross was asked about the school's athletic policies, enforcement, and whether money to athletes ever came from outside the university.

Whatever Cross wrote in reply did not satisfy Byers, and the NCAA continued to investigate OU. On April 26, 1955, one year after Byers' letter to Cross, the NCAA found OU guilty of three violations. The evidence for their verdict came after questioning twenty-six athletes. OU was guilty of offering high-school athletes free education beyond their semesters of eligibility, paying medical bills for the families of athletes, and permitting "university patrons" to give them money and gifts.

The Sooners were placed on probation for two years, but allowed to play in bowl games. It was little more than token punishment, yet irate Sooner fans charged the NCAA with picking on only the better teams in the country. Although the incident happened thirty-five years ago it proves that nothing ever changes when it comes to Sooner boosters. When OU was placed on probation in 1988, the latest generation pointed their blaming fingers in every direction but at the athletic offices in Norman. In the 1954–1955 NCAA investigation of college athletic programs many successful schools were cleared of any violations, while some with losing records were found guilty. OU fans in 1955 didn't appreciate how lucky the school was when it came time for punishment. The school barely suffered compared to the University of Kentucky's basketball team, which was forced to disband for a year.

After the 1955 NCAA ruling Wilkinson and Cross must have

104

breathed a deep sigh of relief. It was like getting charged for driving without your registration, after you had stolen the car. The NCAA had dug, but not deep enough.

By the middle of 1957 Coach Bill Jennings and Coach Bud Wilkinson were not getting along too well. Things were great when the two were at Oklahoma, but Jennings was now the head coach at Nebraska; a bitter OU rival. Each man was familiar with the other's secrets, and so what happened wasn't surprising.

Wilkinson started it all by protesting the eligibility of two Nebraska freshmen. Rather than confront Jennings, Wilkinson sent a letter of inquiry to Nebraska's athletic director and a similar letter to a member of the faculty. It wasn't the accusation that bothered Jennings, but rather that Wilkinson went over his head. Jennings declared war.

The fight began with the battle of Monte Kiffin, a Nebraska high-school tackle both schools wanted for their teams. Jennings reasoned that Wilkinson had no right to enter Nebraska territory to recruit Kiffin, so he wrote a letter to Wilkinson. Wilkinson would later call the letter blackmail. Jennings would protest saying he was only trying to survive. Jennings wrote that he would turn over to the NCAA information about all the infractions he knew about while at OU.

Wilkinson challenged Jennings by telephoning him and asking him to come to Norman and testify to the NCAA. As for Wilkinson, he denied knowing of any infractions or knowing Arthur Wood and his fund for financing recruits. Jennings took Wilkinson up on it.

In the spring of 1959 Byers reopened the NCAA inquiry into OU's football program. His star witness before the infractions committee was Coach Jennings. The NCAA was most interested in Arthur Wood, the mysterious accountant from Oklahoma City. Cross did not wait for the NCAA hearings, and questioned Wood. He learned from Wood that there was a fund to help out the football team and that he handled the money, but denied that any University of Oklahoma alumni organization was involved. He claimed that the money he handled came only from individual supporters of the team. Wood swore to Cross that Jennings was the only coach to know about the fund. He minimized the situation by telling the school president that over the three years the fund was in existence no more than six thousand dollars had been collected. There is no record of whether or not Cross believed Wood, but it was what the president wanted to hear. True, there were violations of the recruitment rules, but no alumni organizations were involved or any coach but Jennings, and he was now in Nebraska. Maybe it was illegal to spend the money on high-school recruits, but after all it was only six thousand dollars over a three-year period.

Cross was satisfied that the matter was resolved, but Byers and the NCAA had a few more questions to be answered, especially of Arthur Wood. If everything Wood had told Cross was true, Byers said to Wood, why not open your books and let us verify it? Wood refused to allow the NCAA to look at his books. Although Byers had promised him that the investigation would be confidential, Wood claimed that allowing the NCAA to look at his books would be a violation of his professional ethics. Byers wasn't buying what Wood was selling, and in 1960 OU was placed on indefinite probation, including no television appearances and no bowl games.

In January 1961 the probation was lifted. Wood and Byers had met several times during the probation and eventually the NCAA was able to look at Wood's records, apparently satisfied that the penalty fit the infraction.

The probation and the scandal were indicators that the Wilkinson glory days were coming to an end. Even in Oklahoma times were a changin' in the sixties. During the 1959 season

106

THE LIFE AND CRIMES OF OKLAHOMA FOOTBALL

OU suffered its worst loss under Wilkinson, Northwestern crushing them 45–13. Also, 1959 was the year Wilkinson lost his first game to a Big 7 team, falling to Nebraska 25–21. In 1960 Wilkinson had his first losing season at Oklahoma with an embarrassing 3–6–1 record. Later, and it's interesting in light of what happened at OU in the mid-eighties, Wilkinson admitted that he had fallen behind the times in the recruitment of high-school players. President Cross thought that his coach had lost enthusiasm for coaching.

If Cross was right about Wilkinson losing his enthusiasm for coaching, there were good reasons for it. The long NCAA investigation into OU's recruitment practices came very close to damaging his squeaky clean image, and he knew that the NCAA would be looking over his shoulder in the future. Also, after the 1960 season Oklahomans realized that Bud Wilkinson was human; he could field losing teams. He was to go to one more bowl game, but only to be blown out by Alabama 48–21 in the Orange Bowl. Perhaps, most difficult of all, it was the sixties, and there was a new kind of student coming to play football at America's colleges. Students were not only rebelling against the Vietnam War and racial discrimination, but authority in general was challenged. It was Bud Wilkinson's misfortune to be the coach of the most extreme example of this type of player, the appropriately named Joe Don Looney.

Every college and professional coach identified Looney as an extraordinary running back. They were right about that, but they were mistaken when they thought they could handle Joe Don. Only in the sixties could a player like Joe Don Looney appear on a football field. By the time he had drifted to OU he had already been enrolled at three other colleges in the past four years. Coaches would recall that, at times, Joe Don would have a faraway look in his eye, as if his body were here, but his mind on another planet. It was impossible for Joe Don to concentrate on football for an entire game. His potential was great, but no coach, not even Bud Wilkinson, could motivate him to fulfill it. Inevitably, the day came when he decided to leave Oklahoma. Wilkinson invited Joe Don to his home to try and change his player's mind. It was reported that the conversation went like this:

Wilkinson: "Do you like Norman?"

Looney: "Oh, yes, Coach. I like it very much."

Wilkinson: "Do you like the University of Oklahoma?"

Looney: "Oh, yes. It's the best school I've ever attended."

Wilkinson: "Do you like the boys you play with?"

Looney: "I sure do. I've been around a lot of teams but these are the best boys I've ever been with."

Wilkinson: "Well, then, Joe Don, why in the world are you talking about leaving?"

Looney: "I can't stand going to class. I don't have time to do my laundry."

In 1962 Wilkinson dismissed Joe Don from the team. But Wilkinson had decided to leave OU, and in January 1964 he made it official. Wishing to name his successor, Wilkinson remained OU athletic director and demanded that the school hire his line coach and friend Gomer Jones as head coach. At the same time Wilkinson had announced his intention to run for the United States Senate as a Republican. He may have been a great football coach, but one has to question his political savvy. Here was the announced Republican candidate for the United States Senate demanding that the Democratic Board of Regents hire the man to replace him. It would have been one thing for Bud Wilkinson, head coach of the University of Oklahoma, to make demands, but once he announced his retirement, he was just another Republican in a year that the GOP would prefer to forget. The Board of Regents refused to name Jones as new head coach and, angrily, Wilkinson resigned from his job as athletic director.

What happened after Wilkinson's resignation is another example of what counts in Oklahoma. A public outcry followed, demanding that Gomer Jones be named head coach at OU. After all, who else but Bud Wilkinson knew what was best for Sooner football? The media didn't miss a beat, and the Board of Regents gave in. The irony is that Wilkinson was badly beaten in his race for the senate. He may have been able to get the public off its asses to name OU's football coach, but when it came to politics it was ho hum time.

The mid-sixties were bad times for Sooner football fans. Gomer Jones proved to be a bust, and after a 9–11–1 record he was replaced in 1966 by Jim MacKenzie from Kentucky. MacKenzie never had a chance to turn the program around at OU. After a so-so year in 1966 he dropped dead of a heart attack at the age of thirty-five. He is best remembered by OU fans as the man who brought Barry Switzer to Norman as an assistant coach.

MacKenzie's replacement was Chuck Fairbanks. The future New England Patriot's coach quickly returned the Sooners to the winning ways of Bud Wilkinson. As head coach for six years at OU, Fairbanks had a 52–15–1 record. In five of those years he took the Sooners to bowl games. He elevated Barry Switzer to offensive coordinator to help implement the wishbone offense at OU.

OU players enjoyed the relaxed atmosphere created by Fairbanks, who recognized that college athletes were a different breed. This was to count most in Fairbanks' desire to bring more blacks to Norman. He cared little about dress codes and wasn't bothered when his players had a good old time. Like Switzer, winning was what it was all about for Chuck Fairbanks.

But there were problems and controversy during his years at Norman. The NCAA was watching OU, and in 1971 the university received a "private reprimand" over the old issue of high-school recruitment. The reprimand amounted to little, but in 1973 the NCAA cracked down and OU was put on probation once again.

The NCAA charged that the high-school transcripts of Kerry Jackson, OU's first black quarterback, and Mike Phillips, a non-varsity player, had been altered. Once again it was an assistant coach who was to take the fall. The athletic department claimed that the only Sooner staff member who knew about the alteration was assistant coach Bill Michael. Michael was forced to resign. Later, Jackson's high-school coach was implicated in the scheme to make the all-state player eligible for college.

Oklahomans were up in arms over the incident, not because OU cheated to get the two players into the school, but because the university was going to be punished for it. OU was forced to forfeit eight games that Jackson played in 1972, including the Sugar Bowl. The school was placed on two years' probation and prohibited from television appearances. Oklahoma's governor protested the action, and two OU boosters from Oklahoma City went so far as to initiate a class-action suit against the NCAA.

Not everyone felt that OU was treated harshly by the NCAA. There were college coaches who thought OU was lucky that the NCAA kept its tradition of never digging as deep as it should. Baylor Coach Teaff said at the time: "If the Republican party comes out of their investigation [Watergate] in Washington as good as Oklahoma did theirs, they will be in the White House forever."

BARRY SWITZER

The probation didn't bother Fairbanks because in 1973 he was out of Norman and into the NFL. The man who inherited his job and OU's probation was Barry Switzer. The Sooners under Switzer were incredible. As head coach he had no losses in his first thirty games. From 1973 to 1988, OU was nationally ranked every year but one. Switzer's teams won more games than those of Wilkinson—157, compared to 145 for Wilkinson, and a winning percentage of .837. Only three times in his sixteen years did the Sooners lose more than three games in any year. He went undefeated in his first two seasons. Under Switzer OU has won three national championships and gone to twelve bowl games, winning eight of them. He would have gone to two more bowls had OU not been on probation.

Barry Switzer grew up dirt poor in Crossett, Arkansas. His father worked in a shipyard, but Switzer loved to boast about Frank Switzer's career as a bootlegger. In fact, his father was doing time in a state prison while Switzer was attending the University of Arkansas. Both in Crossett, and nearby El Dorado, the Switzer family lived without a telephone; not until Barry was in junior high school was there any electricity in the house.

At the University of Arkansas, Switzer played center and linebacker on some great football teams coached by Frank Broyles. Before his senior year, Switzer's mother, who had been ill for several years, committed suicide. Ten years later, in 1969, his father got caught in a love triangle, and one of his two female admirers, finding him in bed with the other, emptied a shotgun into him and the woman. He died en route to the hospital.

In 1961, while Switzer was serving in the army and contem-

111

plating a business career after his discharge, Frank Broyles asked him to return to Arkansas and coach the freshman Razorbacks. Switzer missed football and gladly accepted the two-hundred-dollar-a-month job. When his friend Jim MacKenzie, an assistant under Broyles, left to accept the head coaching job at OU, Switzer was asked to join him and become offensive line coach. When MacKenzie died after his one season at OU, new head coach Chuck Fairbanks asked Switzer to stay with the team and become offensive coordinator. Switzer, more than Fairbanks, was responsible for installing the wishbone and making it one of the most explosive offenses in college football.

Switzer worked under Fairbanks for seven years, the last three as his number one assistant. If Fairbanks did not suddenly shock Oklahomans by going to the NFL, Switzer would probably have landed a head coaching job at some other major university. He was too ambitious to remain an assistant for too long. Switzer was also ambitious in his business dealings. In 1980 he got involved in a get-rich-quick illegal pyramid scheme. During the same year he was reprimanded for soliciting business by using university stationery. A few years after the pyramid scheme he was in trouble again when the SEC filed suit against him and twelve businessmen for insider trading in an energy firm called Phoenix Resources. Switzer's excuse to the SEC in explaining how he earned ninety-seven thousand dollars in trading stock shares was that he had overheard information about the company at a track meet. An investigation also revealed that Switzer had purchased 880,000 shares of an Oklahoma drug company. The value of his shares was ninety-two thousand dollars. Switzer never explained how he accomplished all of this on his fifty-six thousand dollar annual salary from OU.

Barry Switzer is a man who was able to get away with things because of how he was perceived. For a few years I shared that

112

perception. Before I got to OU I thought that if you had to choose a man to be senator or governor, you would want Barry Switzer. He was the most successful man in the state. The people in Oklahoma knew of his business dealings. They knew of his marital problems and his other women, including the wife of an assistant coach. They knew that and more, but were never much concerned about any of it.

Nothing Switzer did bothered them because year in and year out he won football games. Switzer catered to the ego of Oklahomans. The University of Oklahoma's football team was the biggest deal in the state, a football power that wasn't celebrated only in the Southwest but was one of the most successful football programs in America. There are fifty states and I don't know how many universities. That the Sooners were considered one of the best among them was an ego trip for all the people of Oklahoma. They could go to any state in the nation, know nothing about football, but be able to brag about the OU team. This power trip was provided by Barry Switzer.

When I was in high school watching OU football games on television, I got the same feeling from Barry Switzer on the sidelines as I did from Bear Bryant, Tom Landry, or Mike Ditka. They were special people who seemed more than human, people I couldn't dream of associating with on an everyday basis. The biggest reason people in Lawton started to court me when I was being recruited by OU was that I would be playing for Barry Switzer. When he came after me it was almost like being asked by God to play football for him.

Barry Switzer played a psychological game when he first came down to Lawton to visit me, in his fur coat and with almost every championship ring he had won on his fingers. I was seventeen, very impressed with material things, and had never known anyone who owned a fur coat—and here came Barry Switzer wearing beaver. Fucking beaver! There was something amazing about it to me. Switzer knew how to toy with his recruits. They saw the flash, and asked, "Why wouldn't I want that myself?"

I thought he was a great recruiter, and really sold his program. He was like General Eisenhower talking to you about joining the army. You wanted to join Switzer at OU because they never would have been the football power they were without him as the general. But Barry Switzer's greatest selling point was that he knew how to talk to minorities. Black teenagers and their parents related to him because they were aware of all the problems he'd had while growing up, and that his household wasn't perfect like those white families on television.

Switzer did not come from what I thought of as a white family, one where the father was well-paid and wore a nice suit to work every morning, and the kids got cars or motorcycles when they turned sixteen. Switzer fought for what he had. He could come into your house and not feel uptight with your parents. A lot of white athletes ridiculed him because of his relationship with the black players. They thought that if you were white, you weren't one of Switzer's pets. He got a great deal of teasing about it, but he still did more for blacks than white athletes.

Maybe some of it was patronizing, but I felt that Switzer understood that the black players on the team came from backgrounds that made college life more difficult. Most of them did not get any help from home and needed outside assistance and motivation. That's why Switzer had differences with the NCAA. He identified with the black players and their handicaps. He thought that the NCAA was made up of people who had never experienced hard times. They were the people whose families could afford to send them to college, law school, medical school. They did not have to earn their way. Black students did, and they earned it by playing college ball.

114

THE LIFE AND CRIMES OF OKLAHOMA FOOTBALL

Switzer thought that the NCAA rules ignored the black reality, especially when it came to Proposition 48. Part of his opposition to Proposition 48 was self-serving. The rule was aimed at black athletes, and coaches who recruited mostly blacks would suffer the most. But Switzer saw the entrance examination as limiting opportunities for black athletes, as a message that because you're not as educated as the next guy, you can't have a career in sports. He understood the cultural bias in the test, and thought that Proposition 48 had more to do with racism than concern for education.

Black athletes could not write home for a couple of hundred dollars whenever they needed it. Switzer, having visited the families of his black players, knew that they were struggling for their own survival. He had a good heart and couldn't turn his back on people. He frequently violated NCAA regulations by giving his own money to needy players. He also was aware of boosters violating the rules through their financial aid to players, and was responsible for this abuse by allowing the booster network to exist; but Switzer was never a person to worry much about rules.

He was an open, wild coach. To me, he was the outlaw of college football. He was the leader of the black hoodlums who made up the team. He drank hard, loved to run around with women, and his players followed his example. He could out-party any of us. He enjoyed good wine and Scotch. When we drank with him, he put us under the table. At first, I looked up to him for it; later, his behavior puzzled me. It seemed weird that a man more than twice my age was carrying on as he was, going out with women younger than my girlfriends.

During my years at OU, my feelings about Switzer changed. When I was recruited I thought he was *the* football genius of America. But it wasn't long before I noticed how little coaching he actually did. I used to explain his absence from the practice

115

field by thinking he was behind closed doors plotting our next victory. This wasn't the case. At OU, under Switzer, it was the assistant coaches who shaped the football team. I'm sure that Switzer and his coaches got together to discuss strategy, but all of the team's success cannot be credited to its head coach. By the time I got to OU Switzer had too many outside interests to be focused on football. The coaches carried the load for him; in fact, there were times when the assistants thought that Switzer was getting in their way. There were meetings conducted by quarterback coach Jim Donnan when Switzer would make surprise visits. He would start to tell us things opposite to what Donnan had been saying and then leave the room. The players would look at one another in confusion, and Donnan would tell us to forget what we had heard and do what he had been teaching us. We developed a routine: when Switzer talked, we'd listen politely, and when he left, we'd turn our attention to the assistant.

On the other hand, Switzer was a great motivator. He knew how to hype us up for games, a public relations man who knew when and how to push our buttons. He was a supreme bullshit artist and always knew what to say to get us to believe in ourselves. It was when he went into his bullshit mode off the field that I lost respect for him.

He wanted us to think that he was one of the guys. He liked it when we bumped into him at a bar and shared a table with him. He tried to show that he was one of us. He would curse more than any of us—"Fuck this. Fuck that." He thought that by calling someone a "fucking turd" he made us feel more comfortable with him, and that we would think of him as cool because he could use more fucks in a sentence than any of his players. When drunk he was at his worst. He was not the Barry Switzer of television appearances or the Barry Switzer of national press conferences.

116

THE LIFE AND CRIMES OF OKLAHOMA FOOTBALL

He is a complex man, and it has been difficult for me to fully understand him. I know that he cared for his players, black and white, but I doubt that he felt what his supporters claim. Barry Switzer did not love us; more often than not he only tolerated us. He got his position and respect in Oklahoma because of his winning record on the football field. He needed his players, and as long as our behavior did not force his hand, everything was cool.

What he could not tolerate was a player outshining him. When I was at OU, Brian Bosworth was the latest example, but the player who threatened Switzer the most was Marcus Dupree. For his first eight years as head coach everything had gone Barry Switzer's way; after a great 1980 season and trouncing Florida State in the Orange Bowl, the Sooners were facing a rebuilding year. Switzer, looking beyond the 1981 season, entered the contest to recruit the most highly sought after high-school player in history, Marcus Dupree.

There wasn't a college coach in the country who could not have used a back as big and fast as Dupree. Switzer turned on his charm with Dupree's family and was able to recruit him. Dupree had to sit out the mediocre 1981 season at OU, and Switzer looked forward to the following year when Marcus would turn it around for the team. Switzer thought so highly of Dupree's ability that he was willing to get rid of the wishbone to accomodate the power and speed of the big back. Dupree arrived in Norman with much fanfare, but Switzer wanted to keep Marcus in his place and quickly changed his attitude; he came down hard on Marcus in practice and in comments to the media. Marcus was not the type of player who tried hard all the time, and Switzer, at first, took out his disappointment on the team. He began to crack down on team discipline, something he had never been known to do. He thought Dupree was going

117

to make OU a winner, but in 1982 and 1983 they were again mediocre, even with Marcus.

Oklahoma's media, not unlike its citizens, are frontrunners, and began to question Switzer's coaching ability. They quickly forgot the previous eight great seasons. At the same time the media was attacking Switzer, Dupree was being hailed as the second coming of Red Grange. Switzer was frustrated and angry because of his team's poor performances, and directed his feelings toward Marcus Dupree. Switzer missed no opportunity to criticize his running back, claiming that he was out of shape, missed too many practices, etc.

Typically, Switzer showed no concern that his top recruit was having academic problems. Dupree rarely went to class, and one school counselor remarked, after Dupree left OU, that had he stayed he would have flunked out. If Dupree had stayed on, Switzer would have had to explain how his player was able to secure a nine thousand dollar loan to buy a new Oldsmobile. Dupree had no known source of income. Switzer did not care about Marcus Dupree's problems. He couldn't stand the public and media attention focused on him. He wanted the player put in his place.

He never let up on Dupree. Finally, Dupree had had it at OU and decided that OU and Barry Switzer were not for him. He left Norman during the '83 season and later enrolled at Southern Mississippi University. After a few months he decided to try professional football and signed with the New Orleans Breakers of the USFL, but his was a short professional career. Marcus Dupree injured his knee and disappeared from football.

I will never sort out my feelings about Barry Switzer, but for better or worse he has left his mark on my life. I only wish that when I went to play for him in 1986 I had understood that he was a man, not the god that we boys at Oklahoma were given to think he was.

On the other hand, there are some players who see Switzer no differently than when they were seventeen-year-old recruits. No matter what happened during the years they played under him, Barry Switzer remains a god.

Jamelle Holieway

Barry Switzer is a man who knows how to deal with problems. He doesn't put off things and makes decisions right then and there. The man is under incredible pressure to win; I would hate to be in his position and have to produce great teams every year. I liked him. He was cool. To me he was friend, father, and coach. He helped me in many ways and I am very grateful for the opportunity he gave me to be his starting quarterback in my freshman year. He had many critics when he did that and I'm happy I proved him right. As far as what happened in 1989, it can't be changed. Switzer can't be blamed for everything that went wrong.

I'M A SOONER

Damn, I'm a Sooner. I couldn't believe it that August morning when they handed me the uniform with the number 6 on the jersey. I had asked the equipment manager for 1, the number I had worn in high school, but Eric Mitchell, another OU quarterback, had been given it. I didn't feel bad settling for 6, the number my hero Thomas Lott had worn when he played for OU. No matter what I had on my mind it disappeared in the thrill of being where I was. It was the proudest moment of my life. I didn't know it at the time, and I guess it was a kind of omen, but being a Sooner also meant being a bit of a cheat.

When Oklahoma became a United States territory, the government made land available for pennies. The demand was great, and to keep order the authorities established a specific date before settlers could stake their claims. Naturally, there were those who wanted to get a jump on their fellow settlers, and went out to stake their claims before the official date. They became known as "sooners," as in getting there sooner than the other guy. It had a better ring to it than cheater. In Norman I was to meet many present day sooners.

I couldn't wait to get settled at school. For the last week or so at home Rudy had been making my life miserable. My father was forgiving about the incident in Tulsa, but Rudy took it as one more opportunity to settle whatever grievances she had with my mother. Before I left, my father talked to me about why he put up with Rudy and didn't make waves. In failing health, soon to be diagnosed with cancer, he didn't have the strength to fight her. He was getting older, and was frightened to leave Rudy and live on his own. My father believed that Rudy's un-

121

pleasantness was her way of paying him back for all the times he had cheated on her. Taking my side in any battle with her, he feared, could cause her to ask him to leave the house. It was better, he said, to go with the flow.

The first order of business for any college freshman is to find out who your roommate is. The policy at OU is for the athletic office to make all room assignments for the players. They're pretty flexible about it, and it's not too difficult to make changes. I was assigned to live with James Goode, a freshman defensive end, but over the summer I'd become good friends with Artie Guess, another all-state player from Oklahoma. Artie had learned that his roommate was going to be Bernard Hall, a highly touted quarterback from Detroit. In fact, Hall and I were expected to compete for backup quarterback to Jamelle Holieway. Before arriving on campus, Artie and I called the athletic office and received permission to room together.

When potential recruits visit the OU campus, one of the highlights of the trip is Bud Wilkinson House, "Bud Hall." Bud Hall is impressive, and for seventeen-year-old teenagers from poor homes, it is everything big-time football is supposed to be about. Each dorm unit has a living-room area with a small entryway that has a sink and large mirror on one wall and a bathroom on the other. Beyond is a large bedroom with two beds, two closets, and two chests of drawers. Outside the bedroom is a walkway, or balcony, that overlooks the stadium and campus. We referred to the balcony as the "freak area"—the vantage point to view the steady stream of women on campus.

Unfortunately for many who decide to attend OU, there's a surprise waiting when they arrive: freshmen players don't live at Bud Hall but in rundown Jones Hall, which is one of the older dorms on campus and can be a disappointing sight on your first day of school. Each player shares a small room and a community bathroom. I'd been warned before I arrived, but it was funny to look at some of the guys' faces when they learned where they would be living. The coaches who do the recruiting know where the freshmen will live, but unless asked they don't reveal this fact.

The day the freshmen players arrive on campus is news in Oklahoma. The press and television crews are on hand to interview the players, looking for future Sooner stars. Some freshmen come to school with more hype than others. Among us, the player receiving the most attention was Bernard Hall. In Detroit Bernard had been the number two high-school quarterback in the nation, and at OU he was being treated as heir to the throne of Jamelle Holieway. There were even some who thought that Bernard would beat Jamelle out of his job that year. I took a backseat to Bernard that day. Also, in Oklahoma, where most of the players come from two or three adjoining states, it's unusual to have a player from as far away as Detroit. The first time I looked at Bernard I knew that he was not going to be OU's quarterback that year or any year. He was too big, slow, and dumb to run the wishbone.

The wishbone is a distinct, high-scoring offense that requires quality athletes to run the ball. The quarterback is the most important tool in operating the wishbone. Everything is based on his athletic and mental abilities. The average size for a wishbone quarterback is five foot ten and under, and 170–190 pounds. A wishbone quarterback takes a lot of pounding because he is moving or running with the ball on every play. He must possess speed and quickness, not a great passing arm. Great NFL quarterbacks—Steve Walsh, John Elway, Troy Aikman—probably would not be able to take the beatings wishbone quarterbacks have to suffer. Wishbone quarterbacks are more like running backs. In fact, at OU, quarterbacks and running backs are about the same size. Speed and explosiveness are everything, and watching OU play was like observing a

Fourth of July celebration, anxiously waiting for another rocket to take off. It seems that most great wishbone quarterbacks and running backs are black, and at OU the coaches said, "If he's not black, don't bother recruiting him."

Basically, the wishbone is a double or triple option offense. The fullback lines up three feet behind the quarterback and the running backs stand behind the fullback, hands equal to his heels. Although plays are called in the huddle, the quarterback will frequently audible, or change the play, when he goes to the line of scrimmage and sees how the defense is set. For example, we would call "14-5 TED" in the huddle, a triple option where the quarterback can hand off to the fullback, running backs, or keep it himself. If the quarterback chooses to give the ball to the fullback, it will depend on the position of the defensive tackle. If it seems as if he is staying inside and keying on the fullback, the quarterback pulls the ball and looks to a running back to hand off to. If the defensive tackle chooses to move outside, the quarterback hands off to the fullback. It may sound simple, but the quarterback has only split seconds to decide what he is going to do with the ball.

Because the quarterback is changing most plays at the line of scrimmage, at OU we kept our audible codes simple. Even numbers meant the play was going to the right and odd numbers to the left. Color codes were used at the line of scrimmage to indicate a play was being changed. Red and green were "live colors," meaning there was a new play; blue was a decoy to run with the play called in the huddle. The codes also let the linemen know who they were to block on a specific play.

The first thing I looked for when I walked up to the line of scrimmage was how the defensive front line stacked up. The play in the huddle may have been "18-6," a double option to the running backs. The fullback was there to block. However, when I got to the line, if I noticed that the defense was shifted to the right, the direction of the play, I changed the play to "19-6," and ran it to the left side, or I would say: "Set, Red 14-5 TED, Red 14-5 TED, Go," and we would run the triple option with the tight end blocking the opponent's defensive end.

Repetition is the key to learning the wishbone. We would run the same plays so often at practice I began to see them in my sleep. In class my mind would drift off and I would be thinking and seeing shifting defenses. I practiced until it became instinctual. When I walked out on the playing field it was almost automatic.

In fact, I wasn't worried that summer about anyone beating me; including Eric Mitchell, who was also looking to take Jamelle's job away. I had made up my mind that for the first week of practice I was going to go out there and do my thing. The first week of summer practice is about the only time a freshman gets an opportunity to impress the coaches. Once the varsity players arrive everyone's attention is focused on them. The importance of the freshmen's early arrival is so that they can begin to learn the wishbone offense. Also, the coaches don't want you totally lost when the varsity does arrive.

When practice began there was still uncertainty about where I was going to play. Bobby Proctor was urging Switzer to play me as a defensive back. It was only after our first scrimmage, when I played quarterback, that Switzer came to talk to me. "Charles, you're going to be our extra quarterback," he said. "With you at quarterback we can move Eric Mitchell to running back. You'll back up Jamelle, but you're our future quarterback." It was no big deal when Switzer told me this; actually, I thought of it as just talk. Only a week earlier he had told me that whether I played quarterback or defensive back, I was going to be red-shirted, that is, I would sit out my freshman year.

Jim Donnan
Quarterback coach at OU

Coming out of high school, Charles was a guy that we felt had tremendous potential. We were worried about his being so small, how much of a beating he could take, but we knew that he had such great speed to go on top of his quickness that he was going to be a player, if not as a quarterback, then certainly as a defensive back. He had a lot of self-confidence. He always felt that he could get the job done and I always felt that this was one of his better traits.

I think Jamelle was stronger and more durable. He had similar quickness to Charles, but Charles had a lot more straightaway speed. They were both good field generals, they both understood football. Jamelle probably had a stronger arm. Charles was fairly accurate, but you know, he never had a lot of good passing games. In practice you thought he would be fine, but we really never did throw the ball enough for him to get in a groove. I think we could have developed him as a passer.

As a redshirt the only football I would be playing that year would be at practice, but this only made me more determined to learn everything I could to be ready the following season to go after Jamelle's job. Jamelle had experience, and because of it there were two things he could do better: read defenses and run the wishbone. I had seen him at games and at practice, and there was nothing he could do that I couldn't do better. After preparing for my classes, I would stay up three or four hours every evening studying defenses. I was committed.

I demonstrated my commitment on the practice field, in scrimmage against the varsity defense. I wanted to show what I had against the number one college defense in America. All I was to them was "freshman meat." There was a rule that they were to take it easy and not hurt the quarterback, but those animals never obeyed it. In my first scrimmage, I had optioned down the line, looking to cut inside when I saw an opening. Boom, the hole closed as fast as it had opened and I got hit with what felt like a Mack truck. I probably weighed a hundred fifty-five and all of it went flying back five yards, my helmet covering my face and my eyes rolled up into my head. When my senses returned to this world I looked up into the eyes of the modern day road warrior, Brian Bosworth, "The Boz." He stood over me with a grin on his face that said: "Welcome to college football."

It was a big change from high-school football. In high school there are a few talented players on each team, but in college they are all talented and know what they are doing on the field. In high school, if I made a mistake, my speed would compensate for the error. The first time I made the wrong cut in a college scrimmage, Rickey Dixon grabbed me from behind and threw me to the ground. I learned fast not to hesitate before making a move.

Since I was small for a football player, it was important that I show no fear. The defense would hit hard, but I would always get up and smile at them like "Hey, no big deal." When Boz hit me, I got up and let him know, "You ain't no fucking superstar to me." You play a lot of head games in college football.

Off the field, I liked Brian Bosworth. In fact, even though he beat the crap out of me, I liked him on the field. Brian had his own style and was an original. When he played and was on television, or in front of a crowd, he became "The Boz." The character took over: sunglasses, striped bandanna, tight T-shirt with muscles bulging out, saying whatever was on his mind. He loved being the center of attention.

Off the field and away from the cameras and crowds, Brian was a different person—very private, avoiding intimate conversations, protective of his friends. He helped me adjust to college football life. Like Keith Jackson, he advised me about the advantages of being a Sooner, especially when dealing with alumni and boosters. He told me to remember that although there was a great deal I could get from them, they were not my friends, but fans.

Classes did not begin until the second week of September, so there was plenty of time to kill and have some fun. Money wasn't much of a problem for me since I was receiving almost six hundred dollars a month in government benefits because of my stepfather's death. Most important to me were women, and when the other students began to arrive on campus, it was as if I'd died and gone to heaven. I had never seen so many attractive women and it wasn't difficult meeting them. Artie and I ran together, and whenever there was a party, we were there. We would hang out at the dorms waiting for the coeds to drive up so we could help with their luggage. Artie and I were perfect gentlemen, carrying trunks and cartons. When we finished, he or I would get into the car with one of the women and drive to town for beer. All we had to say was that we were on the football team, and we got to know plenty of coeds. We became instant "Mr. Populars." It was fun, and a lot more free and independent than living at home.

Once classes started there was no curfew, but women were not allowed in our rooms past midnight. I don't think any of the freshmen thought twice about breaking the rule. There was a Resident Assistant on each floor at Jones Hall, but he was having too much fun with us to care about enforcing the rules. Nothing very wild went on in Jones Hall, unlike across the road in Bud Hall, but I think this had more to do with the freshmen players still unsure of themselves than any concern about acting like gentlemen.

One promise I had made to my family and myself that first

128

I beat brother Harold to the ball . . . but he made me pay for it.

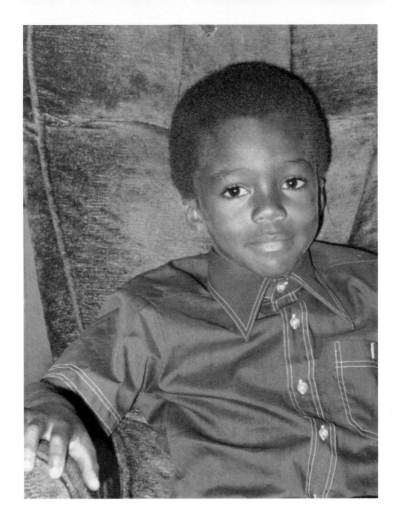

Here I am at five. Now, that's a face that will one day break a lot of hearts.

Charles knows baseball.

Kori visiting me for Thanksgiving Day 1989 at the federal prison camp in Big Springs, Texas.

Kori Kaubin. My Miss Oklahoma.

The two bad black bears. Jamelle Holieway and me, Christmas 1987.

Me and Bernard Hall at an Oklahoma club.

Kori, Mom and Sister Yolanda visiting me in prison.

Big brother Anthony with a firm grip on his teenage brothers, Harold and me.

Jerry Parks celebrating Christmas before the Orange Bowl in Miami, 1988.

Partying in Bud Hall. Ted Long (front), Kim (left), Koquice (center), Monica (right), Artie Guest (rear left), Cedric Davenport (rear center) and me.

Me and Jamelle visiting a teenage patient at Children's Hospital, 1987.

Barry Switzer wearing the ring, the number one reason, that hooked me into going to OU. (Copyright 1988, The Oklahoma Publishing Company.)

Bernard Hall and Nigel Clay with a lot on their minds; like spending the next ten years in prison. (Copyright 1989, The Oklahoma Publishing Company.)

(Opposite page, top) Glen Bell with his attorney Charles Cox. Glen did not take the stand and was acquitted of rape charges. (Copyright 1989, The Oklahoma Publishing Company.)

(Opposite page, bottom) Jerry Parks tries to tell his side of shooting his pal Zarak Peters. (Copyright 1989, The Oklahoma Publishing Company.)

The "Boz". One picture tells a thousand words. In Brian's case, a million words. (Copyright 1986, The Oklahoma Publishing Company.)

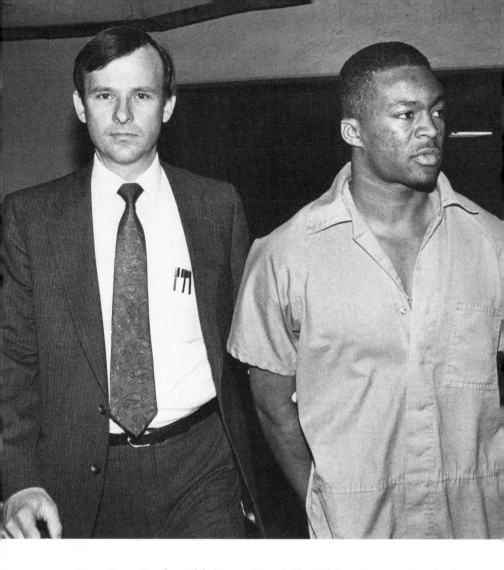

Here I am in the Oklahoma City Jail wishing it was all a bad dream. (Copyright 1989, The Oklahoma Publishing Company.)

Acting President David Swank, Athletic Director Donnie Duncan and Coach Barry Switzer meeting the press. Three men in a tub trying to explain how the baby went down the drain with the water. (Copyright 1988, The Oklahoma Publishing Company.)

Jamelle Holieway's last hurrah in a losing cause against Clemson in the 1989 Citrus Bowl.

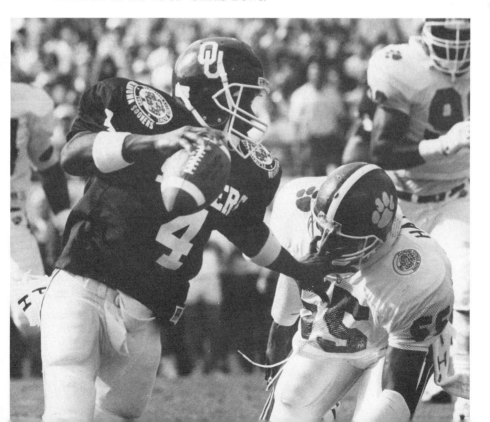

(Page 16) That's me leaving all defenders in the dust. (Copyright 1988, The Oklahoma Publishing Company.)

year was that I was going to get a good education. I was not going to take the gut courses the athletic office enrolled several of the players in—Theory of Coaching, Aerobics, Football Strategy, etc. I took the same course work as any other incoming student—Political Science, Anthropology, Finite Math, Astronomy, and Science. I put in as many hours studying my textbooks as I did OU's playbook.

Throughout the first semester I don't think I missed a day in class. In the back of my head was the idea of being the ideal student/athlete. I had already met guys who went through four years of college playing ball but were unable to read and write. I did everything right my first semester, and was proud to finish with a better than three point index. But this didn't last too long. Everything that I was learning was not in the classroom. I was also getting an education in how to be a football player at the University of Oklahoma.

For the first month or so, the freshmen players pretty much stayed among themselves. The varsity players weren't aloof, but I think we were still intimidated by them. Keith Jackson was the first varsity player I got close to; he wasn't simply an All-American football player but a great human being. It was Keith who took me under his wing, introduced me to "Norman society," and instructed me on the ins and outs of campus life. I think if he hadn't graduated I might never have gotten into trouble. Keith Jackson was a leader like Jamelle and Bosworth, but quieter and understated. He had many other interests besides football, including music, and he played the cello in the school symphony.

Keith was a big guy who often reminded me of the lion in *The Wizard of Oz:* tough and a hardass on the field, but a soft-spoken gentleman everywhere else. The alumni and boosters were crazy about him. Unlike Jamelle, Keith acted with them the way they thought a star should behave. He wasn't cocky or flamboyant, and many of the boosters enjoyed his company more than they did Jamelle's. Keith told me that when Jamelle arrived in Norman he was like a mouse. It wasn't until Troy Aikman broke his ankle in the Miami game, and he beat out Eric Mitchell for the starting quarterback job, that Jamelle began to carry on.

Keith taught me all I needed to know about "freaking"— dealing with boosters and alumni when you attain a certain level of popularity and stature and they want to court you. ("Freaking" was also a term we used when we went out looking for women.) Freaking with boosters and alumni meant they showered you with gifts and money, and sometimes drugs. Former OU running back Stanley Wilson claimed that his cocaine habit was fed by OU boosters. Keith's attitude was that when you are offered gifts from the boosters always show some appreciation and never abuse their generosity. Through him I met many boosters in my first year at OU and I was able to watch how he handled them. He didn't always have his hand out because he believed that he would be able to return to the boosters after his career was over and, should he need it, they would help him. I watched Keith do favors for boosters and receive nothing in return. An example of this occurred when he introduced me to Jackie Cooper, one of the first boosters I met in Oklahoma City.

Cooper owned several automobile dealerships in the Oklahoma City-Norman area. Keith invited me to meet Cooper at one of his car shows and to have dinner and drinks afterward. He told me that Cooper might or might not give me anything for being one of the OU players making an appearance at the show, but that down the road he would do things for me. Keith introduced me to Cooper as he always did: "I want you to meet Oklahoma's next great quarterback."

Keith and I were pretty wasted by the time we got to Jackie

THE LIFE AND CRIMES OF OKLAHOMA FOOTBALL

Cooper's place. We had stopped off on our way at a place called "F.O.P.," where we had drinks with Sugar Smith, a detective, and several other Oklahoma City police officers. When I walked into Cooper's I saw Barry Switzer and tried to sober up. I think Switzer was wasted by that time and didn't notice my condition, at least he didn't say anything.

After the show Jackie Cooper invited Keith and me to dinner at Juniors, a fancy restaurant in the city. There was a party of twelve at the table and Cooper bought dinner and drinks for all. I was underage and not allowed to drink, but every time the waiter asked Cooper ordered two drinks and gave one of them to me. We did a great deal of drinking and Cooper bent my ear by telling me how fortunate I was to be playing for Barry Switzer and that I was going to be taken care of while at OU. I was getting shitfaced and thought about seeing Switzer earlier in the evening. I told Keith that I wanted to leave and got up and went to the bathroom. Cooper joined me in the men's room and asked me if I had a car. When I said I didn't he said, "Well, why don't you get my phone number from Keith and give me a call? You come down to my lot and pick something out. And don't worry, we'll work something out."

I wasn't sure about what he meant by working it out, but I figured that I had nothing to lose by calling, so in a few days I did, and made arrangements to visit the lot. Cooper seemed happy to see me and we discussed how I would pay for a car. I knew it would be expensive because he had classy cars on the lot—BMWs, Mercedes, Jaguars. The car had to be bought in someone else's name, usually a family member. Cooper said this was done because as a student I wasn't working and couldn't show any income. Once that was arranged the bank would approve a loan, but he would have someone take care of the payments. This was the first time I'd heard of anything like

131

that, but it was something I would see several times while I was at OU.

Just as in Lawton, I was picky about the kind of car I wanted. I wasn't interested in an old Chevy, not with all those BMWs on the lot. When I told Cooper the type of car I wanted, he warned against it. He explained to me that the boosters were concerned about the NCAA checking on gifts to students, and even if someone in my family had the car in their name a BMW would be too conspicuous. He told me that there were plenty of OU supporters in Oklahoma who would be happy to take care of the players, but it had to be done the "right way."

I was disappointed, but because I was also naïve I didn't realize that there were other ways to hide my ownership of the car. A year or so later I was able to cover a loan by having one of my high-school teachers take it out in his name. To make me feel better Cooper promised me I could borrow one of his cars when I needed one.

Switzer knew what had happened at my visit with Jackie Cooper, and told me that I could borrow one of his cars. He had a 1987 Nissan 300ZX that I loved, and he let me borrow it to go home to Lawton. He also would loan the car to a running back on the team named Damon Stell. One day Damon got into an accident and totaled the car. Switzer was real nice about the thing and paid for the repairs, but "my" car was in the shop for a long time.

Once I was in school I got to know Switzer a lot better. We talked about various things and I could ask him for help. He might have been breaking NCAA regulations, but I think he was more concerned about taking care of his players than observing NCAA rules he thought were unrealistic. Switzer saw the human side of things, and I think he found it hard to say no to kids who did not have very much money or, like many of us, came from broken homes.

132

I'm sure, also, that it wasn't all altruism. As the year went by Switzer saw and appreciated how much I was developing as a player. He spoke to the press about my future as a quarterback, saying that the difference between Jamelle and me was just experience. Still, the first Christmas I was at OU, when I wanted to visit my mother in Dallas, he paid for the airline ticket. He paid for several pairs of Nike shoes I wanted, and when I needed a few extra dollars he was generous. I don't know if the money was his or the university's, but whether it was fifty, a hundred, two-hundred-fifty dollars, he came up with it. He knew everybody, or so it seemed, and when a concert was sold out in Oklahoma City he was always able to get tickets.

Switzer was like a father, and generally very cordial and cheerful when I was with him. It was as Bobby Proctor had told me about "the family." But I also saw another side of Switzer that first year. Rarely would he get his hands dirty. If anything was wrong, he would have an assistant coach be the bad guy. If you missed practice or weights, it would not be Switzer who bawled you out but another coach. If there were special problems, you knew not to go to Switzer. One typical problem that arose often with the players was their academic incompetence. When a player was failing a course one of the assistants would try to straighten it out with the teacher. The assistant may have had Switzer's clout behind him, but it was never Switzer who directly intervened on the player's behalf.

The first time I had an academic problem was in my second semester. I had started to ease up on my commitment to being an excellent student and was having trouble in one of my courses. It was always my worst subject, and I wasn't exactly hitting the books every night. I had failed a few exams and was in danger of failing the course. Switzer told me to talk about it to Coach Donnan. Donnan spoke to the instructor. I would take

133

one more exam and whatever grade I received it would be my final mark in the course. I passed and got a C.

The next semester I got friendly with an instructor. One evening we met at a basketball game and he felt me out about scoring some grass. I took him to a friend's house, where we smoked some weed. Sitting there, getting high, we agreed to play one-on-one basketball. If I won he would give me an A in the class. If I lost, I would not be able to cut any of his classes. We never played the game, but I stayed friendly with him, stopping by his house with beer and weed, and finished the semester passing his course. I wasn't the only student taking advantage of his loose style; at least one woman student was screwing him for a passing grade.

There were other instructors who were boosters and showed favoritism to the athletes in their classes. Although I didn't expect to have any difficulty in my Business Communication course, the instructor volunteered that because I was busy with football practice I would only have to complete eight of his sixteen assignments. There was a special exam in the course and he prepared me for what was going to be on it. I got a B.

Spring semester I began to change, mostly because my status on the team had changed. Jamelle Holieway had broken his thumb in what was reported as a "freak accident." The only thing freaky about it was that Jamelle had gotten drunk and decided to fight some guy on the wrestling team. Jamelle got in one punch and it was the one that broke his thumb. With him out of action I was the only quarterback. Bernard Hall had been "Proposition 48-ed" and sent to a junior college to try and make up his grades, and Eric Mitchell was at running back. Spring practice is an event in Oklahoma and the press covers it closely. Coverage of the 1987 spring practice was more intense after the "disappointing" 1986 season. OU's records for the 1985 and 1986 seasons were identical, 11-1, including a conclusive 1987 Orange Bowl victory over Arkansas, 42–8; but for Sooner fans there was a big difference in the two seasons: in 1985 OU won the national championship; in 1986, they were ranked a poor third. That may not mean very much elsewhere in the country, but in Oklahoma it's cause for concern. And perhaps as important to Sooner fans was what had happened to Brian Bosworth before the Orange Bowl.

In 1986 the NCAA went all out in their crackdown on steroids. Boz and a reserve guard by the name of Gary Bennett were tested before the Bowl and found guilty of using steroids. As far as the Bowl game went this didn't hurt OU, especially considering the great game played by Dante Jones at Bosworth's position. What made it a big issue was how the Boz reacted. He took a fuck-you attitude toward the NCAA. He thought the NCAA was hypocritical and challenged the accuracy of the steroid test. He never missed an opportunity to express his feelings about it, and Brian, being the Boz, wanted sweeter revenge.

Relegated to watching the Orange Bowl on the sidelines, Bosworth wore his own NCAA T-shirt, which read: NATIONAL COMMUNISTS AGAINST COLLEGE ATHLETES. Switzer and Donnie Duncan, OU's athletic director, were furious and ordered him to get rid of the shirt or leave. This was on national television and Barry Switzer was not going to let Brian Bosworth steal his thunder. It was the final cut that severed their relationship. Although Boz had another year of eligibility, he chose to go to the NFL.

Brian wasn't the only OU player to use steroids. I knew firsthand of five players and was told by others that there were about a dozen. It's interesting that the players I knew who were using steroids were all white.

At spring practice, attention turned to me as OU's starting quarterback. Newspapers in the state were writing about me and there were articles in magazines. But it wasn't only the press who were becoming more interested, and I soon learned that I was the center of booster and alumni attention. The boosters who knew Jamelle, Keith, and other players were constantly asking about me. On campus, students and instructors would introduce themselves to me. Suddenly, Charles Thompson was a name. I wasn't even nineteen years old and I was a celebrity. I liked it. I never really thought it out, about what it meant. It was an end in itself, and seemed so natural. First there was elementary school, then junior and senior high, now college. It was the way I had dreamed it would be.

While I was enjoying all the attention I was realistic enough to know it could disappear in a moment; especially, with a healthy Jamelle Holieway coming back to his role as starting quarterback. With the Boz gone Jamelle would be the biggest name on campus. I knew that Jamelle loved the attention as much as I did. I had a golden opportunity that spring to make an impression with Switzer, so that he would begin to question which quarterback could do him the most good in the 1987 season.

Jamelle was a terrific quarterback. Like me, he wasn't big, but he was quick and fast. He may not have had a great passing arm, but for the wishbone he had more important talents—excellent vision on the field and the ability to really read defenses. He was able to see all eleven defensive players when he had the ball and knew when to run or get rid of it at exactly the right moment. He operated on instinct on the field, something you can't teach a player. When Jamelle Holieway came to OU the team had been in transition. The years 1981, 1982, and 1983 were the worst Barry Switzer ever had; until the 1981 season his teams had never lost more than two games and ranked lower than seventh in the nation. When the Sooners lost four games and went unranked in 1983 there were editorials calling for his resignation.

Things began to change in the 1984 season. OU went 9–2–1

that year and was ranked number six in the nation. But it was the 1985 season that Switzer looked forward to. His hopes centered around a big quarterback named Troy Aikman. Unlike Switzer's wishbone quarterbacks, Aikman was an NFL-styled passer, as he has demonstrated with the Dallas Cowboys. He had an incredible arm that forced Switzer to make a drastic change in his coaching, abandoning the wishbone. Unfortunately, Aikman got hurt early in the year and Switzer was forced to start Jamelle. Misfortune turned to blessing and Jamelle Holieway and the wishbone led the Sooners to their first national championship since 1976.

Jamelle dressed, spoke, and acted the role of a star. He was the city slicker from Los Angeles who was going to show the hicks from Oklahoma a bit of Hollywood. His clothes were as loud as his mouth. Unless the temperature outdoors was a hundred degrees, he pranced around in his fur coat, a Louis Vuitton pouch around his shoulder. His mouth went nonstop; Jamelle would say the damnedest things and never appeared embarrassed by them. He enjoyed partying and was a heavy drinker. When I started hanging around with him that spring he was into cocaine.

Jamelle and I got close when he was hurt and I was named the number one quarterback. When he saw me getting attention and respect from the coaching staff and media he no longer treated me as the green freshman, but more like a person to take seriously. We soon found out that we had a lot in common. I enjoyed going out drinking every night. It took a little time, but Jamelle Holieway decided that Charles Thompson was in his league.

He believed that he was the biggest and baddest man on campus. He was cocky and arrogant because there was nobody in sight who could take his job away; I could be in the same room with him and Jamelle would boast that I had no chance to

137

start while he was on the team. Attention and publicity were very important to him, and when I started to receive my share that spring Jamelle decided there was enough room at OU for two big and bad quarterbacks.

Jamelle and I were friends because both of us had confidence in ourselves. We competed to be the number one quarterback but there were never any petty jealousies. We may have had big egos, but our personalities were so different that we were drawn to one another. I enjoyed Jamelle's style. He was loose and enjoyed showing the rest of us the way things are done in the big city. It amazed me how he could slip into trouble and just as smoothly get himself out. He was a great con man. He loved to get Switzer pissed off, then bullshit: "Gee, Coach, I know I missed practice, but there was this accident. . . ." Or: "It was the strangest thing, Coach, how I broke my thumb. . . ." Whatever he was selling, Switzer bought it.

Jamelle believed that he could get away with anything because of Switzer. He felt that he was too important to a winning team and that it would go downhill without him. He was convinced that he'd saved Switzer's job, and, in turn, that the coach would save his ass. One incident during my freshman year made me a believer about how far an OU player could go without getting into trouble if Barry Switzer needed him.

Jamelle and I knew a girl who would sometimes visit us at school. She was into some weird voodoo cults and strange sex. One day she came to campus and asked me if I knew where Jamelle was. I told her that he was in his room at Bud Hall drinking and gambling with some of the guys. Jamelle loved to gamble on anything. When the girl got to Jamelle's room she told him that she was looking for her girlfriend, who was going out with one of the players. Jamelle told her that her friend was in the player's room and asked her to leave. Sometimes Jamelle wanted to gamble more than fuck.

THE LIFE AND CRIMES OF OKLAHOMA FOOTBALL

He kept asking her to leave, but she wouldn't. "Oh, Jamelle, I want you to fuck me," she kept saying. "You know how I love to be tied up and fucked." There were five or six players in the room. To get rid of her, Jamelle said to the girl, "Okay, but if I fuck you, they have to fuck you, too." So Jamelle took her into the other room and screwed her, and when he was done the other guys came in. It soon started to get out of hand.

Jamelle was wrecked and he began walking around the dorm buck naked knocking on doors with condoms in his hand. "Hey, you wanna get laid? Follow me." It didn't take too long until there were fifteen players in his room. It was turning into a big show.

Jamelle said that at first the girl was getting off on it, that it wasn't anything like the gang rape in 1989 when three Sooners went on trial for an assault in Nigel Clay's room. The lights were on and nobody had to hold the girl down. In fact, she was asking them to beat her, and someone obliged. When he took off his belt and began smacking her she screamed: "No, harder, harder. I want you to hurt me."

The problem came when one of the players, took off his pants. He was big, really big, and when she took a look she screamed: "No, you're too big. I'm afraid." He had been in the room watching for some time and he wasn't going to leave without getting his share of the action. The girl tried to get up, but two of the players threw her down and held her arms while he fucked her. She may have enjoyed pain, but he hurt her bad and she started to get hysterical. The party ended and everyone left Jamelle's room.

She went to get her friend and they left the campus. As soon as it was over, word of what had happened spread to all the dorms. I was still living at Jones Hall and Artie came in that evening to tell me what he heard had happened. He said that it

139

was all over campus and that the coaches had been told. We wondered what would happen; it sounded as if the whole football team would be arrested for rape. I began to imagine the headlines and shuddered. I told Artie that there was no way Jamelle and the rest of them were going to get out of it, and that they would go to jail. I didn't care how weird the girl was, no judge was going to buy it.

The next day nobody was sure about anything. There were all kinds of rumors and the players involved were frightened. When we went to meals you could see how nervous they were. Usually at meals there was a lot of noise and fooling around. Now, it was like death. Jamelle was the only one involved who wasn't worried about the consequences. He told me what had happened and thought it was funny. "CT, you know the bitch. She's a freak," he said. "You know how it is. She came to the room and asked for it."

For the next two days everyone on the football team who knew about what had happened in Jamelle's room waited for the police to raid Bud Hall. Nothing happened. The girl's father was a big booster who was friends with Switzer. When he learned about what had happened to his daughter he was furious and threatened to press charges against the whole football team. Switzer asked him to wait before pressing charges and that he would straighten out the mess. Time went by and nothing happened. There were rumors about the booster being bought off, nobody knows for certain what happened, but the matter died.

Meanwhile, Jamelle was telling me that nothing was going to happen to him. I didn't believe it, and neither did some of the assistant coaches. Coach Donnan came to me one evening and said, "It seems that our boy Jamelle has got himself into some shit. I can't believe he was so stupid. You better get ready to be quarterback." But the days went by and nothing happened. There was nothing in the newspapers or on television, although everyone seemed to know about the incident.

Several weeks later, when Jamelle and I were sitting in a bar talking, he told me that Switzer had taken care of the mess and that nobody was going to get into trouble. "CT," Jamelle explained, "I am a valuable piece of merchandise to this university. If you think Switzer is going to let me be lost, you're crazy." He was convinced that Switzer had done whatever he had to do to cover up the incident.

All this made a deep impression on me. We were not like other students. There were different rules for players. Jamelle was right about our being valuable; we brought glory and millions of dollars to the University of Oklahoma.

Nobody understood that reality better than Jamelle Holieway. During my freshman year I learned that Jamelle, was caught cheating on an exam. It was no secret, and everyone on campus, except Jamelle, waited for his expulsion. It took one visit from one of the coaches to the instructor to correct the matter. All these things are noticed by young people, and while I tried to keep up my grades, part of me was asking: "Why bother?"

Every day brought a new lesson in how to take shortcuts in life. When you're eighteen years old, and people you were taught to respect are handing life to you on a platter, it's hard to resist. I had always thought, growing up, that college was special; yet here I was and everyone was cheating. Whether they were NCAA rules, OU rules, or society's rules, my coaches and instructors were demonstrating to me that they didn't apply to good football players. The worst were the alumni and boosters, successful businessmen who had a warped way of setting examples for young people. I was greedy, Jamelle was greedy, and so were others, but what those who criticized cannot understand

141

are the temptations placed before us. The message isn't "don't take" but "don't get caught."

My family and I got thousands of dollars from OU boosters in exchange for my spending time with them talking about football. I was their toy to show off to their friends and I cost them no more than other gadgets that are the signs of success. I had yet to play in one football game for the University of Oklahoma, but there were at least ten wealthy Sooner businessmen who were prepared to help me at any time. If I sound ungrateful it's only because I've learned how phony they all are. You learn that once you're no longer on the football team, you're no longer someone they need to know.

My wallet grew fat with business cards, and when I needed a few hundred dollars I would pull one of them out and make a phone call. When my mother was having a tough time paying some bills, a booster in Durant named John Massey made the arrangements for her to get the needed money. But Massey came to my aid not only for humanitarian reasons; he also helped me improve my social life.

Although I wasn't eligible to play in the 1987 Orange Bowl, I wanted to impress Monica Huston, a girl I knew in Dallas. I asked Massey to help me get her down to Miami for the game. He paid for her plane ticket and hotel, and threw in the expense money. There was plenty of money for all the players on the team when we went to the Orange Bowl. We would scalp the complimentary tickets for two hundred dollars each. For the guys on the team who didn't get as much attention from the boosters, this was a major source of income. During the season the team loved to play at home, not because of any home field advantage, but because there was money in scalping tickets. Boosters were always available to shell out a hundred or more for a prime seat.

Before my freshman year was over, I couldn't stand not hav-

142

ing a car. If it wasn't going to be an expensive foreign car, I decided, I'd settle for anything with wheels; I was tired of borrowing cars from Switzer and Jackie Cooper. Another OU booster in Norman owned a car dealership, and I chose a white Buick Regal that cost about seventy-five hundred dollars. The deal was for me to put down two thousand, and have a loan taken out by a friend, in this case a former teacher at Lawton High School, for the balance. I was able to get the two thousand from a few boosters and return the same day to pick up the car. The car wasn't in my name, but I owned it, and I didn't give a damn what Rudy would say when she found out.

As the freshman year came to a close, part of me was feeling good about things. The trouble in Tulsa was behind me. I had completed the court-ordered eighty hours of community work at the jail, although it wasn't of much service to the community—I spent most of the time doing my homework and reports, probably one of the reasons I did so well in school that semester. It was quiet at night in the jail, and all I ever had to do was open and close a gate to let people through.

I felt confident about my position on the team. I'd had a great spring practice and had mastered the wishbone. I knew that Jamelle's thumb would heal by the end of summer, but I was certain I could take the job away from him.

It was a good feeling to know that I would have a car for the summer, and that if I visited Lawton I wouldn't have to depend on Rudy. The car gave me an opportunity to visit more often in Dallas with my mother, whom I missed.

Most of all, I enjoyed the life I was living. It was any teenager's wet dream. I had all the girls I wanted—getting laid, going to parties, getting drunk. I had plenty of money in my pocket, and, when there wasn't enough, there were plenty of OU boosters dying to help me out. They were my new companions: big shots, wealthy businessmen who wanted me to eat and drink with them.

Everything was feeling fine, but I knew something was changing. Growing up in Lawton I'd had a great deal of attention because of sports, but it had felt comfortable and under control. In Norman I wasn't so certain that I had it under control. Everything—football, boosters, money—was on a level that was overwhelming. It was fine picking up a telephone when I needed money, airline tickets, or whatever; but when I thought about it I realized I'd been getting thousands of dollars I should not have. I ate and drank for nothing in places I could never have afforded. I never lied to myself about being right; what made me uncomfortable wasn't the right or wrong of it but that I wanted even more of this life. I knew I was going to push it to the limits the following year and the year after that. I knew what a true Sooner was and I wanted to be one.

Jamelle Holieway

It was a lot of fun. It was too bad that things happened that way to Charles. I never turned my back on him. When times were good or bad, it was the same. He had a lot of stuff happening too fast. I was pretty good at having the stardom happen to me, I could handle it, but I think a lot of people misled Charles. He got caught up with some of his old friends back in Lawton and, even though they liked what he was doing, they still brought him down. He couldn't see it because he was just going with the flow. He and I did so much together. He was like my little brother. Everywhere I would go, he would go. Every time a booster would do something, I would want Charles along. He'd do everything like Jamelle, but he still had his own identity.

People who came from Lawton loved him. Growing up

144

they were all his friends, but when it got to the big time, they wanted the same things Charles had and they couldn't have them. They wanted to bring him down to their level. And like everyone young as Charles was, he made mistakes. I suspected Otha. I suspected Otha of a lot of things.

CHARLES VERSUS JAMELLE

Jamelle, Boz, and Keith were the superstars, but the person I felt closest to was Artie Guess. Artie was an excellent wide receiver, but on a team that lived and died by running. OU made the passing game an afterthought, and though Artie was as good a receiver as anybody in college football, at OU he had no chance for the kind of recognition a player of his caliber would get at a school like Miami, for instance. It didn't bother him, and Artie's biggest concern was to be a starter his sophomore year. After our first semester we were able to get private rooms at Jones Hall, but we remained as close as when we shared a room.

Artie is the kind of person other people take a liking to the moment they meet him. He's quiet and more interested in listening to what other people have to say than saying what's on his own mind. He's a natural athlete, as fast and quick as anybody else on the team and has great hands, but because of his laid-back style he rarely gets credit for his ability.

We continued our friendship after our freshman year, and when we weren't working out together we would be hanging out and partying as a team. Unlike Jamelle and me, Artie wasn't much of a drinker. He hated liquor and never developed a taste for beer. I think that the most serious drinking Artie ever did was to finish off a wine cooler or two.

After school ended we decided to rent an apartment in town. Artie and I had the same goal. We wanted to arrive for August practice ready to begin the 1987 season. There is an enthusiasm about Artie that rubs off on anyone around him, and no matter how hungover I was on some mornings after a night of drink-

147

ing, he made me want to go out there and bust my gut running and lifting weights.

Artie and I were also looking forward to sharing a room in Bud Hall the following semester. After an athlete's first year at OU, if you're still on the team, you get to move from the slums of Jones Hall to a third-floor room in Bud Hall. If you stick around another year, you get to move to the second floor. In your final year you get a choice of a first-floor room.

We couldn't wait to move in. Besides the better living conditions at the Bud Wilkinson House—like not worrying who had crabs every time you went to the community bathroom in Jones Hall—there was the prestige associated with living there. Although the apartments were furnished with the basics—beds, dressers, table, and chairs—players were responsible for the extras like televisions, lamps, refrigerators, and decorations. By the time Artie and I were ready to move in we had accumulated most of those things as gifts from boosters. We had stereo equipment, a TV, paintings, and plants we had taken from the athletic office.

The stolen plants had become a mystery on the campus. Our rooms in Jones Hall were so drab and ugly that Artie and I decided that the athletic office should pay for putting us there. Whenever we had the opportunity we would take one or two plants and bring them to the apartment. We weren't master thieves, but nobody in the office could figure out what was happening to their greenery. It became such a major deal—looking for the "plant bandits"—that they had the campus security investigate. When they gave up trying to find the thieves they decided to keep the office locked at night. By that time Artie and I had moved into Bud Hall with enough plants to stock the rain forests.

When August practice began he and I were in better shape than most of the other players. One of the first things the coaches have players do is a running test. For most of them, after fucking off for much of the summer, running in the August heat is a ballbuster. With little rest in between, you have to run a 220, 330, 440, 550, and 660. It was really funny watching the big linemen out there. I loved looking at some of those big, ugly slobs trying to complete the day at the races. Often they would be bent over throwing up or lying on the field gasping for breath. An aide with a hose on a cart would trail them, hosing them down to keep them conscious. Another cart with a stretcher on the back, "the paddy wagon," would be there to carry those who passed out back to the training room.

I won four of the five races that day, Artie winning the other, but more important to me was beating Jamelle every race. It was one thing to be told in the spring, when Jamelle was hurt, that I was the starting quarterback. Now it was August, one month before the 1987 season was to begin, and I was back to being number two. It didn't surprise me, yet, after my impressive spring practice, I thought I had a shot at starting.

I could understand why Jamelle was the number one quarterback, but it pissed me off and made me try even harder. And Donnan and Switzer had played a game with me that summer: Switzer sang Jamelle's praises and talked about what a great leader he was, while Donnan told me that I still had an excellent chance to become the starter.

Their purpose was to use me to push Jamelle. When I beat Jamelle in the races Donnan patted my back and told me how great I was, while Switzer would be telling Jamelle that he shouldn't let a shrimp like me outrun him. If this was only a matter of Switzer keeping Jamelle on his toes I would have accepted it, but it wasn't that way. Switzer never forgot how Jamelle bailed his ass out in the 1985 season after Aikman went down. No matter what Jamelle did after that Switzer was always behind him.

The relationship between Switzer and Holieway went beyond coach and player. As close as Switzer was to me and other players, he was different with Jamelle; they drank together and socialized, not as player and coach, but man to man. If you were with Jamelle and Switzer, you knew the coach had a special place in his heart for the quarterback who delivered the national championship at a time when it looked hopeless. Even a great player like Keith Jackson never got the same treatment as Jamelle.

Once, Keith, Jamelle, and I went to see Switzer to ask him to get tickets to a rock concert. Jamelle did the talking because we knew that if Switzer got us the tickets we would have to leave Norman early and miss practice to catch the show. Switzer looked at me and said, "You don't need a fucking ticket. You're a private. You haven't earned your stripes. Jamelle's a soldier. He's been in combat. But as long as you're going with Jamelle, I'll give you a pass."

It was always shit like that. Jamelle was his boy, and nothing could change it. Because Switzer was rarely at practices, or if he was he never stayed too long, it was difficult for me to change his mind. Donnan kept telling me how good I was, but when Switzer was out there it always seemed he was looking in the wrong direction when I did something great. His eyes were never off Jamelle. If Jamelle tied his laces, Switzer would be going, "Okay, Jamelle, way to be our leader. National championship coming up."

I'm certain that Switzer wanted me to do well, especially if Jamelle got hurt and I had to start. And he tried to motivate me to do better, but in his mind I was always second. When Jamelle fucked up in practice Switzer would yell: "Getum next time, Jamelle." With me, he showed his anger: "How do you expect to win a game against Nebraska, Charles, if you keep fumbling the ball?" Or: "You better get your shit together,

150

Charles. What are you going to do when there are seventy-five thousand in the stands? Fall apart?"

He would use his "seventy-five thousand" comment even when I did something outstanding: "Hope you can do that when there are seventy-five thousand out there. You gotta do it when the band's playing, Charles." Jamelle had played before seventy-five thousand and fucked up, but I never heard Switzer say anything to him about that. On the other hand, Jamelle had done it, pulled off victories, when there were seventy-five thousand out there and the band was playing.

No matter how pissed off I was about the way Switzer favored Jamelle over me it never interfered with our relationship. We knew that to a certain degree everything out on the practice field was a head game. In fact, there was more pressure on Jamelle than me. Switzer and Donnan wanted me to push Jamelle because of what they called the "comfort zone." Both coaches knew that Jamelle had no doubts about being the starting quarterback and were concerned that he would ease up. Before the season began I knew that the only way I would be starting at quarterback was for Jamelle to get hurt.

Both of us knew that competing against one another had nothing to do with our friendship. We were spending more time together; if you saw one of us you saw the other. This surprised many people. Everyone was waiting for a quarterback controversy. They thought 1987 was going to be like 1985 when Eric Mitchell was competing with Jamelle for Troy Aikman's job. They came to OU at the same time, but Eric got more attention than Jamelle. Eric could do amazing things on the football field. Whereas Jamelle was steady and sure, Eric was spectacular. Everyone, myself included (when I was in high school), had heard about Eric Mitchell and thought that Jamelle hadn't a chance to beat him out. In fact, I believed that he was better than Jamelle until I got to OU.

151

When you thought about Eric Mitchell you would think about his fifty, sixty-yard runs. You'd remember the way he would cut and dodge, eluding tacklers. But once you watched him on the field you saw a great runner and an uncertain quarterback. He made costly mistakes. On the next play after he had run for forty yards he would pitch the ball into a defender's hands. When I reported to OU in 1986 I was more concerned about Eric Mitchell than Jamelle Holieway.

The quarterback controversy between Eric and Jamelle had left Holieway bitter. Eric didn't only try to take the job away from Jamelle on the field but in the press as well. There was no love lost between them; they were at each other's throats and made no secret of it. Jamelle and I knew we were in competition but didn't let it become personal. We never spoke about it, and we were not going to let the press get between us. More importantly, we were not going to allow it to divide the team as it had in 1985.

Through August and September I never gave up trying to be the number one quarterback, refusing to accept what everyone else knew. I never lost confidence in myself, and one of the two things Jamelle had over me in my freshman year I had overcome: although he still had more experience than I, I had learned the mental part, reading defenses. So I continued to press him.

One of the problems I faced was scrimmaging against the second-team defense; worse was playing offense with the second team. If, on offense, I moved the ball down field and scored a touchdown, Switzer would say: "Nice going, but can you do it against Nebraska's defense?" If I moved the ball down to the ten-yard line and somebody fumbled on the next play, or some other screw up, he would yell: "You gotta get it into the end zone, Charles." It was a no-win situation.

There is a night-and-day difference between the first and

152

second teams, yet our second team could compete with most college teams. When you're playing with or against the first team, you're playing with people who have proven themselves. They have the edge of having been there before, a savvy about how you win close games. I resented not getting the opportunity to show Switzer that I belonged with the first team; and as we got closer to our opening game that season, it didn't look as if I would have that chance. When I complained to Donnan he would shrug his shoulders and promise me that I would get my opportunity.

Our first game of the 1987 season was against a weak North Texas State team. Everyone at OU couldn't wait. We thought we could win another national championship, and before our first game we were ranked number three in the nation. Nobody on the team, including Switzer, was worried about kicking North Texas State's ass, but there was some concern about Jamelle. For a week or so before the game Jamelle wasn't working hard and was jerking off in practice. He didn't seem to take the game seriously, nor did he think for a second that I was going to start. He was right: he started at quarterback and we murdered North Texas State 69–14.

The game was a blowout, 28–0, by the end of the first quarter. I knew that I was going to get in, and kept looking at Switzer for the signal to go out there. There were seventy-five thousand people in the stands, including my family and friends. I might not be starting, but I was going to show them all why I should be. In the second quarter Donnan signaled me to go in. I couldn't believe the moment had arrived.

We were on North Texas's eight-yard line facing the south end zone. The play from the sidelines was an option, right. As soon as I heard the play my first thought was, "Run with the ball, Charles." I wanted to show something the first time I handled the football in a regular season game. But I also wanted to do the right thing. It was a play we had run hundreds of times in practice and I knew in my sleep when to keep the ball and when to get rid of it.

I looked at the stands. There was a sea of people and the noise was deafening. With my hands under the center I saw that the right end had overplayed me. I knew what to do. I got the ball, looked to my left, and then cut inside the end. It was over and I was in the end zone. The first time I had touched the ball in a college game, we had six points. "Unbelievable," I screamed and ran to the sideline—no thoughts of slamming the ball in the end zone, I'm keeping this one!

I was in a dream. I don't remember which coach met me when I got off the field, but my hand was sore from high fives. A hundred voices were yelling: "Okay, CT, atta way, CT, put it here, CT." When I used to break dance I wore a black hat with the initials "CT," and a few of my friends and teammates at Lawton would call me CT. But it was after that touchdown against North Texas that the name began to stick. I liked it.

I couldn't wait to get back in the game. I felt as though I owned the field that day. In the third quarter I scored another touchdown, a four-yard run around the right end again. I prayed that Switzer wouldn't take me out, and in the last quarter I threw a twenty-yard pass to Carl Cabbiness for a touchdown. It may have been North Texas State out there, but I felt like Paul Hornung. There was nothing I could do wrong. I didn't realize just how true that was when with about seven minutes left in the game I was running an option play, following Rotnei Anderson, when the ball fell out of my hand. It bounced right back up to me and I ran it in for my third touchdown of the game.

I walked on air for several days after the North Texas State game. It didn't mean I would start the next week against North Carolina, but no matter how weak North Texas was, I had outperformed Jamelle. I was proud of myself, and knew that people would pay more attention to me. They had heard about me all last spring; now, in the first game of the season, I showed my stuff.

Of course the boosters took notice. To those who had been taking care of me, the Bentleys and Coopers, I'd proven that they were making the right investment. And now, I knew, there would be others looking to meet me. Sure enough, the following week they were at practice looking to shake my hand, a few leaving a fifty or a hundred dollar bill in my palm. One of them, whose name I never got, summed it up: "Kid, you are the man of the future. If you need anything, we're there for you." One person, however, wasn't carried away with my performance against North Texas State—Barry Switzer.

I was hoping that after the game he would say to me, "Charles, I was wrong. You can do it when the band is playing and there are seventy-five thousand out there." But Switzer shook my hand after the game and said: "Nice job, Charles. You know that North Texas State wasn't on our level. Hell, our third-string players walked all over them. Can you do it against the Cornhuskers?"

Switzer had made it clear: I was going to be his "mop-up" quarterback. Outplaying, outrunning, and outscoring Jamelle was not going to change a thing. Jamelle was his man and my job was to clean up after him. But I wasn't going to let it defeat me. If I couldn't prove it to Switzer, I was determined to prove to everyone else in Oklahoma who was the better quarterback.

The following week we were at home to play against North Carolina, another ordinary team. I thought I would see a lot of action in what should have been a one-sided game, but I was disappointed. We were expected to beat North Carolina by twenty-five points, but, outside of the second quarter when we scored three touchdowns, the Tar Heels hung tough, losing 28–

0. Jamelle had a great game, scoring all four touchdowns, and looked sharper than we had seen him in a long time. I played for a few minutes, rushing for fourteen yards on four carries. If I was going to make any headway against Jamelle, I would need more playing time. If I had been walking on air after the North Texas game, I was depressed after playing North Carolina.

Our next game was against Tulsa on their field.

I was certain that we would run all over them, and Donnan told me during the week before the game that I would be seeing more action. Personally, I had a score to settle with Tulsa after what had happened to me there two summers before. Because I never had the chance to show my stuff at the all-star high-school game, I'd show them now what they had missed.

We were ahead by about forty points when I got into the game in the third quarter. Jamelle had run for sixty-five yards and scored two touchdowns. On our first possession I moved the team thirty-two yards before I ran in from the seven for a touchdown, my fourth of the year. I couldn't wait to get my hands on the ball again.

Three minutes later I made the highlights film with OU's longest touchdown run of the season, sixty-eight yards from scrimmage. It was an exciting play that Donnan had had me practice for weeks. Jamelle had never called it and when I had gone back in Donnan said: "Go do it, Charles. Run the forty-two." The forty-two was a variation on the bootleg, where we lined up in the wishbone, reversed out, and I faked to the left running back. It was a perfect fake because everyone on the defensive line went for the running back, and I turned around sprinting in the opposite direction. There were two defenders between me and the goal and I put my best moves on them. Six points.

I got back into the game with less than a minute in the quarter and moved the team downfield again. With thirty seconds left Donnan called in a passing play. In the huddle I winked at Artie and he smiled. We had practiced it often enough so that he knew what I was planning to do. I rolled out right and hit Artie right up the middle for a twenty-two yard touchdown. I had played a perfect quarter of football—three possessions and three touchdowns. Before the game ended I scored one more touchdown on an eleven-yard run.

The 65–0 final score was no surprise, but my performance in the game got a lot of attention. Even Jamelle stood up and took notice when he was asked to comment on me: "What he'd run for, sixty-eight yards? I wish I could do that sometime." It was after the Tulsa game that a new OU quarterback controversy began, although most who got involved chose Jamelle. One writer for the *Daily Oklahoman* sang my praises but concluded, "Considering how well Holieway has performed, there appears no need for a quarterback change." Digging the nail in deeper he added, "Besides, Holieway has played teacher for Thompson."

Jamelle and I stayed out of it, saying nothing but polite things about each other, but Switzer spelled it out to the press about my standing on the team: "Both are excellent players. Both have great quickness. When you have someone like Charles Thompson coming off the bench, your talent doesn't drop off." The one person who gave me the edge on Jamelle was Tulsa's defensive tackle Dennis Byrd, who had played against both of us. "I've never seen anybody with moves like him (Thompson). That includes Holieway. That includes anybody."

The team was on a roll and there was no need for personality clashes. We believed that we were headed to an undefeated season and a national championship. We weren't worried about winning, but winning by the largest margin possible. To move up in the ratings we'd have to win conclusively. We didn't care how embarrassing it was for the other teams, we never stopped trying to put points up on the board. I felt the same way as did Switzer and the others about scoring fifty, sixty, or seventy points in a game. When I got into a game it usually was history. All I wanted to do was outperform Jamelle. I wanted to keep the fans in the stadium no matter what the score was. I was doing it, and it became a big deal at home games to stay through the fourth quarter to watch me play. I was becoming Mr. Touchdown, and after playing a few quarters in three games had already run for six touchdowns, more than anyone on the team.

I began to notice another reason why some people had an interest in seeing us run the score up. I knew that there was a betting line on football games, but when I thought of the spreads it was more in terms of our being that much better than the other team. Boosters mentioned to me that they hoped I got to play a lot in the next game because OU had to cover forty or forty-five points. Former OU defensive backfield coach Scott Hill, who was there when I played, approached me before a game and said, "Your ass better score three fucking touchdowns because I got money on you." There was one game where Hill got so excited he blurted out, "Come on, you can do it. One more score and we beat the spread." Next season, I would learn that some of the guys on the team were betting on OU games.

The next game we traveled to play Iowa State and it was a rerun of our earlier efforts. By the half Iowa State was blown out and I came in to do my weekly mop-up job. I played for a little more than a quarter and ran for 137 yards, my career high at that point. The final score was 56–3, and besides running for the most yardage in the game, I gave the best post-game quote to the press: "Iowa State hit pretty good and pursued pretty good. This was a tune-up for the Texas game, but Tulsa was a tune-up for Iowa State. Each game is a tune-up for the next game."

THE LIFE AND CRIMES OF OKLAHOMA FOOTBALL

The team was flying high, telling one another that we were going to go undefeated that season. We hadn't beaten any team of our caliber, but nobody was as good as OU. We were scheduled to play Texas the following week, and although it was a mediocre Longhorns team, everyone was up for the game. The OU–Texas rivalry was one of the oldest in college sports, and, important to Switzer and us, the game was going to be on national television. I was looking forward to showing the country how good I was.

The Texas game was the first one I had seen Switzer excited about, making more appearances during practice week than before. Usually, during practice, he'd come out on the field for a few minutes, but before the Texas game he was out there every day, all day. He ended each practice with a pep talk: "You gotta get ready. They're gonna play your ass. They'll be out there shooting the gun." He was pumped up and tense. To get us in a frame of mind for the game he had all the songs we would be hearing played over the P.A. It really was intense.

Switzer was worried that we might lose some of our edge because he had heard players talking about how weak the Texas team was that year. Everyone knew that we were favored by thirty points. Before we left for Dallas he called us together and said, "Boys, we're going to Dallas to kick some fucking Longhorn ass. They may not be much of a team this year, but they're gonna play your ass." He told us about past OU–Texas games in which one of the teams were underdogs but pulled off upsets. "Remember," he warned us, "they have as much tradition as we do."

It was an exciting week. I had never experienced anything like it. We flew to Dallas on the Friday before the game. The next day hundreds of Sooner fans were waiting for us when we boarded the buses that would take us to the stadium. I had

159

never been so pumped up as I was sitting on that bus heading to the Cotton Bowl.

The Cotton Bowl was packed with seventy-five thousand screaming Longhorn and Sooner fans. The school colors of burnt orange for Texas and red for OU lit up the bowl. As we dressed in the locker room you could hear the thunder of the crowd. Everyone was nervous. We had several players from Texas who wanted to impress their home state, let them know that Texas recruiters should have tried a little harder to keep them at home. But the most nervous person was Barry Switzer.

Switzer was as tense as I had ever seen him. Always a nervous smoker, at one point he was walking around the dressing room with two lit cigarettes in his hand. The NCAA had asked him not to smoke on the sidelines, especially when a game was on national television, but whenever he was tense he would forget and light up. It was time to go out on the field and Switzer gave us one more motivational speech:

"Here is your chance to show the people in the nation what kind of team you are, what kind of players you are." Addressing the players from Texas he added: "It's a chance for you to go home and say you did the right thing by going to the University of Oklahoma."

We headed toward the tunnel that led out to the field. We were psyched up and raring to go. Both teams converged at the tunnel and started to taunt one another. "You are fucking dead, Longhorn. I got your number in my head, watch your ass out there." And the Texas players were going, "We gonna get us some Sooner ass today. Gonna kick your ass and then fuck your cheerleaders." When we hit the field there was a roar so loud that I got shivers. It was an incredible feeling.

The game began and for the first half everything Switzer had been warning us about came true. Texas played as if they were the undefeated team. We had a 13–6 lead, but Texas believed they could beat us. Jamelle played the whole first half and had one big play, a thirty-two-yard pass to Keith Jackson to the Texas seven from where we scored. Switzer gathered his troops in the dressing room at the half. He was lighting one cigarette after the other.

"Let's go, let's go, settle down. Look, they're not doing anything special out there. We'll make a few changes, nothing to worry about." I wasn't so sure. It was the first time I had ever heard Switzer give a talk when we came in at halftime. Usually, we'd just separate into offensive and defensive teams and hear from the assistant coaches. Before going back on the field Switzer would then talk briefly and that was it. Now, he was pacing up and down, two cigarettes in his hand, telling us not to worry.

In the third quarter we calmed down and got down to business. Rickey Dixon turned it around with an exciting interception and fifty-yard run. The Sooners started to roll. The third quarter was almost over when Donnan told me to go in. He was upstairs and got me on the headphone. "There's millions watching on TV, Charles," he said. "Go show them who you are."

And that's exactly what I did. I played the rest of the game and made my case for best OU quarterback. I led the team on one fifty-yard drive for a field goal, and an eighty-one-yard drive for OU's final touchdown. I was out there for sixteen or seventeen minutes, but I led everyone with 114 yards rushing, including one sixty-yard run for a touchdown. I felt great. I had done it on national television. Switzer told me that I was the first OU quarterback in several years to rush against Texas for more than a hundred yards. I reminded him that I had done it all in the fourth quarter.

The Texas game not only put me on the map, but kept the quarterback controversy alive. The newspapers made a big deal of the fact that I rushed against Texas for more yards than any other previous OU quarterback, not just in a long time, as Switzer had told me, but ever, and they were asking me if I felt frustrated playing only one or two quarters. I was very careful what I said, always telling reporters that Jamelle was a great player and that I would have to wait my turn. However, I think after the Texas game Switzer found himself answering tougher questions about his starting quarterback, and was more defensive about starting Jamelle.

When he spoke to me about my performance on the field, he had a new line. No longer, "Can you do it when the band is playing?" or "Can you do it on national television?" but "Can you do it when Jamelle hasn't softened them up?" This was also what he told alumni and boosters when they started questioning him about not starting me. "Well, Charles is a great, natural athlete," he'd say, "but Jamelle has that experience, that savvy. Charles hasn't been in a game when it was on the line."

In a game or at practice, after a play, Switzer would say to me: "Now, that's a good play, Charles, but it could have been a little bit better if you had . . . See, Jamelle would know how to read the defense a little better." He wasn't completely wrong. Jamelle did have more experience on the field and could read defenses better, but I wasn't getting enough credit from Switzer. After the Texas game I felt that I was getting fucked over, that Switzer was acting as if I was shit. There were times after long touchdown runs when he wouldn't even acknowledge me, although I saw him applaud Jamelle for five-yard pitchouts.

It was frustrating, but I couldn't complain to Jamelle, Switzer, or the press. The only person I complained to was Artie. "Don't worry, CT," he would console me, "they can't keep doing that to you. People are gonna raise questions. You're too good."

What was as strange to most people was how close Jamelle and I remained. In fact, after the Texas game, a couple of boosters asked us to stay and party with them in Dallas. They paid our bills at the Fairmont Hotel that weekend. Jamelle and I had a great time and drove back to Oklahoma on Sunday night. We loaded the car up with liquor and beer and stayed drunk until we crashed in Norman.

What people who were surprised about our friendship did not understand was the amount of respect Jamelle and I had for each other. He believed that we were an exclusive club, the Sooner quarterbacks. His philosophy was that they couldn't get along without us, but if anyone came along who was better they'd throw us to the wolves.

Switzer resented our friendship, and tried to keep me away from Jamelle. He warned me about Jamelle being a bad influence. The other coaches detested Jamelle's flamboyant style—the clothes, the ring in his ear, the Louis Vuitton pouch. For Oklahoma, Jamelle was too loud, a ghetto nigger, the wrong image. I saw Switzer's hypocrisy about Jamelle. In private he warned me off, but on the field he'd do all but suck his cock.

Later, when Jamelle and I decided to share an apartment off campus, Switzer and Donnan went so far as to ask my high-school coach to come to Norman to try and talk me out of it.

Our next game was with Kansas State. Switzer decided to change the game plan, maybe because we were favored to beat them by fifty-seven points. Rather than wait until the fourth quarter when we would be ahead by fifty points, he was going to have Jamelle and me alternate on a series of downs. I suspected Switzer's motives for making the change. I think what he wanted to do was to push Jamelle a little harder, while at the same time get those who favored starting me to think he was seriously considering a quarterback change.

The Kansas State game was a perfect one for him to play around without hurting the team. Kansas State was terrible and we could have beat them blindfolded. By alternating us at quarterback Switzer tried to keep the alumni, boosters, Jamelle, and me all happy.

Jamelle ran for 102 yards, more than in any of our earlier games. I was able to play for the first time in the first quarter. What Switzer didn't do was put me back in the game when it was a blowout. Most of my seventy-seven rushing yards were in the first half and Switzer was not going to allow me to have another better game than Jamelle. And he could point out to the Charles Thompson fans that he had played me as much as Jamelle in the first half, but kept Holieway in the second half because I wasn't getting the job done. Right, it was real close at the half, 31–10, and the final score of the game was 59–10. At practice the next week Switzer knew I was wondering about what was going on, and he promised me that I would see more action in the Colorado game the following Saturday night.

The Colorado game turned out to be a disaster for me. The only time I got in was to return punts. The game was a lot closer than its thirty-seven point spread predicted, with OU winning 24–6. By not putting me in Switzer was sending a message—telling me he had no faith in me. If the going got tough, he didn't think that Charles Thompson was good enough to play. Standing on the sidelines in the Colorado game I began to stew. By the last quarter I was more pissed at Switzer than I had ever been at anyone in my life.

With about six minutes remaining in the game, Coach Mike Jones (running back coach) told me to warm up. I didn't move. Fuck you, I thought, I ain't your mop. I'm sick of this game. I've earned a lot more respect than that. Jones couldn't believe what he was seeing. "Charles," he said, "aren't you going to get warm?" I looked at him and said I wasn't going to go in and turned away. After the game I told Donnan that I didn't care what the fuck they wanted to do, that I didn't care. I told Donnan that I knew there were other schools who wanted me to play for them and I would transfer if I had to.

I knew that Switzer would punish me for my refusal to play, but I didn't know how. He found the way that would hurt me the most—to play me as little as possible. It was the easiest and best way to fuck me and he knew it. I don't know if he told Donnan what he planned to do, but all week before the following game against Kansas, Donnan swore I would see a lot of action. We beat Kansas 71–10 and I only saw one quarter or so of action. Switzer kept up the punishment in the Oklahoma State game the week after. I saw even less action and we beat OSU by 29–10. However, I wasn't angry at the end of the game. I knew that in spite of Switzer's tactics I would be getting the biggest opportunity of my life. Jamelle Holieway had gone down with an injury.

When Jamelle went off the field in the OSU game I thought he had just twisted something. By the end of the game we knew it was more serious, and that he would be out for the rest of the year with torn ligaments in his knee. I was the starting quarterback. I was thrilled, not because Jamelle was hurt, but because this gave me the opportunity to prove to Switzer that I deserved to be the starting quarterback. Switzer was still pissed off at me and showed very little confidence when he spoke to the press. "He's (Charles) a very talented player, but he's not a Jamelle Holieway. Jamelle Holieway has been a great player for three years and this kid is just a freshman."

The win over OSU was very costly to us. Not only Jamelle was hurt, but also Lydell Carr, the team's second leading rusher. There were two games left in the season and we would have to win both of them if we were to have a chance to be the national champions again that year. We were undefeated and nobody was worried about the following week's game against

Missouri. It was the next game that Sooner fans were thinking about, our last game of the season against our bitterest rival and strongest challenger for the national championship—Nebraska. Now I would have to do it when the band was playing.

WHEN THE BAND PLAYS

For the few days after the game against Oklahoma State I had mixed emotions about becoming the starting quarterback. In fact OU almost lost both its quarterbacks that day, and I finished the game only because of the seriousness of Jamelle's injury. Early in the fourth quarter I'd been scrambling when one of their linebackers grabbed me and swung my body around. As I went down another player hit me and I started to gasp for air. I was sure he had cracked my ribs. It was a fourth down and I hobbled to the sidelines.

When Donnan told me I'd be finishing the game I thought he was nuts, but then he told me we were out of quarterbacks, that Jamelle was probably finished for the season. Holy shit, I thought, I'm the fucking starting quarterback—suddenly I was no longer hurting.

Still I felt bad about Jamelle. I had prayed to God for this opportunity but I know that I never wished harm to Jamelle. I wished I could have gotten the starting job some other way, but I was also honest with myself: I'd wanted it too long to let any guilt get between Jamelle's injury and my performance. If Jamelle Holieway hadn't been hurt there was no way Barry Switzer would have started Charles Thompson at quarterback.

Switzer didn't want Eric Mitchell to back me up. Eric was used to playing running back in the wishbone and Switzer thought changing his position would only be a disadvantage. Switzer asked Glenn Sullivan from the baseball team to become a backup quarterback. Sullivan had been a backup at that position before he left the team to play baseball. He wasn't very good, but he understood the wishbone.

167

Practice the week before the Missouri game was weird. I had all the confidence in the world that I would get the job done, but there were doubters. Switzer's comments to the newspapers about my "not being a Jamelle Holieway" didn't help matters. For many of the players it was strange not having Jamelle take charge. They had played with me, had seen what I could do, and knew I had the authority and confidence of a winning quarterback—but that was when I was the mop-up player. Jamelle had been their leader all year.

There were legitimate reasons for them to worry. Not only was their starting quarterback out, but Rotnei Anderson was replacing Lydell Carr. Both lost players were team leaders. There was concern about Rotnei's timing on plays, and mine, and, as important to winning games, the sound and cadence of my voice, not as familiar as Jamelle's in the huddle and at the line. The team worried about offsides penalties and exchanges from the center, but they were great that week of practice. Normally, against a team like Missouri, where we were favored to win by five touchdowns, practice would be light and loose. Now, everyone practiced hard and didn't complain. A quarterback option play that I wasn't too familiar with was run a hundred times that week. It was fortunate that the Missouri game was coming up; had it been the Nebraska game, Switzer would have been walking around practice with a dozen cigarettes smoking in his hand.

I understood the problems we were facing with two key players injured, but I wasn't troubled about doing my job. Still, I appreciated Keith Jackson expressing his confidence in me. He told me to take charge and not be intimidated, and said that if I thought any of the players were fucking up, not to be afraid to open my mouth, that he would back me up. Coach Donnan gave me motivational talks all week. Switzer watched and said little.

The Missouri game was played before a full house at Owen Field, and I was thankful that I was starting my first game at home. Missouri may have looked like nothing in the game films we watched during the week, but they came to Norman to win. For four quarters they played as if they were the number one ranked team in the country.

On our first possession, it looked as if the game would be over by the end of the quarter. We took the ball on our twenty-two-yard line and moved up the field. We made a few first downs, and then I hit Artie over the middle with a nineteen-yard pass. We stalled on their nineteen-yard line, but kicked a field goal to lead 3–0. I was disappointed in not getting the touchdown, but figured we'd get it next time.

We couldn't do much in the second quarter. Missouri was able to score a field goal and their defense toughened. Toward the end of the first half we mounted a drive and got to the one yard line with less than a minute to go. Anthony Stafford ran it in but we were a sobered Sooner team headed to the dressing room, leading Missouri by only 10–3.

I don't know whether it was because we were shocked at the score, or that Switzer really never believed we could lose the game, but nothing unusual was said to us. The offense went to one side of the room, the defense to the other; adjustments were made, and out we came for the second half. Everybody started screaming that it was time to kick ass and nobody panicked.

Missouri hung in there. A little less than midway through the third quarter we got a good drive going, taking the ball at our twenty-two yard line and moving down to their fourteen after Keith had caught a big twenty-five-yarder. Donnan called in the option play we had practiced all week, and it was just like practice: I held on to the ball and went fourteen yards un-touched into the end zone. The score was 17–3 and it looked as though Missouri had run out of steam. There was no way they were going to make up fourteen points against the number one defense in the nation.

With a little more than a minute left in the third quarter we fumbled the ball on our twenty-yard line. It was one of six OU fumbles that day. One play later Missouri scored, making things tight again—17–10. Missouri scored another field goal in the last quarter and our defense stopped them with a few minutes left in the game when they were deep in our territory. The final score was 17–13. I had to agree with Missouri's cornerback Adrian Jones, who said afterward: "I feel like Oklahoma is glad to get off the field with us today because we outplayed them."

It was not a game I was very proud of. If you look only at my statistics—124 yards rushing, 104 yards passing, and a touchdown—it doesn't seem bad. But I had fumbled a couple of snaps and screwed up one of my handoffs to Rotnei Anderson. There were also three running plays where I lost yards. But we had won the game and I wasn't going to make excuses about my performance. In fact, some people thought I was arrogant when I told a reporter that I rated my performance "about eight." What pissed off the press, boosters, and alumni was that our small margin of victory knocked us down to number two from number one in the ratings. Worse, Nebraska, next week's opponent, was now number one. No matter what was in my future, by many I'd be remembered for what I did against Nebraska.

It was billed as "The Game Of The Century, II." Number I was the Nebraska–OU game in 1971. This would be the biggest game I'd ever play in; I don't think a World Series or Superbowl could be bigger. The game was for the right to play for the national championship, for an undefeated season, and for what the game is all about. It's what you work for all your life if you are a football player. Every player dreams of playing in "the big one," and it comes to very few of them. Our performance in the

Missouri game made OU an underdog for the first time that season.

The week before the battle is a war of words. The media lives for it as much as the players. They can't find enough to write about. Actually, they don't have to look too hard because everyone shoots his mouth off. OU players weren't the models of modesty, but the Nebraska players were total assholes; especially Steve Taylor, their quarterback. Taylor and Jamelle were always mouthing off about one another. Now that Jamelle and Lydell were out, Taylor was talking about this little shit, Charles Thompson. There was no way, Taylor told the press, that a first-year quarterback was going to move the Sooner offense against the mighty Cornhuskers. Taylor laughed at this low-caliber quarterback who was replacing Jamelle Holieway—who, Taylor claimed, had been lucky to beat Nebraska a year earlier. The Sooner luck was gone and he was going to blow us off the field.

I read and heard all the bullshit, but kept quiet. I got my mind to another level, moving up a notch at practice so that by game time I would be like a robot. I would be a machine in Lincoln, unstoppable. Switzer noticed the change in me. He watched me and said: "Charles Thompson, I'll tell you, son, if you play like you practice, you'll stun the nation. I swear, boy, if you play with the same intensity, the same execution, you will fucking stun the country."

One of the symbols for the game was the "key"; OU had the key to be number one in the nation. We psyched ourselves with that all week: only we had the key to the championship. Personally, I saw Nebraska as a key—the key to my future. Nobody would ever doubt Charles Thompson if we beat the Cornhuskers. I would never have to worry about living in the shadow of Jamelle Holieway. I could lose to Miami because Jamelle lost to

171

Miami, but I could never lose to Nebraska because Jamelle had beaten them.

I focused on the game. I spoke to our players, especially those who played against Nebraska in 1986, only about the game. I asked about the Nebraska weather, the stadium, the fans. I spent a lot of time talking to Keith Jackson. When I asked him about beating them he told me the truth. "Yeah, we can beat them," he said, "but it's going to be tough. But this is why you came to the University of Oklahoma. You can make your future in one game. I haven't caught too many passes in my years here, but a few against Texas, Penn State, and Nebraska made my future. This can be one of those games for you."

Keith knew what was on my mind that week and told me, "This is the kind of game that separates the winners from the losers, the people who believe from those who don't."

I believed everything he said. I had grown up watching Oklahoma play Texas and Nebraska; this was why I wanted to come here. I concentrated only on the game; I didn't drink or party; I stopped studying and going to classes. My mind was completely preoccupied with Nebraska. It was nothing less than the greatest challenge of my life. True, I was in college and eighteen years old, but for that week I was a professional football player. I wasn't being paid millions of dollars, but I was no different than any NFL quarterback. I was in college to make my school the best team in America.

At night, I went to sleep thinking and dreaming about the game. I believed that God was with me. I dreamed of breaking eighty-yard touchdown runs. I put pictures in my mind of what I wanted to do in Nebraska that Saturday. I had a philosophy that if you pictured yourself doing something, it became easier when the time came to do it. I believed in myself.

My brothers Curtis and Anthony spoke to me all that week.

THE LIFE AND CRIMES OF OKLAHOMA FOOTBALL

Anthony told me, "Charles, you know you can do it. This is your first step to the Heisman. Two years from now, when you're up for the Heisman Trophy, you'll remember this phone call and what I said to you. I told you that you were gonna get there. You go out there and remember what I've taught you. It's gonna be no different than any other game you've played in."

The whole campus was crazy by the end of the week. There were rallies every day. Switzer wanted to win so badly that he gave me a speech every day after practice. He pumped me up with how I would be shocking the nation and how he always believed in me. He knew how to get to my heart when he said, "Charles, Steve Taylor can't carry your jock."

Everyone on the plane to Lincoln, Nebraska, and the bus that took us directly to the stadium to practice was loose. Keith Jackson sat next to me on the plane. "You look for me out there tomorrow," he told me. "You throw the ball and I don't give a fuck where it is, I'll catch it." On the bus Damon Stell kept us laughing by staring at me and saying, "Oh yeah, I can see it in your eyes, CT. You gonna do some mean shit to them." They could see how much I was concentrating on the game, and they wanted me to relax. I wanted to treat it as a job that I had to get done, but it felt more like my life was on the line.

In a way it was like that. This was a war and I was going into battle against the enemy in Nebraska. When the plane landed, I felt the cold Nebraska air and shuddered. I was in enemy territory, close enough to smell the war. Time to get the rifle and gear to do battle. It was eerie driving into town, a cold and windy day and the roads were deserted. I imagined myself in a Clint Eastwood film. I was the good guy, a gunslinger coming to town to find my man while all the townsfolk were hiding indoors. I pictured myself not on a bus but a horse, hat covering my eyes, rolling a cigarette, real cool. Nebraska quarterback

173

Steve Taylor was the bad, defensive end Broderick Thomas, the ugly.

Earlier in the week there had been a press conference before the national media in the Big Red Room at Owen Field. I had never seen so many television and newspaper reporters in one room. I was in the spotlight and it wasn't Oklahoma versus Nebraska, but Charles Thompson versus Steve Taylor. There I was, eighteen years old, with everyone hanging on my every word. They asked the typical questions: "Are you nervous about starting in the biggest game of the year?" And I gave the typical answers: "Well, it's a great honor to be given the opportunity to prove . . ."

I snapped out of my Clint Eastwood movie when we got to the stadium in Lincoln to practice. Both teams were out on the field, and the reporters were running around for more interviews. So much had already been said that both questions and answers were mostly repetitious. But I loved it all.

In the past, I had quietly watched Bosworth and Jamelle get all the media attention. Now that it was my turn, I wasn't going to be outdone, and acted my coolest, pretending not to notice the cameras snapping pictures of me everywhere I went, as if this were something I did every day of the week. When the network television reporters interviewed me I responded, "Well, Brent, I think . . ." All in all the media was very kind to me. I was the shrimp substitute quarterback who looked as if he'd be eaten up by the powerful Nebraska machine. Once I saw Steve Taylor smirking at me while I was being interviewed. Fuck you, I thought, we'll see who eats dogshit tomorrow.

CBS was broadcasting the game and although they said some nice things about me, they didn't feel we had a shot in hell to win the game with me at quarterback. Earlier in the year, Pat Haydn had said I had the "quickest feet in football," but I don't think he believed they would be quick enough against Ne-

174

braska. Still, while I acted cocky for the television cameras, inside I was one very nervous young man.

After our final practice we returned to the hotel. The guys were nervous, and tried to keep busy to get tomorrow off their minds. I played a lot of ping pong games with Keith and Artie, but couldn't get rid of the butterflies in my stomach. I wanted to go to sleep and wake up tomorrow, but Keith and I were so wired we stayed up late talking. It was a big game for Keith. His college career would be over and he'd be off to the NFL, and he wanted one more win against Nebraska.

"We're gonna beat those mothers, Charles," he said. "I ain't never lost to Nebraska since I've been here, and I'm not about to lose to them now. It's gonna be Sooner magic out there tomorrow; you'll see." Keith sat silent for a few minutes, looking at me. "Tomorrow, Charles," he said. "I'm going to be out there for you. I'm going to catch everything you throw. You throw it; I'll catch it."

I believed him. Keith Jackson was the greatest pass receiver I have ever seen. OU didn't threw the ball all that much, but Keith made every one thrown to him count. The first time I practiced with the varsity my freshman summer, I threw a ball so wild I could have sworn it would wipe out the first row of the stands. I was looking at it, embarrassed, when Keith jumped up and with one hand palmed the ball.

Ever since, I'd believed in Keith Jackson. He always told me to throw it out there and he would catch it, and most of the time he did. So we passed the hours that night talking about what we expected to happen in the game. As though I needed any more encouragement, Keith had some final words for me before he went to sleep. "All we have to do is jump on them quick and they'll quit," he said. "They're talking a lot of shit, but believe me, they don't think they can beat us. They have never been able to put us away and they won't tomorrow."

175

He was snoring in five minutes. I don't know how he was able to put it out of his mind so quickly. I spent the next hours tossing and turning, remembering some point Donnan or Switzer had made about the Nebraska defense. I thought the night would last forever. I don't remember when I dozed off, but when I jumped up and looked at the clock it was five-thirty in the morning. I wasn't going to get any more sleep. Fuck it, I said to myself, let's get it over with. I got up and took a shower. Keith was still sleeping so I put on the television very low and watched the news.

The morning crawled. At seven-thirty Keith and I went downstairs to have breakfast with the team. All the fans were in the dining room wide awake and gung ho. "Hey, Charles, we know you're going to do it. Let's bring the championship back to Oklahoma. We got the key, we got the key."

The team was pretty quiet and the coaches did most of the talking. Switzer kept telling us that it was just another game. He told me to go back to the room and relax before we went to the stadium. Back in the room I lay on the bed watching ESPN football experts try to shake whatever confidence I may have had. They all agreed that I was too inexperienced to carry the load, and without Jamelle Holieway, OU was doomed. I wondered whether Rotnei Anderson was watching ESPN that morning because the commentators never missed a beat in doubting his ability to replace Lydell Carr.

It was partly anger that motivated me to go out there and, as Switzer had said, "stun the nation." Nobody in the nation believed in me. Only my family, my friends, and the team knew I could do it. Suddenly there was no more nervousness, no butterflies in the stomach. I was beyond all that. It was time to get it done. It was fuck-you time. OU was going to stick Charles Thompson up those Cornhuskers' asses. OU had the key and it was Charles Thompson who was going to turn it in the lock for the national championship.

There was nothing unusual about the bus ride to the stadium. We chatted among ourselves as we always did heading to the park. Whatever had to be said had been said hundreds of times. After we got dressed, Switzer made the same speech he had been making the whole week of practice: "It's gonna be a tough four-quarters game. We gotta pound them, beat them up. We win today and we go to the Orange Bowl. In a few hours you'll be the number one team in America. Offense, go out there and establish yourselves. Defense, do what you've been doing all year. Let's go get them."

There was one bit of good advice Switzer gave us before we went out on the field—to put on our helmets because the Nebraska fans could get out of hand. When we left the tunnel they were waiting for us. "Fuck you, Sooners," they screamed, and threw all kinds of shit at us. They pelted us with bottles, cans, whatever they had in their hands. You could tell they were pretty well wasted by that time. We never looked at them and ran onto the field.

Memorial Stadium was packed. There were more than seventy-six thousand people in the stands. The sound was deafening. All around the stadium there were Cornhusker signs: THE LOCK HAS BEEN CHANGED, THE KEY DOESN'T FIT. I tuned it all out, but my heart was beating so hard I could hear it. I knew that we were to be receiving, and I walked off to the side and said a silent prayer. I was ready to do it.

There were many thoughts running through my mind when I led the offense out to the field after the kickoff, holding on to the ball not the least of them, since we had been giving the ball up more than usual that season. Switzer warned us about fumbles because Nebraska was not Missouri and would capitalize on our mistakes. But my foremost thought was wanting to do something dramatic early in the game. Before we went into the huddle I knew what I was going to do.

The noise level was beyond belief, but I decided to put it to my advantage. I walked to the line of scrimmage, bent down over the center, paused, and looked up at the referee: "It's too loud," I said, and calmly walked away. They called a timeout. I think it stunned the crowd and they got quiet. Broderick Thomas, Nebraska's big defensive end, looked at me and smirked. He was letting me know that I was going to pay for my little stunt. He pointed at me, a signal that he was going to be my worst nightmare that afternoon.

The game got going and I moved the team downfield into Nebraska territory. I carried the ball for a few first downs and thought we were headed for six points. I knew Rotnei was nervous, but on the Nebraska eight-yard line I called his number. He got hit and coughed up the ball. It was the first of his three fumbles that game. I was upset, but I felt good knowing we could move against them. After only a few minutes I had taken a pounding, especially from Thomas, who found reason to hit me whether or not I had the ball. Each time I got up and gave him a look that said, "Hey, no big deal."

The game became a defensive struggle. We would begin to move the ball, but whether we fumbled it away or Nebraska got tougher, we couldn't get near the end zone. Nebraska was able to mount one long drive at the end of the first quarter, and on a beautiful twenty-five-yard run by Keith Jones the Cornhuskers led 7–0. It was to be the only score in the first half. Despite our failure to put points on the board, we thought that we had outplayed them. Our biggest problem was bad luck. Poor field position, four of our six possessions began inside our twenty-yard line, and two fumbles had hurt us. After Nebraska's long drive for a touchdown we toughened. We went to the dressing room pretty happy about how the game was going.

178

Even Switzer felt good at halftime. He told us that our luck was going to change in the next half. He thought that once we started to move the ball the game would belong to us. The coaches and players were calm and nobody panicked. I had some time to think about Nebraska's defense and was certain we'd nail them the next half. Nebraska's luck wasn't going to last the whole game.

It didn't take too long. Less than three minutes into the third quarter, Rickey Dixon intercepted a Steve Taylor pass and returned it twenty-four yards to their thirteen-yard line. It was time for me to work the wishbone magic. On our second play I pitched the ball to Anthony Stafford and he ran around right end for eleven yards and the touchdown. The score was tied at 7–7. Our defense shut Nebraska out for the quarter and with about two minutes left Patrick Collins got off a sixty-five yard run for another score. We went into the last quarter leading them 14–7.

Our defense played as if they were on a mission for God. Dante Williams and Dante Jones were immovable. Steve Taylor couldn't do shit. When he ran they were all over him. When he was able to get a pass off, Rickey Dixon either intercepted it or smothered his receivers. All in all we simply beat them up.

We didn't run up a score, adding only a final field goal in the last quarter to win the game 17–7, but our offense ran their asses off the field. Patrick Collins, Rotnei Anderson, and I each ran for more than a hundred yards, for a total of 429 rushing yards. We beat them in every aspect of the game, except maybe punting. We played like we were the number one team in the country.

There was madness in the dressing room after the game. We had taken so much shit all week from Nebraska and the media that it was our time to get even. Jamelle had a four-foot cardboard key he had brought along to tease Nebraska fans and in the dressing room he shouted, "We don't need any key to beat Nebraska. We just kicked the door to their house down." When a reporter noticed that the towel I wore around my uniform read, "King Charles VI," he asked Switzer how he felt about it. Switzer was so high on winning the game that he answered, "Clothes, hair, what the hell does any of that have to do with winning? Earrings, sunglasses. Does any of that tell you whether a player is a great athlete, what kind of competitor he is?" Of course I didn't remind him about what he had been saying to me about Jamelle's earrings and jewelry.

I felt so proud of myself. I had proven to Switzer that I deserved to be the starting quarterback. I had led them to a tough victory. It wasn't like the previous year, when Jamelle had pulled off a big play to win the game. It wasn't a lucky win, but a game in which we dominated Nebraska. I had run for 126 yards, but that was over the long haul of four quarters, in twenty-one carries. And the band was playing when I did it.

My body ached, though. I had paid a price to play well; Broderick Thomas had given me a licking. After the game he came over to shake my hand and tell me how tough he thought I was, because he had sworn to break me. He hadn't broken me, but he sure had left a few parts rattling. That was another thing that made me proud to have beat Nebraska: one criticism had been my size, and whether my 165-pound body would be able to take the pounding of Big 8 football.

We were one happy bunch of Sooners that afternoon. We were number one and we were going to the Orange Bowl to play Miami on New Year's Day. If we won there, we'd be the national champions. That was something else to look forward to, but all we wanted to do after the Nebraska game was celebrate the moment. We were going home to party.

When I got home there were dozens of messages on my answering machine. Relatives, friends, boosters had all called to congratulate me. My brothers, Curtis and Raymond and my sister Lorna were coming to Norman that night to celebrate with me. I called my mother back and spoke to her. I couldn't wait to get Anthony on the phone and when I did he bubbled, "Charles, you are the man now. Nobody has got shit on you. The Heisman comes next." Everybody has that one exquisite moment in their life and this was mine. No matter what has happened since, they can't take that game away from me.

The Nebraska game changed things for me on the team. I was now Switzer's starting quarterback and he treated me differently. I had nothing more to prove to him and this was a turning point in our relationship. He didn't relegate Jamelle to second-class citizenship, but he let it be known that he had two great quarterbacks. For several years I had been in awe of Switzer's fur coat, and when Jamelle and I wanted to pose for Christmas cards wearing fur coats, Switzer let me borrow his. He let me hold on to it, and I wore it to parties and other events. And it wasn't only Switzer who appreciated my performance against Nebraska. If there were ten boosters a month ago, there were another twenty now who wanted to take care of me.

Jamelle Holieway

A friend of mine by the name of Eric Polk, who was at OU before Charles or I got there, told me that when certain people do things for you, just carry on the tradition, don't be selfish with it, tell somebody else. He asked me to pass that down to certain people. So when Charles got there, I did.

Some boosters might feel sorry for you because you come from poverty and they just want to help you because they know it's rough at school. Shit, they should pay college players. I came from California to Oklahoma and it was culture

181

shock. A lot of them felt sorry for me. A lot of them do it because they've been doing it ever since they can think about it, or their fathers before them did it. They would buy your tickets. There were all kinds of ways you could get money, not just people giving you cash outright. I was never a person to say no if people wanted to give me money. I mean, thank you. I do my job on the field. If I had to do it again, I'd ask for more.

The Orange Bowl was going to be a Mardi Gras for the boosters and alumni. Although the game against Miami was for the national championship, the players and coaches looked forward to fun and games after a long, difficult season. I was still going out with Monica Huston, who lived in Dallas, and I asked one of the boosters if he could work out arrangements to get her down to Miami for a few days before the game. He told me that there was no reason why it couldn't be taken care of and gave me the name of another booster to call.

I called John Massey, the booster, who was owner and president of a bank in Durant, and he told me to have Monica call him and he would make arrangements through a friend's bank in Dallas to give her money for the flight and expenses.

I flew to Miami two weeks before the game. The team stayed at the Fontainebleau Hotel on Collins Avenue in Miami Beach. I had been there the previous year for the Orange Bowl, but now I wasn't the red-shirted freshman coming along for the ride. I was the Sooner starting quarterback who had led his team to a stunning victory against the nation's number one Nebraska team. The media was waiting for me with open arms and microphones. There also were plenty of other perks in Miami.

The boosters and alumni were already there when I arrived, and you could tell the good old boys had been whooping it up. They approached me in the hotel lobby with gifts of fifty and

182

hundred dollar bills, telling me to have a good time. The players weren't supposed to drink, but boosters took us by our elbows and dragged us into the lounges. Of course, we never paid for the drinks.

Barry Switzer had a car available that he left at my disposal. Switzer's kids were with him for the trip and I went shopping with them while being chauffeured around in the car. I called John Massey in Oklahoma and he told me that everything had been arranged for Monica's flight the following week. John said that Monica had asked if she might bring her friend Koquice with her, and he had paid for her ticket, too.

Visitors weren't allowed to stay in the players' rooms, and John asked me if I wanted him to put Monica up at the Eden Roc Hotel next door to the Fontainebleau. He was surprised when I said she'd be staying with me at my hotel. Shit, why did he think I wanted her down there? My brother Ronnie had planned to come down for the game and I got some tickets for him.

It was an exciting time and although it was hard for me to believe, there was more coverage of this game than the one in Nebraska. I remember seeing a camera crew from Japanese television in the lobby one afternoon. The hype was that there were now two teams remaining in America who were un-defeated and battling for the national championship. I knew that it meant a lot, but my heart was never in it as much as it was for the Nebraska game. It was anticlimactic. I couldn't make the same commitment I had for the Nebraska game. The team practiced hard and wanted to win, but there were too many distractions in Miami to concentrate on why we were there.

For example, some of the players took a cruise before the game, on a gambling ship that left Miami every day and once outside United States waters became a floating Las Vegas. Jamelle, who loved to gamble, went with me and we got shitfaced. We went to the craps table and everybody kept passing the dice to us. We played for hours, raking in money and having a great time. We were fed so many drinks that Jamelle and I began taking our clothes off. I don't know how much Jamelle won, but I left the ship with four hundred dollars.

Not only Jamelle and I were distracted. All the players were out partying until the wee hours, and it was vacation time for the coaches, who had brought their families or girlfriends with them to Miami. It was no big deal for the Miami players to be in the same city they lived in all year. On the other hand, it seemed that Switzer was going all out to win. Our game plan for Miami was entirely different from any developed earlier in the year.

Switzer and Jimmy Johnson, Miami's coach, knew everything about each other. Switzer wanted to fool Johnson and developed a new offense for us. The players liked it, as it would open up our game and exploit our talents. We were going to do more passing, sprintouts and roll outs, trying to get the ball to Keith Jackson as often as we could. We were going to hit our backs with quick passes and open up the Miami defense. It would be Switzer's version of a run-and-shoot offense. For a week we did nothing but practice the new offense. We were going to surprise Johnson and the Hurricanes.

The Orange Bowl was a complete disaster for OU. Miami beat us 20–14, becoming the national champions and knocking us down in the ratings to number four. Their quarterback Steve Walsh played a great game, passing for 209 yards and two touchdowns. I did nothing out there, running for twenty-nine yards on nineteen carries. Our offense, which had been averaging four hundred yards on the ground, finished the game with

176. From the opening drive, when Walsh hit one of his receivers for a thirty-yard touchdown, I saw it coming. I saw it coming the first time Lydell Carr, who was back in the lineup, stopped without gaining a yard. Throughout the game it was Stubbs, McDowell, Clark, Shannon, or Hawkins hanging all over me no matter where I tried to run. Our defense kept the score close, but we were headed nowhere on that first day of 1988.

Losing was one thing, but the big mystery was Switzer. He failed to call the plays we had been practicing all week. I can think of only two occasions when he tried them. The rest of the time it was back to the same old wishbone. After the game there was a great deal of grumbling by the players. What the fuck was going on? Had Switzer been serious about winning? All the players had noticed Switzer on the sidelines laughing it up with Bobby Bell, one of his good old boys, while we were getting beaten. When the television cameras were on the fun-loving coach the nation must have been wondering if this was indeed the "win at all costs" Barry Switzer.

After the game, in the locker room, he wasn't upset and we still couldn't believe it. OU had just lost its bid for the national championship and Switzer was parading around like he was at a victory party. We knew that we had played poorly, but why didn't Switzer call in those plays? Later, there was a great deal of gossip and rumor, and all of it had to do with gambling. A close friend of my brother Anthony had come to Miami for the game and told me that he had been at a Miami Dolphins game with a gambler friend. When the friend asked who he was betting on in the Orange Bowl, he told him Oklahoma. The friend told him to save his money.

Artie and I talked about the game, and he said people had called him to ask if we were dumping it. Artie reminded me of an incident during the game. We had a trick play called the "fumble rooski," where I lined up behind the center as usual, but didn't open my hands to get the snap. When he hiked the ball it didn't go to me but lay on the ground until a lineman picked it up and ran with it.

During the game I went to Switzer and asked him to put in the play. After hesitating, he said I could run it. But he told me to put Keith Jackson in the guard's position to run with the ball. I couldn't believe what he was telling me. If we put Keith in at guard, the whole fucking world would know what we were doing. I looked at him to see if he was joking, but he was serious. This game has got to be a fucking joke, I thought, and walked away from him.

I'm not saying that Barry Switzer dumped the Orange Bowl, nor am I saying that he bet on football games. But Barry Switzer was no stranger to gamblers. Jamelle and I met several gamblers and bookies who were Switzer's friends, and they freely and openly discussed point spreads on OU games. It was no secret that Jamelle bet on football games, and Switzer's friends simply assumed, as a friend of the coach and Jamelle, that I also bet on games. I didn't, but I sat in many restaurants with Switzer's buddies talking about gambling. One close friend of Switzer's, an alumnus, approached Jamelle and me about point shaving an OU game. I should have told him to go fuck himself, but he put it in a way that didn't seem so bad. "Hey, I'm not asking you to lose," he said, "just to keep the game close."

As disappointed as I was over losing the Orange Bowl, and particularly about my performance in it, I felt good when the season was completed. I had gone a long way from September's mop-up boy to the starting quarterback who beat Nebraska in their own backyard. I would have liked to do more in Miami, but I had a few more years up the road to get even better at my

186

job. Things had changed. Next season it would be Jamelle coming after me for the job. I would have to prove myself one more time to Switzer. But for now he knew one thing: Charles Thompson could do it when the band was playing.

GETTING OUT OF HAND

Barry Switzer tried his hardest to keep Jamelle Holieway and me apart. Jamelle may have been Switzer's favorite player, but he believed him to be a bad influence on the rest of the team. It was bad enough that we had Bernard Hall from Detroit on the team, but Jamelle was the big city boy from Los Angeles who was going to corrupt the Oklahoma bumpkins who thought Tulsa was the center of the universe. Most of the players were born and raised in Oklahoma, where Barry Switzer was more important than the governor, and he didn't want any city slickers coming around disillusioning us about a world outside Norman. Whatever was bad about Los Angeles Switzer saw in Jamelle, and he did not want his other quarterback close to him. It didn't work, and the two of us became best friends.

Jamelle was also friendly with Lonnie Finch, another player on the team. Lonnie enjoyed living off Jamelle's popularity and contacts. When he was with Jamelle he ate and drank for free, and, when he was lucky, got laid with his friend's rejects. Because of Jamelle I tolerated Lonnie, and when we agreed to share an apartment off campus I didn't object to Finch moving in with us. Lonnie and I were not supposed to live off campus, so we needed Switzer's permission to make the move. Switzer flipped out about the idea when I asked him and refused to make an exception. No matter how many times I asked him about it he found a reason to turn me down. His biggest excuse was money. He told me that too many players were living off campus and that the budget for rent money was exhausted. This was bullshit, but I could do nothing to change his mind. He did not want Jamelle Holieway and Charles Thompson living together.

A certain Sooner booster was a wealthy businessman who had made his millions in oil and drilling. Switzer and he were close drinking buddies. They were so close that he would make his private jet available to Switzer whenever the coach had somewhere to travel. He got off on hanging out with the players, and was especially fond of Jamelle, so we thought that he was the person who could change Switzer's mind about the move off campus. We went to him about the problem we were having with the coach. He thought it was a good idea that OU's two quarterbacks should live together and promised us that he would talk to Switzer about it. Jamelle and I explained to him how much OU would benefit from having us spend hours together talking about football. Not only was he going to explain the benefits of the move, he was going to help us find an apartment. When I told him that Switzer would bring up the budgetary problems, he laughed and said he would work out the financing of the apartment.

This booster lived up to his word and found us a new condominium at 423 West Comanche, less than a mile from the campus. It was a small complex, each unit with three levels, had a nice backyard, and was completely modern. There were two bedrooms on the top floor and one at ground level. The condo was owned by a friend of his who was asking four hundred fifty dollars rent monthly. He promised he would contribute two hundred every month to help out. It was perfect. All we needed was Switzer's permission.

One evening he, Jamelle, and I were having drinks at the Interurban, a restaurant down the street from the campus. Although it was close to campus and we were underage, we often got drunk there and nobody ever bothered us. Lonnie joined us later in the evening and we sat around getting drunk, flirting with some girls at the bar. Suddenly, the front door crashed open and someone came running through the restaurant and headed toward the men's room in the back. It had happened so quickly that we weren't certain who it was. "I think that was the coach," Jamelle said.

Jamelle and I were feeling giddy and went to the bathroom to check it out. At first we didn't see anyone, but Jamelle noticed that one of the stalls was closed and peeked in. There was Switzer. High on booze and "primo," a smokable form of cocaine Jamelle had introduced me to, we decided to have some fun, and began to kick and bang on the stall.

"What the fuck is going on?" Switzer screamed. "Who the fuck is out there? Can't you see I'm trying to take a shit?" His screaming only made the two of us laugh more, and Switzer recognized Jamelle's loud laughter. "Oh no, it's the two little turds," Switzer said, slurring his words. Coach had been doing his share of drinking that evening.

Coach was feeling no pain and the three of us returned to the booster and Lonnie at the table. It was only a few minutes past nine, but the restaurant was pretty empty and the help had started to clean up. Switzer gave one of the guys cleaning up a dirty look and yelled, "Hey, we're not leaving so soon. Get me another Scotch." The booster saw his opportunity and started to work on Switzer about the move off campus, telling him all about the condominium and what a great deal it was for us. Switzer sat there drinking, mumbling some nonsense about his midget quarterbacks. The booster realized that he would be better off talking to Switzer with us out of the room. "Hey," he said, with a wink at me, "why don't you guys go take another look at the place?"

We were gone about forty-five minutes and when we returned to the restaurant the chairs were on the tables and the help was standing around waiting for the booster and Switzer to leave. The booster ordered another round of drinks and a nasty look at one of the waiters from Switzer was enough to keep the restaurant open. The booster had a look on his face that said everything was cool and that Switzer was going to allow us to make the move. Hell, Switzer was so drunk by this time we could have asked him for his car keys and the deed to his house and he would have handed them over.

Meanwhile, Lonnie and Jamelle were having a drunken argument about who would get the bedroom with the private bathroom. It wasn't too long before I got into the fight. Switzer put up his hands to quiet us. "Enough, the three of you shut the fuck up," he said. "I got an idea." He took someone's hat and placed it on the table and told us to write our names on pieces of paper. "The first name I pick from the hat gets the room with the private bathroom. The second name . . ." We screamed that this wasn't fair, that we should put the names of the *bedrooms* on paper and draw from the hat. We were so wasted we didn't know what we were talking about. When we did agree about what to write we argued about cheating when we pulled out the slips. Finally, Switzer said: "Okay, here's how it's going to be. The three of you turn around. I'm going to put in three slips of paper marked *A, B,* and *C. A* is the bedroom downstairs. *B* is the large room upstairs, and *C* is the smaller room. Now, turn around." We turned and waited for him to tell us to begin picking. When we did there was a surprise: in addition to the three pieces of paper there were six hundred dollar bills inside the hat. It was Switzer's way of wishing us good luck on our move.

We couldn't wait to get into the apartment and wanted everything to be perfect. The first order of business was to furnish it. Earlier in the season we had met a booster named Frank Vale, Sr. in the lobby of a Tulsa hotel. Frank was a short, chubby guy in his fifties who had a great sense of humor. He wined and dined us that weekend in Tulsa, and told us that any time we wanted to spend a few days in the city with our girlfriends he would pay for everything. Jamelle and I took him up on it later that season and Frank was true to his word. He paid for everything and threw in a couple of hundred dollars in cash. Now that we had the new apartment we decided to take him up on another offer: Frank Vale owned a large furniture store.

Whatever we needed to furnish the apartment—couches, tables, chairs, waterbeds—Frank gave to us. All he wanted in return was to hang out with us and have us sign the pictures he had hanging in the windows of his store. I have no doubt about Frank's sincere desire to help us out, but it remains a mystery why he and other wealthy businessmen went out of their way to please teenagers with whom they had little in common. It was more than supporting your neighborhood football team, when you consider that they were endangering the team by violating NCAA regulations. Even after OU was put on suspension by the NCAA in December 1988, Frank continued to wire Jamelle and me money from Tulsa. Of course, players like Jamelle and myself were too greedy to worry about NCAA regulations, except to make sure we didn't get caught breaking them.

Frank was not the only booster or fan who flaunted the rules to make our life at the condo as comfortable as possible. Once every month we were invited to shop at a local supermarket. The first couple of months we lived in the apartment we were like a family. We cooked dinners every night and invited some of the other players from the team to join us. It takes a lot of food to feed football players and the supermarket was a blessing. There was no limit on how much food we could put in our shopping carts, nor did we have to pay. To make it look good, in case the NCAA was looking, we would write a check at the checkout counter. The cashier took the check, usually for two hundred dollars, to the manager. He would return with an envelope holding our change, usually two hundred dollars.

We rarely paid for anything. Beer and booze was supplied to us by Switzer. All we had to do was go to his house and he would load up the trunk of our car. Ken Henderson, another booster, owned a large drugstore in town and would never charge us when we went shopping there. Ken had a Cadillac stretch limousine and would chauffeur Jamelle and me wherever we wanted to go. We even stopped paying rent to the landlord. All we did was go to Frank Vale or some other booster and they would make up the two hundred fifty we owed each month. We found none of this strange and, in fact, only expected things to get better. I think Jamelle's greatest goal in life was to one day be an OU booster.

Jamelle Holieway

Ken Henderson. That is a friend. He didn't care whether we played football or not. Because it was like this: we would do stuff for him, and this is how he would show his appreciation, by doing little stuff for us. We went to Hands Across America for the handicapped kids; he was one of their big sponsors, that's how I met him. He asked us to get a few football players and I organized them. He got a big kick being around us young people, just like we got a kick out of him, because he acted like himself. There was no front to him. I hope when I get to that age I'm still in communication with the "in" crowd.

Every day more people came into my life offering favors. It was like a line in a bakery shop where each customer takes a number to be served, except that they were patiently waiting their turns to serve me. I questioned none of it. I never asked

194

myself why so many adults were doing flipflops over a black teenager from Lawton. It didn't even seem strange to me that most of the few blacks on campus were athletes. As a teenager I was vain enough to believe that all these people loved Charles Thompson the person.

Jean Yarbrough—Charles Thompson's mother

I always tried to tell Charles not to let things go to his head. It started in junior high when the coaches from three high schools began hanging around to get me to move to their district so he could play on their team. As for the boosters, there's got to be something wrong with their giving all that money to the players. It affects the kids. It makes them think they're better than other kids. It swells their heads. I would see it, sometimes, in Charles, and I talked to him about it. When I was around he would act the way I taught him, but when I wasn't around he acted completely different.

I knew he was getting all that money from the boosters. I told him to keep a level head and not let the money influence him. Charles didn't need their money. He was getting a lot of money because of my husband's death benefits. Still, the boosters were matching the money Charles had from the government. The boosters are playing a game. They're very rich, belong to the same country clubs, and like to show one another who can spend more money on the players.

What they did was make stars like Jamelle and Charles believe that they could get away with anything. Whatever they did wrong would be overlooked, and most of the time it was.

One evening Jamelle and I were chauffeured by Ken Henderson to a club in Norman called The Fox, owned by "R.W.," a

195

booster. It was another club where I was underage to drink but was always served, not unlike any other player on the team. R.W. took us to a table where I was introduced to a young guy named Brett, a friend of Marshall Brackin, Jr., whose father was a millionaire businessman. My date that night was a beautiful woman named Jolly. Brett couldn't keep his eyes off her, and by the time all of us were drunk he invited Jolly and me back to his apartment. Brett could tell I had no interest in Jolly and was hoping he would score with her that night. To entice us back to the apartment he let us know there was plenty of booze and weed there.

Marshall owned an apartment called Tree House in the wealthy Forest Pointe complex. He referred to the pad as "The Z," after the letter on the door. The Z was everything you can imagine a bachelor's apartment to be. Everything inside it told you that Marshall, or at least Marshall's father, had money. The furniture was modern and expensive. There were thousands of dollars' worth of electronic equipment, and a hot tub that sat eight and looked like a small swimming pool on the back balcony by the patio. The Z was soon to be my home away from home.

When we got to the apartment Marshall had returned from work. I liked him immediately. Brett took out some grass and cocaine which I refused. I had been doing a lot of drugs, but when Jamelle and I were around strangers we were discreet and would use a code we'd developed. One of us would say, "It's time to get in a mobile stage," and off we'd disappear to do some primo.

That night Brett couldn't care less about getting me high. He wanted to get Jolly high and in bed. It was a fun night, and when I left, Jolly stayed behind. It was the beginning of a long friendship between Marshall, Brett, and me. In fact, Marshall gave me a key to the Z that night and told me it was mine whenever I wanted to use it.

The hot tub fascinated me, and I began turning up at the Z almost every night with my girlfriends. Marshall was out of town a great deal and got a kick out of coming home and seeing me in the tub with a different girl each time. "Jesus, CT," he would say, laughing, "your dick is going to fall off. Man, I've never seen anybody fuck as much as you." Any night was party time at the Z. We got drunk and high all the time. I did more and more primo, and less and less of everything else. I rarely went to class, knowing that Donnan or some other coach would square it for me if there were trouble, and as long as there was no football practice until April I spent the months after the Orange Bowl getting wrecked and laid. Hell, I was living the letters I used to read about in *Penthouse.* It was orgy time at the Z, although sometimes it did get weird.

One night, Marshall, Brett, Jamelle, four girls, and myself were sitting in the hot tub. We all were naked as there was a sign, NO BATHING SUITS ALLOWED. It was getting too crowded to have sex and Jamelle, Brett, and two girls left to go back to my apartment. Marshall took his girlfriend to his room. I figured that Brett would stay overnight at my place, so I took the girl I was with into his room.

She was wrecked, and when we got to the room she asked, "Charles, did you ever do it there?"

I didn't know what she was talking about and said, "Where's there?"

She started to giggle and looked me right in the eye. "My ass, Charles. I want you to fuck me in the ass."

We got it on and after a few minutes I knew that something was wrong. "What is that smell?" I asked. There was a terrible odor in the room. I didn't want to look, but I knew what had happened. She was so whacked out on drugs that she'd lost

197

control of herself. There was shit all over the place. I didn't know what to do. I was afraid to move, but there was no way that Brett was going to come back to the room he was staying in to this mess and be happy. "Hey, come on," I yelled, "we gotta clean this up before Brett gets home."

No sooner had I said it, when the door to the bedroom opened and Brett walked in. "Oh, God, no," he screamed. "Tell me it's not so. Please, CT, please tell me I'm dreaming all of this."

I jumped out of bed: "Brett, it's okay, I'll take care of everything. It's okay, I swear."

Brett walked out of the room, saying to nobody in particular, "No, I didn't see what I just saw. That's not shit all over my silk sheets. It can't be."

I was more embarrassed than I'd ever been in my life, but when I looked at the girl she had a big shit-eating—no pun intended—grin all over her face. We took the sheets off the bed, went into the bathroom, rinsed them off, and took a shower. I told her to get her ass back there the next day and take the sheets to the cleaners.

We went back to the bedroom to get dressed and have a few more drinks, but when it was time to go, she refused to leave until I fucked her the traditional way. We got back into bed and had begun to screw when Brett, calmer than he'd been earlier, walked in. He saw us fucking and flipped out. "No, this ain't real. You're fucking her. You're fucking her. The girl just shit all over the place and you're fucking her."

We broke up laughing. The next morning she returned to pick up the dirty sheets. I wasn't there, but Brett told me that she acted as though this were something she did every morning after getting laid—return to the scene to pick up her soiled bed clothes.

Although I had smoked grass in high school, I never felt that

198

THE LIFE AND CRIMES OF OKLAHOMA FOOTBALL

I was part of a drug scene. But after the Orange Bowl I was high almost every day, doing primo with Jamelle and cocaine with others. There were other drugs. Jamelle had a contact who supplied us with speed, and a girl I knew scored drugs from a clinic where her father was a physician. Most of the time we got Percodan, but when that wasn't available we would get some other kind of painkiller. And no matter how many drugs we did, we continued to drink every evening. R.W. was the owner of Chrystal's, a big restaurant at the country club. Jamelle, a few other players, and I would get there early in the evening and drink until the place closed. R.W. made a drink he called the "blue motherfucker," a blue liqueur, and Everclear served in a shot glass. It was a potent drink and we would slam them down one after another. When we had some speed or painkillers we would wash them down with blue motherfuckers.

When we weren't at the clubs or Marshall's apartment, we were back at our place to welcome a steady stream of friends, teammates, and girls. There was always food and drink for everyone. We played cards and shot craps, turning the apartment into a mini-casino. Jamelle had a girlfriend and I was still going out with Monica, but this never stopped us from bringing other girls to the house. Monica always complained about how badly I treated her, but she wasn't important enough to me to care about her feelings. Because of my inflated ego and immaturity I enjoyed being a womanizer and Monica was forced to put up with it. My mother, who knew Monica, was upset about the way I was treating her, but this did nothing to change my behavior.

My on-and-off relationship with Monica Huston can best be described as rocky. I did have feelings for her, but I was never in love with her. I enjoyed the company of other women, and Monica, while never accepting this, knew I wasn't going to change. Sometimes her frustration would explode in rage. Once she went so far as to get me thrown off the team. There were a

199

few weeks left in the spring semester when one afternoon I walked into the apartment and heard someone screaming, and throwing and kicking things all over the place. I didn't know what was going on, but Lonnie was in the living room and gave me a look that said something bad was happening. The commotion was coming from my bedroom, and when I ran inside there was Monica going completely mad. She was throwing pictures, tearing up cards and letters, knocking down stereo speakers, screaming and cursing.

I yelled, "What is this shit?"

Her eyes were bulging when she turned to me and yelled back, "You are a sorry motherfucker!" I didn't know what she was talking about and tried to calm her, but she snapped, "Don't play that stupid game with me, Charles. I'm sick and tired of you fucking around." She turned away from me and continued her rampage through the room, picking up a book and throwing it at one of the windows. I tried to grab her, but she began to hit me and kick me in the balls. I tackled her and we wrestled on the bed for a few minutes until she stopped struggling and said that she would stop acting like a wild woman. I let her go, but as soon as she got up she picked up a picture and slammed it to the floor. I lost my temper and slapped her on the side of her head, which made her angrier, and she picked up the television and threw it.

Now there were two crazy people in the room. I slapped her twice; she stumbled into the living room where Lonnie was sitting. He didn't make a move to stop what was going on. The way the three of us were living, nothing that happened in the apartment would have surprised any of us. Maybe it was Lonnie's lack of concern that did it, but Monica finally calmed down. I took her home.

I thought that was the end of the incident, and went home and forgot about it. The next day, however, Monica's mother, sister, and brother who worked for the FBI came to Norman. Monica had told them what had happened, as well as a few other things that were going on with some of the players, and the family was determined to get me kicked off the team. I learned that they had spoken to Switzer and were planning to talk to Donnie Duncan and school officials.

They had been in town for two days when I decided to stop them. I was out with Quinn Grovey, quarterback for the University of Arkansas, and a few other people, and I was drunk. I went to a telephone and called Mrs. Huston to ask her to stop what she was doing because I didn't want any problems with Switzer. She told me to return to my apartment, because someone was coming to talk to me. I went home and waited.

When Monica and her mother arrived I was still drunk, slouched in a chair with my shirt off. It was not the right impression to make for the occasion. Mrs. Huston was livid, and ordered me to stay away from her daughter. I kept looking at Monica, wondering why she was letting her mother do this to me, because in two weeks she'd be running back to me.

The next morning Mrs. Huston and Monica went to the athletic office and spoke to a few of the coaches. They said that Charles Thompson was "coked out" and in another world. I found out about this a day later when I was called in and tested for drugs. I was clean at the time and passed the test. I told the coaches I didn't use drugs and was believed. Mrs. Huston was told about it and was asked to drop the matter. Monica told her mother that it was useless to press the issue because at OU the football players were gods. By that time she had lost any enthusiasm she had to get me into trouble, and wanted things to return to normal. But her mother wouldn't quit.

Mrs. Huston wrote a letter to Barry Switzer and Donnie Duncan, conveying her disgust about how they allowed the football players to carry on as they did. She accused the school of using young men for their own selfish ends, and tolerating drunkenness and womanizing to win football games and championships. If the purpose of the university is to give students a vision in life, at OU it goes no further than the end zone. She wrote that she refused to send her daughter to a university lacking in morals and character. In fact, Monica did not return to OU the following year.

At the time of the incident I hated Monica's mother, thinking she wanted to do anything in her power to keep me away from her daughter. I didn't understand that what she was trying to do was for my benefit as much as her daughter's. Mrs. Huston knew that I was living in a glass world waiting to be shattered. The people I admired—Switzer, Duncan, alumni, and boosters —were nothing but hypocrites and users; and if Monica Huston was a casualty along the way, so be it.

We were sitting at the bar in Chrystal's one day when I turned to Jamelle with an idea: "How about throwing the biggest party in the history of the University of Oklahoma?"

"What the fuck are you talking about?" Jamelle asked, and looked at me as if I were crazy. "We fucking party every night. Why do we need a special party?"

I explained to him that I was thinking about a party for everyone in Norman, for a special occasion, to celebrate the departure of Keith Jackson and the other seniors on the team who wouldn't be playing for OU the next season. "Jamelle, think of it," I went on, "we rent the whole country club from R.W. and throw the party on the golf course. We'd have all the space in the world, and if you wanted to get laid on the eighteenth hole, nobody would notice."

Jamelle got interested and we began to work out the details. We would get money from the boosters to pay for everything— food, booze, music, security, radio commercials to advertise the party. "And," I added, "we'll make money out of the deal. We'll charge two dollars a head." We decided to have the party in two weeks and began to work on it at once. We had fliers all over the school, radio commercials, and good old-fashioned word of mouth to announce the event. Everything went smoothly except for the weather. It rained and we had to hold the party inside.

Hundreds of people showed up. The crowd lined up was so huge that R.W. had to have the security guards turn away more than a hundred. Outside the door people fought to get in. Jamelle had made the situation worse by inviting every girl he met—and her friends—to come to the party as his guests. When the security guards asked about them he didn't have a clue who they were and they were not allowed in. Besides, the two of us had gotten so fucked up on dope before the party that we were on another planet. We arrived late, making a grand entrance, wearing double breasted suits underneath our fur coats. We looked like two pimps, wearing sunglasses and with small cherry-tipped cigars hanging out of our mouths.

We spent most of the party in the back seat of Ken's limousine getting blowjobs. We would get done with two girls, go back inside, smoke some more primo, and return to the car with another two girls. That night was the highest I had ever been on drugs. At times I would drift off and not know where I was. Later I was annoyed with myself because I had wanted to impress a special person and almost blew it.

Kori Kaubin was the most beautiful girl I had ever met. Her father was full-blooded native American and her mother white. Her features and coloring resembled those of her father, and she never went out with black guys. I had met her in one of my classes and immediately tried to hit on her. Hey, I was Charles Thompson, OU's quarterback. But Kori would not have been less impressed with me than if I'd been the hunchback of Notre Dame. She had a boyfriend and did not cheat on him. She

203

quickly let me know that she was aware of my reputation with women and thought it disgusting. The more she resisted me the more I wanted her. In class, I would pass her dumb love notes she found amusing, but which didn't change her mind about going out with me.

I invited her to the party and she said she'd think about it. At the last minute she decided to come with a few of her friends. It was late when I saw her, and I forgot about everything and everyone else. I talked her into taking a ride with me in the limousine, but all we did was talk. It was going to be a long time before we ever did anything else, but that night I fell in love with Kori, although I was too stupid to know what to do about it.

The morning after the party Jamelle and I were in terrible shape. We were so hung over we thought we'd die. To make things worse, we had promised to go with Ken Henderson to do some volunteer work at the Children's Hospital. Mike Gundy, Oklahoma State University's quarterback, had also agreed to visit and try to cheer up some of the kids in the hospital. What started as a plan to do something nice for the children was later to cause OU problems with the NCAA.

Ken picked us up early and then drove to the city to get Gundy. It was a rough trip. Throughout the ride Jamelle was sick; when he wasn't throwing up the two of us in our fur coats and sunglasses sat quietly in the back wishing the day was over. When we picked up Gundy, Jamelle asked Ken to stop at his drugstore so he could get some aspirin.

Whenever we needed something at Ken's store, Jamelle and I would take it without paying. Gundy watched Jamelle walk up and down the aisles, picking up all kinds of stuff. Pretty soon he realized what was going on. Why not, he figured, and began to take a few items for himself. Nobody thought anything about this until a few months later, when the NCAA visited the Norman campus to investigate various allegations about OU violating recruitment and other regulations. Gundy had spilled the beans about our drugstore stop on the way to the hospital.

The NCAA had been investigating OU for most of the year, and the athletic department had been warning us to be careful. I knew that I would be questioned about what had happened when Gundy was with us, and had time to prepare myself for the NCAA investigator. I told him that Gundy was wrong about getting items free at Ken's store. If Gundy didn't pay for what he took, I said, then that was something I knew nothing about. I was asked about the fur coat I had worn that day, and simply said it was a coat Coach Switzer had let me borrow for a party I had gone to the night before. The NCAA didn't press me too hard; in fact, it was almost as if they didn't want to know too much. All they had to do, to nail OU and me, was to walk outside the athletic building where I had parked a new Cougar Jackie Cooper was letting me use while my Regal was in the repair shop. After the NCAA left we thought everything was cool, but eight months later, in December 1988, we learned differently.

What I had discovered since the Orange Bowl, unfortunately, was that an OU football player could get away with murder. Our role models—Switzer, alumni, and boosters—were not only indulging us with money and gifts, but were showing us a side of their lives that said: this is what successful people do—drink, do drugs, and cheat. I knew right from wrong, but I saw very little right being done. Even so-called right things, like civic activities, were done the wrong way. For example, the players were often asked to make appearances at various functions as representatives of OU. According to NCAA regulations we were not allowed to be paid for them. In reality, doing something for nothing was the exception to that rule. Once, Steve Bentley, my first OU booster, gave a banquet in Norman for Oklahoma athletes. In addition to Keith Jackson and some others who had played out their eligibility and were permitted to receive money, he invited Jamelle and me to the dinner. Afterward Keith was given a thousand-dollar check, but when nobody was looking Bentley slipped both Jamelle and me five hundred in cash.

Even the visit to the Children's Hospital was paid for by gifts from Ken Henderson's drugstore. Bentley and Henderson at least tried to be discreet, but on one occasion Jackie Cooper pulled a stunt that could have shut down the whole football program. He was doing a big promotion for his auto dealership and had asked a few players to make an appearance. I showed up and shook a few hands, and then Jackie asked me to step outside. There was a van from the local radio station parked out front. Jackie asked me to go inside and say a few words about what a great deal you could get when you bought a car from Cooper's. I did it. It's one thing for Joe Montana to make a paid pitch for a car dealership, another thing for a college quarterback to play huckster.

Although I can rationalize and excuse myself for allowing the Bentleys, Hendersons, and Coopers into my life, I also allowed some lowlives to enter or reenter. About the time of the Orange Bowl Otha Armstrong, "Big O," moved to Norman. I hadn't seen or heard from Otha since the summer I graduated high school, but one day he popped up at Bud Hall with an armful of stolen VCR's in his arms. He soon became the retailer of hot merchandise to OU's football team—VCRs for twenty dollars; stereos for two hundred, etc. Otha sold me one stereo system for two hundred twenty-five; I priced it in the store for three thousand. Before I knew it, Otha was hanging around with us, and when we moved to the new apartment he showed up all the time.

Otha wasn't the only creep who came around. Jamelle's L.A.

homeboys also visited and brought dope; in fact, there was a parade of weird characters from Los Angeles and Lawton at the apartment, and neither Jamelle nor myself was smart enough to throw them out. We knew that most of them were slimeballs and dopers, but because of who we were we felt invincible. Even when our apartment was watched by either the police or OU security, we continued to carry on as usual. For several nights I saw the same car with tinted windows parked outside the apartment, and when I finally went outside to see who was in it, the driver took off. This was a warning I chose to disregard.

Trouble was brewing and it came to a boil during April practice. During football season the procedure at OU was to test the players for drugs once or twice a month. Because the tests were random I kept clean throughout the season. The first time I smoked primo with Jamelle was right after the Orange Bowl and I was caught by surprise when trainer Dan Pickett called for urine tests. I was scared silly, but we were able to get one of the assistants to switch the urine samples and I slid by.

When practice began in April I stayed clean for the period because they were going to test us once before the Red and White game, the final scrimmage between the varsity teams, played at Owen Field. A few days before the game we had been tested and were in what the players called "a comfort zone"; meaning no more drug tests until we returned to school in August. That had been the procedure for the last eight or nine years.

Once, when I was a freshman and not doing drugs, I got booted out of a car by some players before the Red and White game, because they were in the comfort zone and wanted to do some drugs. That's when it was explained to me that the comfort zone meant "time to run wild." The attitude of the players was, "Okay, now we can get fucked up." After the Red and

White game the coaches rarely saw us because we were studying for final exams, and soon after would be going home for the summer. Jamelle and I felt very safe before the game because both of us had minor injuries that prevented us from playing.

The night before I joined a few of the guys who decided to get high. We were in the comfort zone and nothing could happen. The next day we arrived at Owen Field in the back of Ken Henderson's limo, hung over and hiding our glassy, red eyes behind sunglasses. Back at the apartment were friends and family, including my mother, whom we'd invited for a big barbeque to celebrate the end of the school year. Two hundred dollars worth of steaks, chickens, four trashcans full of beer, and cabinets full of liquor were on hand, none of it, of course, paid for by us. We were all looking forward to the end of the scrimmage, and to the party, when trouble appeared in the form of Barry Switzer.

We were on the field when the coach pulled us off to the side to say, "I want a urine sample from you all before you leave today. If it's the last thing you do, don't leave without a urine sample." Jamelle and I looked at each other in disbelief. This was something they'd never done before, and there was no way we were going to pass it. As an afterthought Switzer told us that he wanted Lonnie Finch to leave a urine sample also.

Out on the field we walked around talking to ourselves. Jamelle was at one end of the field, and I was at the other, when Dan Pickett came to me with a big dumb grin on his face, and said: "CT, don't forget now. You come see me after the scrimmage." Then he walked down the sidelines and said the same thing to Jamelle. There was no doubt that he knew we were not going to pass any drug test. Every twenty minutes Pickett came back with that big fucking grin and repeated himself. Whoever had been watching the house had told Switzer what was going on inside. We were doomed.

THE LIFE AND CRIMES OF OKLAHOMA FOOTBALL

Jamelle was more shaken than I. He had already failed one drug test and couldn't afford to fail a second. A few minutes before the end of the scrimmage we decided to sneak away, hoping that Switzer would forget the whole thing. We wanted to figure out how to get the coke out of our systems. We'd heard about different methods, and were so desperate we were ready to try anything. Our plan was to go back to the apartment, drink water, vinegar, and beer, and smoke grass. We reasoned that it would be better to test positive for marijuana than cocaine.

At the apartment Lonnie Finch was waiting for us. "Oh, man, are you guys in trouble," he said. "Switzer is looking all over for you." Lonnie had stayed around after the game and had given a urine sample to Pickett. While Lonnie was talking, the phone kept ringing; Switzer was on the line demanding to know where we were. Jamelle's cousin Clint insisted nobody had seen us, but Switzer told him he was full of shit. Meanwhile, I was worried about my mother finding out. Ken Henderson had taken her for a ride to see someone's house and I prayed she wouldn't return until this was all over. Jamelle and I were in the backyard when we heard the front doorbell. It was Switzer.

"Shit," Jamelle said, "I might as well go inside." I hid out back, but I could hear Switzer screaming at him: "What the fuck's wrong with you, Jamelle? Didn't I tell you to wait around until after the game? Where is that little shit buddy of yours?" It was Switzer at his wildest: "Jamelle, you got twenty minutes to find that little turd and the two of you get your asses back to Pickett. I don't give a shit if the two of you have to sit there all night you're going to piss in those bottles. Don't fucking leave until you do so."

Switzer left in his Lincoln town car and Jamelle came back outside. He repeated to me what I'd already heard and we sat there trying to figure out what to do. After about thirty minutes

Jamelle said: "Fuck it, I gotta go. He's already seen me. What's the use?" I agreed with him and we got into the car to drive to the school. Pickett was there waiting for us with that same grin on his face: "How nice to see you boys again. I've been waiting for you."

Before I left the house I had put salt in my pockets, since I had heard that salt in the urine fucks up the test. But Pickett was watching us like a hawk: "Charles, get your fingers out of that bottle. I'm watching you, boy."

We knew it was hopeless and pissed into the bottles and left. "They got us," I said to Jamelle.

"Right, CT," he answered. "There's only one thing to do now until Switzer calls us in."

"What's that?" I asked.

Jamelle smiled. "Might as well really get fucked up. Nothing to lose now."

Monday morning, the phone rang. "Charles," Switzer said, "get Jamelle's, Lonnie's, and your ass down to the office now." When we walked in he was fairly calm. The three of us had cocaine in our systems, Lonnie the most and I the least. Switzer told Lonnie he'd deal with him later, that now he wanted to talk to Jamelle and me. As soon as the door closed behind Lonnie, he went crazy:

"Look at you, my two quarterbacks, my leaders. What kinda fucking leaders are you? How could you fuck around with this shit? I'm disappointed. I'm . . ." and Switzer began to cry. Jamelle and I looked down and refused to meet his eyes. I think this was the first and only time we felt we'd hurt him.

"I love coaching," Switzer went on, "but I ain't gonna do it anymore. Jamelle, you're my leader. Charles, you're my leader of the future. Your teammates look up to you. You gotta slow down. I know about the drinking and I know that you're young guys, but maybe you have drinking problems." I don't know how long the tirade lasted, but Switzer kept saying how much he had been hearing about us. He never mentioned what he saw when he drank with us, but I wasn't going to correct him at that moment. "Now it's coke," he said, shaking his head. "It's getting out of hand."

Jamelle and I promised Switzer that we would get our act together and that we had learned our lesson. We'd known he was going to rip into us, but we weren't certain how. What he was supposed to do was report us to the NCAA, but neither of us thought Switzer would risk losing us for the next season. The coach did have standards, but the overriding one was winning football games.

"Okay," he decided, "here's what's going to happen. I want the two of you and Lonnie to spend the summer in Norman. I want you tested every week for drugs. Charles, I'm going to call your father and tell him about this and I also want you to see the school psychologist."

That was it. You could hear our sighs of relief clear across the campus. He was going to let us skate, Jamelle would get away with even more than I. One of his girlfriends had given birth, and when he asked Switzer to let him spend the summer in California to be near his new baby, he was given permission. As far as my staying in Norman, that was what I had planned to do anyway. I wasn't too thrilled about my father finding out about the cocaine, but I knew I could make him feel better by telling him it was the first time I had ever tried drugs. He might see through that, but it was what he wanted to hear. I did have to see Dr. Wayne, the school shrink, but that was nothing more than Switzer covering his and the school's ass. In fact, Switzer was such a bullshit artist that he never released the drug test until the following March after I was arrested for dealing cocaine. Nothing ever changes at OU: do what you got to do to win those football games.

211

I walked out of Barry Switzer's office that April day pissed off only because I had to be tested for drugs once a week and that would be an inconvenience. Oddly enough, I did not have a drug problem. It didn't bother me that I couldn't do drugs, but I was annoyed at being treated like a common druggie. It is easy to say that most addicts have a problem with denial, but physicians who tested me later agreed that I did not have a physical dependency. It was stupid of me to do all the drinking and drugs that year, but I did them not because I had to, but wanted to. I believe that if Switzer had really cracked down on me that day I would have stayed away from drugs. What I realized was that Barry Switzer had given me a license to do anything, as long as I didn't get caught.

OUT OF HAND

The worst prospect about the coming summer was that Jamelle would be in California. Although hundreds of people had come into my life that spring, he was the only one who was a real friend. Five months of living with Lonnie Finch had not developed our friendship; in fact, I looked forward to moving back on campus the next semester only because I wouldn't be living with Lonnie.

Although I liked him, Lonnie Finch never came up with an idea of his own, but would wait for Jamelle or me to decide to do something and then ride on our shirttails. Lonnie knew a lot of people, alumni and boosters, through us. Most of the players resented the attention Jamelle and I got and did a lot of talking behind our backs. The white players said we had Switzer in the bag, and tolerated us only on the football field or when we threw a party and they could get free booze. Lonnie got women, booze, drugs, and other perks because of us. By the end of spring I wanted him out of my sight.

People who had known Lonnie earlier claimed that Jamelle changed him. There was some truth in this. Lonnie did everything Jamelle did or asked him to do. I don't think he would have tried drugs if he hadn't wanted to impress Jamelle.

Jamelle himself believed Coach Donnan bad mouthed him to Switzer as a bad influence on the other players. He thought Donnan did it because he was jealous.

Jamelle Holieway
Coach Donnan said I did everything to lead Charles on. This goes back to when I first came to Oklahoma to play.

213

Donnan would call fucked-up plays, and everyone would look at everyone else like, damn, why did you call that play? So it made him look bad when I called better plays. I always tried to be one step ahead. And when I did this, it belittled him. They'd go into meetings and they'd see the films. There would be a sheet with the plays we checked off. And I checked off a lot during the game that would work, and they'd marvel at this and look at Donnan as if he should've done that. Donnan felt as if I had something on him. I couldn't help knowing the wishbone better than he did. When Charles arrived, he told him to stay away from me. Then Donnan came to me and said, well, try to get in good with Charles.

People also said Jamelle had corrupted me. What they didn't seem to understand was that I had my own personality. Of course you're influenced when you hang around with one person most of the time, but, I was always my own man. If there was something I wanted to do, nobody, including Jamelle Holieway, was going to change my mind. But Jamelle could talk Lonnie out of anything, and he often did. If I said to Jamelle: "Let's go to Chrystal's and get us some women," Lonnie would pipe up, "Yeah, let's go." If I said to Jamelle, "Let's go to Tulsa and see Frank Vale," Lonnie would say, "Okay, I'll come with you." For a while I didn't let it get to me. I thought Lonnie and other players should share in some of the good things available to Sooner footballers, but when he began to act like a hot shot I lost my patience with him. When his Mr. Hyde personality took over, Lonnie not only bothered me, he hurt himself.

He drank when he wasn't a drinker, and he did himself little good when he started with drugs. He also had a really nice girlfriend who loved him, but because of Jamelle or me or both of us, he thought he should have three or four. He wound up making a fool of himself with the others, and worst of all he lost a woman who loved him dearly.

People sometimes misunderstood me because I was the shyest and quietest of the three. They were wrong thinking I was under Jamelle's thumb, and soon learned that Charles Thompson could and would assert himself without any prodding.

One of our neighbors on Comanche Drive was a middle-aged woman who liked me very much and called me "baby face." She was aware of all the partying at the apartment, but thought I was the little brother who was being led astray by his two older, wilder brothers. What she didn't know until one evening was that I was the one who kept order, that whenever there were problems, I was the one who dealt with them. I was very proud of the apartment, it being the first one I had away from my parents, and I wanted people to respect it as my home. Despite the parties it wasn't a crash pad. We kept it neat, clean, and as quiet as possible. It became my job to kick out anyone who thought differently.

One evening when Jamelle and I were home watching television a girlfriend of his came to visit. After a few minutes it became obvious that Jamelle didn't want her there but she wouldn't take the hint, wouldn't shut her mouth, and was disturbing us. "Michelle," I said, "why don't you sit over there and watch the show with us?" She ignored me and went on talking. I asked her again, but she went on talking as before, only louder. "Look," I told her, "either chill out and watch television or else you're going to have to leave." It made no difference to me if she was a friend of Jamelle's; this was my home. I got up and led her outside.

But Michelle wouldn't quit, and stood banging on the glass door with her fists. "You better get her to quit or I'm going to do something," I said to Jamelle, who shrugged his shoulders and went back to the television. I got a big pail, filled it with hot

215

water, and went upstairs, opened the window, and emptied the water on Michelle still banging on the door. "Now," I said, "you'll leave."

The next day I bumped into my neighbor. "Baby face," she said with a big smile, "I guess I was wrong about you. You are the bad brother." She was joking, but like other people she had misjudged the relationship between Jamelle and me and was surprised to learn I wasn't a clone of OU's other quarterback.

Unfortunately, Jamelle had to pay a price for how people felt about the two of us. After we failed the drug test the coaches placed the blame on Jamelle. He had led sweet Charles Thompson astray, and thank goodness, Charles wouldn't be living with him any longer. The big city boy had taken the nice small-town boy down the road to ruin. Even today there are people at OU who think that I wouldn't have gotten into trouble if I hadn't met Jamelle Holieway. There is no truth in it, I am responsible for myself. It is to Jamelle's credit that he has never complained to me about it.

I knew I'd be seeing a great deal of Otha Armstrong that summer because by the end of the semester he was at our apartment almost every day. Jamelle got along well with Otha, but never missed an opportunity to break his balls. Otha was washed up as a football player, cut from the Washington Redskins, but he still loved to play the role of big shot. He would drive up to the house in his new maroon Nissan 300ZX like some high paid NFL star, and empty his trunk of hot merchandise. I knew that Otha was a thief, but he swore the merchandise wasn't stolen, and claimed to be working for a drug dealer who used him as a strong armed man to collect money. When the debtor had no cash, Otha would take merchandise. Otha claimed the dealer only wanted the amounts owed him and that he'd told Otha to keep the rest. He may not have been lying; a friend who was a police officer in Norman checked out the serial numbers on a stereo I bought from Otha, and told me that the set had not been reported stolen. However Otha got the stuff, it was his only known means of income.

Otha was dark complected and Jamelle loved to call him "Black Ass." "Otha," Jamelle would rag on him, "there ain't no way any respectable woman is going to go out with a nigger like you." Otha would protest: "Jamelle, if you were no quarterback, you'd never get laid." One day, Jamelle told Otha that he was going to prove him wrong. "Otha, you know that dumb bitch you live with?" he said. "I'm going to take her away from you. Once I fuck her she'll never want to see your black ass again." True to his word, Jamelle got Otha's girlfriend over to the apartment and fucked her. To rub it in, Jamelle passed her along to Lonnie. She never went back to Otha.

Otha would often appear at the apartment with other people I had known in Lawton. One of them was John Douglas, who had played baseball with me in high school. John also was a good football player, but had decided to concentrate on baseball and attended Seminole Junior College before accepting a scholarship to play at OU. I was happy to see John, but two other characters from Lawton that Otha brought around—Moses and Flip (not their real names)—made me nervous. They were associates of Snowman and probably never earned an honest dollar in their lives. They were older than I and had criminal records. Although I was suspicious of them, I couldn't figure out what they wanted from me.

They were sharp street people and I warned Jamelle about them, but of course Jamelle thought nobody was smarter than the dumbest person from Los Angeles and underestimated Moses and Flip. Once he asked them to shoot craps, thinking this would be an easy way to make a few hundred dollars. Two hours later Jamelle handed over six hundred to the two rubes from Lawton. Pissed off, he left the house. Flip and Moses thought this was funny and gave all the money to John Douglas and me. It was obvious that they had more than six hundred dollars on their minds, but I didn't know what, except that it had something to do with Snowman.

A few days after the incident Flip and Snowman called me. Snowman talked about Dallas and reminded me to visit him when I came down there to see my mother. We talked about the summer I won all the foot races and he ended the call by saying, "Charles, if there is anything, I mean anything, I can do for you, don't hesitate to call me." It was to be an offer I should have refused.

Another OU player in Norman that summer was defensive back, Jerry Parks. Jerry was a weird, volatile red-shirted freshman from Houston, who had to attend summer school to make up some failed courses and was also being tested for drugs. Jerry had never been caught doing drugs; rather, he'd volunteered his drug use to Switzer. His confession left a lot of players nervous about him; Jerry Parks had an attitude of not giving a damn about anything. If something was on his mind, he said it. I liked Jerry and knew that we would spend time together that summer.

My only plan for the summer was to get a new car. I was driving the Cougar Jackie Cooper had loaned me after I'd wrecked my new Regal, which was still in the shop and which I doubted would ever be the same, even after repairs. A month earlier, I'd been driving back to the apartment, drunk and speeding, when the rear wheels hit the curb and the car spun around and crashed into a pole. I got out to take a look at the damage. The car was pointed in the opposite direction from the way I'd been headed, its tires flat and axle broken. "Fuck it," I screamed and decided to leave it there and to walk the three blocks back to the apartment.

When I got home there were several people waiting for me. I

218

must have been shaking all over because someone remarked that it looked as if I'd been in an accident. I laughed and tried not to make a big deal out of it and said that I'd had a minor accident.

"You can't leave it there," Jamelle said. "Your registration is in the car." A few of us decided to return to the scene and found five police cars there. I was too drunk to talk to them and went back to the house.

A few hours later the police called to tell me that they'd towed the car to the station house. They weren't too concerned that I had left the scene and asked only whether I had been drinking and had I been wearing my seatbelt. Of course I wasn't drinking. Yes, I was wearing my seatbelt. As far as the police were concerned everything was cool, but when I went to the shop where the car was eventually towed, I knew I'd never want to drive it again. I liked Otha's car and decided to buy a new Nissan 300ZX. What I wasn't certain about was how I was going to pay for the purchase.

The Regal had been registered in my high-school teacher's name. I knew, to avoid NCAA scrutiny, that I had to put a new car in someone else's name, but I wanted to avoid asking boosters, taking out loans, and all the rest of it.

The question was how to get fifteen thousand dollars. There was only one person I knew who could lend it to me—Snowman. My intention was to visit him and ask to borrow the money. Later, somehow, I would repay him with interest. I wasn't thinking about drugs until I discussed my plan to borrow money from Snowman with Otha.

Otha thought I was a fool to borrow money when there was an easier way. "CT, you're talking about, what, fifteen thousand?" he said. "In a month—no, two or three weeks—you can make that and more without worrying about paying it back.

Fifteen thousand is sucker money to someone like Snowman. Let him front you some coke and you'll have the money."

At first I refused: "Otha, there ain't no fucking way I'm gonna get involved with that shit. I got a reputation here. It ain't gonna look good for the fucking quarterback of Oklahoma going around Norman dealing coke."

"Shit, Charles, you don't have to deal it," Otha argued. "You just get the shit and I'll get rid of it. You know, CT, you'll also be helping me out. I sorta got a cash flow problem and could use a few bucks. Look, you got nothing to worry about. You can sit back and I'll be the one walking around with the shit. I ain't gonna let anything happen to your career. If there's any trouble, it'll be me they'll come after. Would I ever fuck you, CT?"

That is when the idea was born. There were several discussions about it with Otha, but I continued to turn down the idea. If I had given him a final "no," nothing would have come of it, but I was greedy and he was convincing. Soon, rather than saying no, I began to ask him questions about how we could do it, lying to myself that I wasn't really going to sell drugs, but curious about what Otha would say. Otha knew he had me after a while and began to appeal to my greed: "CT, think of it: fifteen thousand and you won't owe anyone a penny. All you do is make a trip to Dallas, see your mom, and pick up the coke on the way home. It's a piece of cake. Hey, I don't mind being the man out in front. If I have to take the rap for you, no big deal."

Why did I decide to sell drugs? I've thought about it every day for more than a year, and I'm still not certain why I would do something I always knew was wrong. Even when I was smoking primo with Jamelle I knew I was breaking the law and made a big deal of hiding it from other people—not because I could get into trouble with the law, but I felt that it was the worst lesson the quarterback of OU should be giving to other people. Yet by the end of that spring I was psyched up with this drug shit. It was bad, but it was exciting. It was something new to do, another challenge. My life had been filled with things that people never expected me to accomplish, but I had proven them wrong. When I got to OU nobody thought I would take Jamelle Holieway's quarterback job, but I did. Nobody in the nation thought I could lead OU to victory over Nebraska, but I did. Now, I felt, everything was easy.

Whenever I needed anything—money, girls, gifts—all I had to do was pick up the telephone and dial. I saw the selling of drugs as a new adventure, something to keep me going. In a perverted sense I saw a moral in it. For the first time in a long time I would be earning my own money. I wanted to get things without being beholden to other people. When I decided to sell cocaine to make money for the car I never thought I was doing the right thing, but I did believe I was breaking away from a system that I felt was strangling me.

At the end of June, I telephoned Snowman. I didn't tell him what was on my mind, just that I wanted to talk to him. I was driving to Dallas over the weekend to see my mother and I thought he and I should have dinner together. I told Otha I would talk to Snowman and feel him out. Snowman's reaction surprised me; he tried to talk me out of it: "Charles, this not kid stuff. You know that people recognize you up there. I want you to think about it a little more. I'm not saying no, but I want you to be sure you know what you're getting into. Go back, think some more, check it all out and come back and see me." I didn't tell Snowman about Otha's involvement because he didn't trust him and would have refused then and there to have anything to do with the idea.

A few days later I called Snowman from Norman. I told him that I had thought it out and was ready to move some cocaine. He didn't argue with me and said that it would be there when I visited Dallas the following week. And so it started. I picked up two ounces of cocaine and returned to Norman and Otha with it. Now, I thought, let Otha take care of business. But it wasn't so simple. Otha promised me he would get rid of the coke quickly, but I found myself chasing him all over town for days. He always had an excuse for why things were taking so long. Sometimes there were other people at his house looking for him because he owed them money or drugs.

I realized I wasn't going to get my car the way I had planned, and in the middle of July I did what I could have done two months earlier: I asked Shelly, the friend who got me drugs from her father's clinic, to take out a loan and register the Nissan 300ZX in her name. Then I prayed that Otha would get enough money so I could pay off the loan; if not, I'd have to turn to the boosters.

While I waited for Otha to move the cocaine I was bringing back from Dallas, I spent most of my time hanging out with Jerry Parks, John Green, and a few other guys from the team. We did nothing but drink, and decided to formalize our association by starting the "Winos," the Sooner football fraternity. Although Jerry and I were supposed to be tested for drugs regularly, things had cooled down since April and the trainers had become lax. I was able to control the days of the drug testing and made sure I was clean on those dates.

Jerry drove to Dallas with me, but knew nothing about my visits with Snowman. He did suspect Otha of drug dealing, but only because so many strange people were coming around asking for him. When Jerry asked me about it I told him that Otha was moving a little stuff, nothing heavy. A few weeks in the cocaine business with Otha had convinced me that it was not for me. He disappeared for periods of time and was always behind in the money, which was insignificant for what I was risking and came in dribs and drabs.

I could never get hold of Otha when I needed him. Everyone

else on the team would see him, but Otha was doing a great job of ducking me. This pissed me off, and I got so angry with him that I failed to see how he was setting me up.

Otha had the stupid practice of bringing his customers over to my house. I told him this was dangerous, but he said, "Come on, CT, they know that you're my friend and they're big fans of yours. They don't know that we're in business together." Al was one of the characters he brought to my house. Otha said, "Oh, Al's real cool. Shit, you can do anything around him, CT."

One day I went to Otha's house; it was a week since I'd seen him and I wanted my money. Al was also there looking for Otha, and we began to complain to one another about him, how he wasn't a dependable guy and only seemed to be around when he wanted a favor. Al told me that Otha had been promising him coke. What he hid from me was that he was a member of the OSBI (Oklahoma State Bureau of Investigation) and was getting ready to set me up.

Right after that meeting with Al, I heard from Otha, who told me some bullshit story about why he and I weren't connecting, and that we would be able to make some money off Al. At the time I had a little more than four grams of cocaine in the trunk of my car. Otha told me to give it to Al and that Al would pay for another four grams of coke Otha had given him earlier. The situation sounded weird to me, but I wanted to get the money to repay Snowman. I told Otha: "Okay, I'll give it to him, but you collect the money," thinking I was avoiding actual dealing by not taking any money for the cocaine. I should have recognized that something was really bad about the deal when Otha added, "CT, you know that five hundred I owe you? Al will give it to you." There was no reason in the world why a "legitimate" drug buyer would lay out five hundred dollars. But when you're not thinking, just trying to get out of a bad situation, you do things you would not do any other time.

I was to meet Al on two occasions, which I later learned were videotaped and recorded. At the first meeting Al went all out to get me: "Look, man," he said, "I know that you're the one who can get the coke. I want to deal directly with you. You seem pretty straight; shit, I spend half my time looking for Otha. You're a smart guy. You know how it is in this business. When you need the shit, you need it now. You don't need it next week, next year. I lose my clientele that way. You're reliable and I want to deal only with you."

Al asked me for another ounce of coke for the following week. I told him I would get it, but I wanted the money up front. When I returned to Snowman a week later with the money, he wasn't angry but warned me not to try to get the money from customers before I gave them the drugs. Again, that sale was videotaped. But why wasn't I arrested? To understand the answer to that question I have to explain two other events, which took place within a month of each other.

A few days before the end of July, Barry Switzer called me to his office. When I got there he was boiling. "We got a real problem, Charles. I know everything that is going on," he said. "You're fucking with drugs again. You're not only fucking with them, you're selling them. Don't deny anything. You know I got a lot of friends in Oklahoma police and they've told me. I can't believe it. My quarterback selling drugs."

Then he got off the drug dealing and asked me, "Do you have a drug problem? I think you do. I don't give a fuck what the school shrinks said last time. I think you got a problem. We're gonna settle this once and for all. And this time I want your whole family down here to help straighten it out." It seemed a little bit more serious this time; Switzer let me know that I had failed another drug test. I wondered why he didn't tell me until now, but I kept my mouth shut. He told me that he was going to wait until my family got to Norman before he discussed it any

224

further with me. I was so upset about my parents finding out about the drugs that I never worried that Switzer knew about my dealings with Otha. You could say that Switzer was sticking his neck out to save me, but that was never the case. It was as Jamelle had told me in April: "Nothing is gonna come of this, CT. The man needs his quarterbacks to win."

Jamelle was correct, but this time Switzer had caught only one of his two quarterbacks. Maybe Switzer would throw me off the team? Maybe he would even report us to the NCAA, which he was required to do in April and never did. But no, Switzer was going to do what was best for him and OU, and when my family arrived for the meeting, I was certain about it.

They sat in his office while he confronted me about everything. I didn't deny anything, but I tried to soften some of what he said. "Yeah, Coach, I was involved with coke, but I never actually sold any of it. No, Coach, I've tried cocaine, but I don't have a problem. I don't need it, I just do it to have a good time. I'm definitely not addicted to it." When Switzer looked dubious since I had continued to do coke even though I knew I was going to be tested, I said nothing. I wasn't going to tell him that his trainers had become so lenient in testing us that I thought I could get away with it.

Finally, Switzer got to the bottom line. "Charles," he said, looking at my parents, "we're going to have to take different measures. Apparently, you need help because you are going to continue this behavior. We are at the point that we have to show that we're making some effort to correct this problem. If you show no effort, you cannot be on the team any longer. I want you to go to drug rehabilitation."

Switzer was full of shit, but there was nothing I could say with my mother and father sitting there. I knew that he wasn't concerned about whether or not I had a drug problem, but rather covering his ass with the NCAA and making sure he had two quarterbacks available the following season. I saw right through him when he told my mother, "I don't want the school involved in Charles's drug rehabilitation (meaning it will look like the school knows nothing about Charles failing another drug test and no reason to notify the NCAA). I want the family to pay for it (meaning you'll probably get a booster to pay for it). And I want Charles here on the first day of practice (meaning I don't give a shit where he goes for rehabilitation, but it better be over in ten days so he can play football)."

I realized that my parents were deeply concerned about their son having gotten involved with drugs, but it still surprised me how they were taken in by Switzer. It took them a long time to understand that if Barry Switzer was really concerned about their son's drug problem, he would be sending me somewhere for real treatment. But Barry Switzer is in a class by himself when it comes to dealing with the parents of black athletes. They think he cares about their children. When I was arrested in February, Switzer went public for the first time, and tried to make a big deal about how he had tried to help me back in August.

Switzer milked the meeting with my family and me for as much as he could. I was made to admit how lucky I was that Coach Switzer was giving me a chance to play football for OU, and to promise that I would never get involved with drugs again. Dan Pickett provided my mother with a list of drug rehabilitation places, but the school was not to know which one the family chose to send me. Because I had to be back for practice in two weeks there weren't too many options. My mother called around and she was told either thirty or sixty days were the minimum stays for drug admissions. We finally found some place in a rundown section of Oklahoma City that would take me in for a few weeks. The cost was fourteen hundred dollars and Frank Vale paid for it.

The rehabilitation was a joke. There were some tests, but I can't recall any type of therapy. I was admitted under my mother's family name, Lamont Yarbrough, but most of the guys there knew who I was. They sat around talking about Oklahoma football and a few of the patients called me "Charles." When I told them they were calling me by the wrong name, they would say: "Man, you sure do look like Charles Thompson." Still, they were nice to me and said things like, "It's okay, man, everybody fucks up." The hospital released me ten days after I was admitted and suggested that I have follow-up visits. They concluded that I wasn't addicted to drugs, but that I had a background of chemical dependency and should be cautious in the future.

As for why I hadn't been arrested, I thought Switzer had something to do with it. From what he'd told me it seemed that the Oklahoma police not only knew I was dealing drugs, but where I was getting them from. I did feel lucky, and while I was not going to sell drugs anymore, Otha still owed me money and I was going to collect it. When I caught up with him he invited me to his house. When I got there he introduced me to the guy I got to know as "Tony." In court the following year I would learn his real name and that he was with the FBI. Otha began bullshitting to me about the problems he was having collecting from a guy he had sold to. He said that Tony was helping him collect. Otha said that Tony was great in tracking down guys who owed money to bookies and that we could depend on him.

One afternoon on campus Otha and Tony approached me as I sat in my car with Kori. "Hey, Charles," Tony said, "Otha tells me you still got a problem." I thought it strange and told Tony that I had no problem. But Tony continued, "It's okay, Otha explained the whole deal. I'm gonna get it for you." I was suspicious of Otha and told Tony, "If you get something that belongs to me, bring it to my house." It was a mistake for me to even talk to Tony. From that day on he did everything possible to get me to score drugs from Snowman in Dallas.

What I wasn't able to figure out back then was simple: Otha was a snitch for Al from the Oklahoma State Police. Al had used Otha to set me up for a drug bust, but when the police realized that the drugs came from a big-time dealer in Dallas they turned over the case to the FBI. Otha was assigned to work with Tony in using me to set up Snowman. Oklahoma police had warned Switzer about what was going on, but not about the FBI investigation to nail Snowman. Switzer, like I, thought it had ended in August. But it was not going to be over until the FBI realized that I would never get drugs from Snowman again and decided to get me in some other way. By that time something even more disturbing than drugs was going on in Norman.

BEFORE THE STORM

I returned to Norman in the middle of August determined to put everything behind me. Too much had been happening since the Orange Bowl and I wanted to take control of my life, to get away from a lot of things, nothing more than drugs. I knew that I wasn't a drug addict and was going to prove it to anyone who might have had doubts. It's a good thing I wasn't an addict because a few days at a rehab clinic wouldn't have solved anyone's problem. Over the next six months, I was tested some twenty-odd times and passed each time. I wanted to play football and wasn't going to push Switzer to the point where he'd be forced to throw me off the team.

I moved back on campus and roomed at Bud Hall with Jerry Parks. Jamelle and Lonnie moved out of the apartment on Comanche Drive. Jamelle found a new place where the rent was paid by a booster, and he asked me to live with him, but I refused. I wanted to be away from him. Besides being burnt out from what had happened, I wanted to prepare myself mentally for the fight for the starting quarterback job. It was Jamelle's final year at OU and I knew he wanted to go out as the starter.

Jamelle and I never argued, but there was a change in our relationship after the summer, which had more to do with football than anything personal. For the first time since he'd become starting quarterback, he was being pressured for the job. The coaches had a theory that if they played us off one another we would try harder. In a way this worked. On the field I felt different about Jamelle, to survive I had to do better than he did.

What I didn't understand when I returned for August practice was that Switzer had already made up his mind. He had no plan to give me a fair chance to win the starting job and was going to hand it to Jamelle because he felt he owed it to him. It was payback time for Switzer for all that Jamelle had done for him and fuck Charles Thompson. I was hurt because I had done everything on the field Jamelle had done. Donnan told me that Switzer would go with Jamelle until he proved he couldn't do the job. Before the first game of the season I began to lose my enthusiasm.

It was difficult to go all out in practice when I knew it was going to get me no further than if I did nothing at all. Donnan tried hard to keep my spirits up, but I wasn't sure whether he was encouraging me because he believed in me or because he hated Jamelle Holieway. Making matters worse for the team was that there were only nine returning starters for the 1988 season, the fewest number in fifteen years. There was a great deal of uncertainty about how the players would perform. The younger, inexperienced players were good athletes, but as Switzer was fond of saying: Can they do it when the band is playing?

We were fine in the backfield at running back and quarterback, but our offensive line was inexperienced and weak at tight end. Bernard Hall was back, but he was a big question mark. The biggest question was our defensive line which was big but young. Our first game was against North Carolina. The odds-makers had made us a 23½-point favorite, and OU was ranked number four in the national polls. It looked as if the bookies and newspapers had more confidence in OU than the team had in itself.

I played more than I'd expected to in the game, but it still felt like a back-up role. Jamelle was in for forty-nine plays and I got in the game for twenty-five snaps from center. Our defensive line proved itself as we beat North Carolina 28–0. Jamelle played well, leading the team on three long scoring drives, but when he ran it seemed as if he was still having trouble with his knee. It was not a good game for me. Though I ran for sixty-three yards, I fumbled the ball four times. I couldn't get myself up for the game and felt sluggish.

Although Switzer had decided to start Jamelle, he was going to alternate his two quarterbacks in the game. If that was the way it was going to be, I decided I'd better stop acting like a baby and go out there and do my job. The following week's game was against a tough but underrated Arizona team. We were favored by twenty-three points, but I don't think the Arizona players knew it. They were a physical team and came out hitting. It was a good game, but fumbles and penalties helped both sides more than any outstanding plays. I took some good licks in the third quarter and was knocked out of the game. I thought my back was broken, but it proved to be nothing more than a bad bruise. Jamelle played for the first time like the Holieway of old and led the team to a 28–10 victory.

The team, especially Jamelle, looked forward to our next game against USC in Los Angeles. Everyone expected Jamelle to have a great game as he returned to his hometown. We were a one-point favorite against number five ranked USC, and it was to be the first time OU was tested that season. The coaches and sports press made a big deal about Jamelle's coming home to Los Angeles in his final season as Oklahoma's quarterback. Watching him during practice that week I had doubts about it. Although he'd played well in the Arizona game, he didn't have the spark he used to display on the field. There was nothing wrong with his mechanics, but the quickness was not there. Emotionally, he was not the same player. Donnan saw it, but there was no changing Switzer's mind.

USC began kicking our asses from the start. If any quarter-back was going to be the star of the game, it was not going to be

Jamelle Holieway. Rodney Peete took charge of USC's offense and led them to twenty quick points by the half. Jamelle was horrible. Two of his fumbles deep in OU territory led to USC scores. On the field he looked as if he were moving in slow motion. At halftime we hadn't put a point on the board.

We had to make a change, and Donnan said to me, "Get ready because we're going to put you in, probably the first or second series of the quarter. We'll let Jamelle start, see if he can turn it around, but if nothing happens you go in." The coaches were worried. In three previous games OU hadn't beaten USC and Switzer was already seeing tomorrow's sports pages. He came to talk to me at the half and also told me to get ready. He was not going to lose again to USC.

Switzer may have wanted to win, but he had his head up his ass in the second half. I was ready to go in, but he kept waiting for Jamelle to do something to turn the game around. I couldn't believe it. He kept Jamelle in for the whole third quarter, and five minutes into the last quarter, before he sent me in with USC winning 23–7. The only way we could catch up was by throwing the ball and we were not a passing team. There were ten minutes remaining in the game and they wanted me to pull a miracle. There was little I could do but drop straight back and throw the ball. That was no big surprise for USC and their defensive backs sat back and played centerfield for the rest of the game. I completed four passes for thirty-seven yards but had three interceptions. I was disgusted about the whole thing, and angry that Switzer hadn't put me in earlier. By the time I came in OU had given up the wishbone and wound up being embarrassed before eighty-six thousand fans in the Los Angeles Coliseum. It was a quiet flight back to Oklahoma.

After the USC game we all knew that Jamelle was not the same player. We had an easy schedule the next few games, and I knew Switzer would start Jamelle, but I was certain that before the season ended I was going to be the starting quarterback. What was troubling me about Jamelle was that he didn't seem to care. He was still partying as hard as ever and drinking more than he should. If there wasn't a party over at his apartment he'd have guys coming over to shoot craps and play cards. He'd invite me to his place, but I'd tell him I was too busy. I wanted no part of that life. Also, there was something else going on that was more important to me than either Jamelle or football.

When I returned to school in August I knew that I wanted Kori in my life, but I knew that to win her over I would have to change. She was not impressed with the glamorous side of Oklahoma football and even less impressed with many of the people around me. Kori was one of the most beautiful women on campus and I was not the only one interested in her. She would speak to me and exchange notes in class, but we never had a real date, partly because she was seeing someone else, and also because of the racial factor. She didn't like to date black guys. She wasn't a bigot—quite the opposite, she had many black friends—but she knew how strongly her father, a full-blooded American Indian, felt about the subject. It made me wonder about the guy, since he was married to a white woman. Also, I think Kori was simply playing hard to get. It was her way of letting me know that though I dated some of the most beautiful women on campus because I was a hot dog quarterback, I would have to work harder if I expected her to go out with me.

I talked about her all the time to my roommate, Jerry Parks, who laughed at me when I told him that if Kori went out with me I wouldn't run around as in the past. "Shit," Jerry said, "I give you one month and you'll be back fucking every girl you meet. You can't change, CT."

I knew what Jerry was saying, and that was one of the problems I was having with Kori. I was a womanizer. I didn't think

233

of it as a problem, though, but rather a stage in life I had gone through. I didn't feel it was abnormal, but that now was the time to move on and grow up. I had gone out with several women for long periods of time, but I didn't love any of them. Monica understood that I was going to fool around, and that if she wanted to see other guys, that too was fine with me. With Kori everything was different. She was somebody I wanted to be a major part of my life. I was happy just to sit and talk to her about everyday things. I liked thinking about her all the time. I knew that she was special, and because of that I did not want to see anybody else.

Our relationship developed slowly, neither one of us certain what it would lead to. Kori said later that she didn't think it would turn out to be as serious. At first I wasn't too sure myself what was happening. It was one thing to want her because she was beautiful and aloof, another to court her.

Kori was not a total innocent. She'd had her flings when she first came to college, no different from most other young people away from home for the first time; but she never let herself get out of control. She had gone through drinking and drugs, and now that those were behind her she didn't want to get caught up again because of me. I told her a little about the previous summer, but nothing about the drug dealing. She knew that I had been caught using drugs and that was all. I would eventually tell her, but I was having enough trouble winning her over and thought certain things could wait.

Jamelle doubted Kori's sincerity and thought her just another starfucker no different from other women on campus. He couldn't see that she was a serious person, concerned about her pre-med studies and her future. It wasn't until I was in serious trouble, convicted, and imprisoned, and Kori had stood by me throughout the ordeal, that he understood what she was all about. Still, it made no difference to me what Jamelle or any of my teammates thought of Kori, I had found the person I wanted to share my life with.

We won our next two games against Iowa State and Texas. Iowa State was a blowout, 35–7, but Texas at home played us tough, losing 28–13. Jamelle was not looking any better, and in the Texas game Switzer knew he had to make a change at quarterback. Early in the game Jamelle had hurt his ankle, and although it wasn't a serious injury it gave Switzer an excuse to keep me in for the rest of the game. I was feeling better than I had all season and ran the wishbone as if I'd been born to it. I was so confident that I began to change plays at the line of scrimmage, something I'd never done before. I wasn't thinking on the field as much as reacting. I felt relaxed and able to read defenses as though viewing them as a spectator. After the game the coaches saw the difference. Donnan said, "Well, we made a decision. Jamelle doesn't have it any more. Switzer wants you to start."

Now that I had won the starting quarterback job again I wasn't going to lose it. I was on fire for the following week's game against Kansas State. Jamelle was going to play, but I was the starter. It was the perfect opportunity to end the quarterback controversy. On our first four possessions, I led the team to four touchdowns. In the first half I completed five out of seven passes, one of them a touchdown to Adrian Cooper. By the end of the game I had rushed for 123 yards including a seventy-seven yard touchdown run. It felt as if I owned the field and could do no wrong. I also felt good that Jamelle was able to play, so that everybody could watch both quarterbacks and draw their own conclusions as to who should be the starter. The final score of the game was OU 70, Kansas State 24.

The Kansas State game demonstrated how explosive the wishbone could be, but unlike the previous year our defense was giving up a lot of points. It was not the great Oklahoma defense of years past. For the past eleven years we had played Colorado and each game we blew them out. When we went to play them everybody expected another easy victory. OU was favored by fourteen points and we thought we'd win the game by twenty or more. We were in for a surprise. Not only was Colorado's defense tough, but they showed how shaky ours was. They ran up almost as much total yardage as we did (339 yards to 379 yards), and it took a twenty-two-yard field goal in the middle of the fourth quarter for us to eke out a 17–14 victory.

We were happy for the win against a determined team, and for me personally, the game was vindication against a few Jamelle Holieway fans who did not believe I could win in the dramatic, closing-minutes style he had become famous for. With the game tied in the last quarter Switzer had the option of taking me out and going with Jamelle. There was a moment after we got the ball back that Switzer looked at Jamelle and he got up and put on his helmet. But then Switzer turned away and I went out on the field, moving the team seventy-one yards down the field for R.D. Lasher's field goal and the victory. One more time Charles Thompson had proven he could do anything Jamelle Holieway did.

We suffered several key injuries in the Colorado game, and were playing with more and more inexperienced players. We were ranked number eight in the nation, but we had four more games to go in the season. Three of those four were against tough Oklahoma State, Nebraska, and Missouri teams. I knew that we would have to remain healthy if we were going to end the year with only the one loss against USC.

We caught a breather the next week against Kansas and won 63–14. Kansas was the worst team in the conference and nobody expected the score to be different. The most noteworthy event of the game was that it allowed Jamelle Holieway to become Oklahoma's all-time career yardage leader. It was a great accomplishment for Jamelle because it put him in a category with such OU greats as Billy Vessels, Billy Sims, and Joe Washington. Although I had a good game and was overlooked because of his record, I was happy for Jamelle. It was the only bright moment for him in a disappointing senior year. What pissed me off about the game was that I ran ninety-seven yards from scrimmage on a play that was called back because of a penalty. It was one hell of a long distance to run for nothing!

The next game, against Oklahoma State, was our first big one since the USC game. It was the best OSU team in several years and they were ranked twelfth in the nation. We were a 3½-point favorite, but playing them at home in Stillwater. They had some top players, especially Barry Sanders, NCAA leader in rushing and scoring, and were up for the game. I knew Mike Gundy, OSU's quarterback, who was having a great year, and it was an extra incentive to outshine him. Mike had all the incentive he needed because it was the first time an OSU game was on national television.

At first it looked as if the game was going to be a piece of cake. We scored touchdowns on our first two possessions, and after the first quarter led them 21–7. But suddenly things turned around, and Gundy and Sanders went on a roll. Before OU knew what had happened there were eight minutes remaining in the game and OSU was winning 28–24. It was the first time since 1984 that OSU was leading OU in a football game. The fifty thousand OSU fans in the stadium were screaming, "Defense! Defense!" when I led OU back out on the field. I tuned them out. It was time to show them some Charles Thompson magic.

We had eighty yards to go for a touchdown. A field goal wouldn't be enough. Slowly and calmly we drove down the field. Thirteen plays later we were on their eighteen-yard line, when I kept the ball on an option play and headed left before cutting back and sidestepping two OSU defenders. There was one defender left and I just ran past him into the end zone for the touchdown. I went crazy and improvised a victory dance, taunting the OSU fans. It was a great victory for OU. We'd been tested and had proven ourselves. The final score was 31–28. Barry Sanders had run for 215 yards and Mike Gundy passed for 228 more, but it wasn't enough to beat a determined OU football team. I think that we were prouder of ourselves after that comeback victory than at any other time.

Jamelle and I kept drifting apart during the season. We talked to one another, but it wasn't the same relationship we had once enjoyed. We were still hurting after a tough game against Missouri when he came to see me after practice the following Thursday. I'd had a good game against Missouri, winning 16–7, but like most of the other players I was disappointed that we had allowed them to play us so tough. We should have beaten them by three touchdowns, but after scoring sixteen points in the first half they shut us down in the last two quarters. If we were going to beat Nebraska in our last game, we would have to play a lot better. Jamelle didn't say what he wanted, just that he would meet me back at my room at Bud Hall.

When he came over he had three people with him, John Douglas and Snowman's friends from Lawton, Moses and Flip. I knew immediately that something was up because nobody seemed to have anything to say, although Moses and Flip hadn't driven from Lawton to wish me good luck in the Nebraska game.

"What's going on, Jamelle?" I asked. He didn't answer me, but turned to Moses and Flip.

"Charles," Flip began, "some friends of mind are thinking

238

about making a big bet on the Nebraska game. They're looking to bet Nebraska. What do you think?"

I didn't know what he was getting at. "I don't know," I answered, "it's gonna be tough, but I think we can beat them. What's the problem?" There was silence in the room.

Finally, Moses picked up the conversation. "Well, we were talking to Jamelle about how our friends want to make sure Oklahoma loses. They're willing to pay a lot of money for it. We've got thirty thousand dollars for you and Jamelle to make sure you guys lose."

What I should have done at that moment was throw them all out of the room, but I could not believe I was hearing what I was hearing. I knew that there was a lot of betting on the games, even by players and coaches, but nobody had talked about shaving points or dumping games. I looked at Jamelle and asked: "What do you think?" Jamelle shrugged his shoulders and said: "It's all up to you, CT." I sat there without saying a word.

"Well, what do you say?" Flip asked.

This was crazy. They had to be kidding me. I asked them to repeat the offer and they did: "Thirty thousand for Jamelle and you to lose the game against Nebraska." Suddenly I felt sick. I may have done a lot of things I shouldn't have while at OU, but I always felt that I owed it to the school to go out and win football games. There was no way, not for thirty thousand, not for one million dollars, that I was going to dump a football game. Forget about right or wrong—I hated losing. I asked them to leave and said I would speak to Jamelle later. It was a stupid thing to do because I think they left the room believing I was considering the offer. But I wanted them out of my sight. I called Jamelle later to tell them my answer was no. He said he'd told them I would probably turn them down, and that he thought it was the wise thing to do.

Jamelle Holieway
The Bribe Offer. "I know what you're talking about. I shoulda took it."

I was shaken by the whole incident. I questioned myself. How had I become involved with people who would dare ask me to throw a football game? Now I understood why Snowman wanted me to stay in touch with him. It had nothing to do with drugs. They wanted a hook on me, and when they thought the moment was right they were going to try and reel me in. It was a fucked-up situation. All OU needed was to dump a football game. It was bad enough that the gamblers in Norman and Oklahoma City were pissing and moaning that we hadn't covered the point spread in any but one or two of our games. If Moses and Flip's offer to dump the Nebraska game ever got out I could imagine the talk. It would seem that the team was point shaving all season: "Sure, they won nine out of ten games, but they kept the score down." Maybe I should have reported the bribe offer, but at the time it seemed wiser to forget about the whole thing.

Kori Kaubin—Charles Thompson's Girlfriend
Charles told me about the bribe offer. At first I was shocked, because it was so much money. But when I thought about it, it wasn't much different from some of the things I had been seeing since we'd started going out. I'd seen Charles pick up the phone and call someone whenever he needed five or six hundred dollars. He always got it. Still, the idea of losing a football game for money shocked me.

We sat there and talked about how weird it was that a person would give Charles thirty thousand dollars to lose a game. Charles said that it was only money, and that he was

240

too devoted to football and OU to take the offer. He said that he would let too many people down and that he couldn't do it to himself.

As it turned out, Moses and Flip should have gone ahead and bet Nebraska. We played the game at home, but the rain-slicked home field turned out to be a disadvantage to OU. Our defense was great, but so was theirs and they held us to a field goal as Nebraska beat us 7–3. It was our lowest point total against Nebraska in forty-six years. We did nothing on offense and rushed for less than a hundred yards all game, pretty bad when our season average had been 367 yards per game. The victory sent Nebraska to the Orange Bowl and OU to the Citrus Bowl. Worst of all, it sent me to the hospital. On our last offensive play of the game I was scrambling when I slipped on the wet field. I got hit as I fell and heard a strange sound in my leg and screamed out in agony. I didn't have to look to know that my leg was broken. My season was over. It was the last time I would play for the University of Oklahoma.

Jim Donnan

I heard about the bribe offer, what was it, the Nebraska game. I don't think there is anything to it. We lost the game not because someone took a bribe, we just played poorly that day. There were also rumors of a bribe in the Citrus Bowl, but I don't believe it. We just didn't play well. The school had just been put on probation, and the players were not very emotional for the game. It had nothing to do with a bribe.

Coach Ahlschlager

I don't think Charles would influence the outcome of a football game. He was so competitive. I've heard some stories about Holieway. That's been a rumor down here about the Citrus Bowl. Charles was so competitive. But people get in a financial bind, you don't know what they would or wouldn't do.

The 7–3 loss to Nebraska is significant to me because it was the beginning of the end for the University of Oklahoma's football team and Barry Switzer. Nothing good seemed to happen after that loss. It knocked us out of the Orange Bowl where we wanted to return to avenge the previous year's loss to Miami. If that was the worst thing to happen, I think everyone in Oklahoma today would be happy. But there was more to come. About one month after the Nebraska game the NCAA delivered its bad news to OU. They were putting the football program on suspension for three years.

We all knew back in August that they were investigating the program, but nobody thought they would be able to nail us on anything. We were wrong. The list of violations included:

A booster had provided a recruit with an automobile at no cost.

An assistant coach had promised a recruit that he would be "taken care of" if he enrolled at OU.

An assistant coach gave a prospective recruit a thousand dollars to induce him to come to OU.

Players on the football team were given cash for their complimentary tickets to games.

Shirley Vaughn, Switzer's assistant, had provided free airline tickets to recruits and players.

Switzer had supplemented the salaries of his coaches and paid for rental cars for students out of his personal checking account.

Transportation, entertainment, and inducements were provided to prospective players.

THE LIFE AND CRIMES OF OKLAHOMA FOOTBALL

The NCAA penalties for the violations included no televised games and bowl games for the next three years. The NCAA also warned that should OU commit any of these violations again within the next five years, the school would receive the "death penalty," barring the program from competition for three years.

Every player and coach knew that we were guilty as sin. What we also knew was that the NCAA had no grip on reality. Bosworth wasn't the first and I'm not the last college football player to condemn NCAA rules and regulations because they were formulated for another time. A great many of today's athletes are poor and minority students. They are brought in to major universities only because of their athletic abilities. It's because of these abilities that the athletic programs are earning millions of dollars, little or none of it going to education. It's one thing to pay for room, board, and tuition for these students, but another to expect them to exist financially when they come from homes with little or no income. The NCAA is living in a decade when most college students were white males who could afford a college education and could afford to be amateur athletes. To those who say that many blacks get into college only because they can play sports, I say fine, then pay them. When you look at the size of television contracts colleges are getting to broadcast their football and basketball games, you realize it's a crime that the athletes get nothing out of it.

It makes me angry to hear that athletes are getting a free college education and that they should show some appreciation. A free education for athletes is a joke. Just take a look at some of the courses we take—Theories of Coaching, Physical Education I, II, and III, etc. Nobody guides this free education.

Nothing changed at OU after the NCAA suspension in December 1988. I continued to receive money from boosters, as did Jamelle Holieway. When recruits came to visit the school after the suspension I was given money to show them a good time. Nothing will change until the NCAA decides to recognize reality. When I was in prison an official of the NCAA came to visit me to learn about allegations of OU abuse after December 1988. I told the representative that I wanted time to think before talking to the NCAA. There was a great deal going on in my life and I wanted to straighten out my legal problems before talking to them. A few months later they were contacted about information that I had for this book. David Berst, head of enforcement for the organization, made it clear that he no longer was interested in abuses at the University of Oklahoma.

There wasn't much enthusiasm before the game against Clemson in the Citrus Bowl. I was out of it with my broken leg, but made the trip to Orlando to be with the team. Both coaches and players seemed more interested in having a good time in Florida than worrying about beating Clemson. I had made plans with one of the boosters to fly Kori down there the week after I arrived. It was party time. One of the players was from Orlando and he scored cocaine for the team. I hadn't done any drugs since the summer, but like the rest of the team said what the hell. It was a mistake to carry on in Orlando as we had in Miami the previous year. Orlando is a family town and we brought a lot of attention to ourselves. When a few players wrecked a hotel room, it was front page news. Orlando is a city known for Disneyworld, not cocaine.

Scott Hill, one of our coaches, spent most of the time getting drunk and violent. He was in a fight at a nightclub and the school had to pay damages. Hill was later fired and was arrested by the FBI for drug use and other crimes. The leader of the wild band in Orlando was Barry Switzer. He outdid himself at the Citrus Bowl.

One night after curfew I went down to the bar and there were a booster pal and Switzer, who was drunk as hell and didn't notice me as he had two girls sitting on his lap. How could any of the players take the game seriously when their head coach was outpartying them? It was the drunkest I had ever seen him; I thought of him asking me in August if *I* had a substance-abuse problem.

Watching Clemson kick our ass that day, I was disgusted with the team. We lost even though we had people on the field talented enough to walk all over Clemson on our worst days. We were supposed to be a football machine, but you wouldn't know it by the way we played in Orlando. Jamelle had a horrible game and it was sad to see him end his career on such a sorry note. Oklahoma fans were so shocked by the loss that soon afterward all sorts of wild rumors began to fly. There was talk that we'd dumped the game, but, regardless of what happened before the Nebraska game, there was no evidence to prove it. It was simply one of those times Oklahoma fans had to face up to the fact that Barry Switzer was not God.

CAMPUS GONE AMOK

If you had toured the players' rooms in Bud Hall, you might have thought yourself in an armory. Many of the guys on the team had guns. There were handguns, hunting rifles, and shotguns all over the place. The scene was an accident waiting to happen. Given the drinking, drugs, women running in and out, and the presence of physical men with volatile tempers, it was only a matter of time before something exploded.

Jerry Parks

It was wild. There were times when players would trash the bathrooms and overflow the toilets, and get us all in trouble. They would pop firecrackers and set them under your door, not knowing if something was going to catch on fire. One time they shot a bottle rocket under my door when I was sleeping. I heard the noise and woke up, trying to figure out what was going on. I went out and they were all white guys.

Defensive end Proctor Lane and I didn't get along because I thought he was a racist. He was the one doing all the pranks on me. He thought they were funny. Once Nigel Clay and Lane had a fight. There were seven white guys up in the dorm getting drunk. They had about two cases of beer. One of them got the brilliant idea to get into cars and throw eggs at the dorm. They began throwing eggs and hit everyone walking into the dorm. Nigel saw them when they were ready to throw one at him and warned them not to. They figured he was alone and couldn't do anything and threw the eggs at him anyway. Nigel responded and it almost started a racial battle on the team.

There were at least eight ballplayers selling cocaine or crack or weed. I knew many—thirty, forty guys on the team —who used it. Some of the coaches knew, but they were just covering their asses.

Zarak Peters was a big, strong lineman who came to OU a year before Jerry Parks. Jerry was rooming with me, and Zarak had the apartment above us on the third floor. Jerry and Zarak had gone to the same high school in Houston and got along well. They were different types—Jerry highstrung and volatile, Zarak laid back and easygoing. To earn spending money Zarak was the team barber, charging the players two or three dollars for haircuts. He was a good barber, but also unreliable and not too good at keeping appointments.

After I broke my leg, Coach Donnan gave me a Nintendo game to keep me busy. Zarak came down to my room every night to play the game, and for about a week I'd been asking him to cut my hair. Every night he made an appointment for the next day, but when I went to his room he said, "Oh, man, CT, I can't do it today. I forgot about something I have to take care of." I was getting pissed off at him because I paid him more than the other players. I knew he didn't have much money and wanted to help him out.

Finally, Zarak promised, "CT, you come up here at seven and you'll be the first haircut I give." But at seven he was busy with another player.

"What's going on, Zarak?" I asked. "You told me you'd cut my hair first."

Zarak shrugged and said: "Yeah, I know, but I can put your name on a list. You're number six."

"Six," I screamed, "you ain't shit, man. You tell me to come up here at seven and now you tell me this shit. For the whole fucking week you been promising me to cut my hair. I come in here and you got five people in front of me. That's fucked up. You know, Zarak, you come down to my place anytime you want to play my Nintendo game. If I'm ready to leave my room, I let you stay to listen to my music, whatever."

I went downstairs on my crutches and Jerry was there with Rod Fisher, another teammate. Kori was in the bedroom studying. Jerry and Rod had been drinking. I was furious and Jerry asked me what the problem was. "Jerry," I said, "why don't you go upstairs and jump all over your homeboy's ass and straighten him out. I can't believe how that fat bastard played me for a fool."

Jerry said that he'd go and get the whole thing squared away. While we were waiting for him to get back we called to order a pizza. While we were waiting for the delivery, the telephone rang and it was Billy Dykes from the team. "Charles," he said frantically, "you better get up here. Jerry's going crazy." In the background I could hear screaming and cursing. I told Rod what was happening and he said that we'd better get up there. I got my crutches and had limped out the door when Jerry came flying down the stairs. Jerry and I used to call one another "Po," short for Protege, and when he ran into me he screamed: "Po, where's the motherfucking gun? Where's my gun at?"

Weeks before I'd learned that Jerry had taken Zarak's gun. He had gotten into a confrontation with some guy and was going to get the gun to shoot him. I took the gun away from Jerry and hid it in my car. That's where it was when he asked me for it. I tried to stop him, but Jerry was wild, his eyes bulging. "Fuck you, Po, where are the keys to the car? I'm gonna bust a cap in that fucker," he said, and rushed past me into the apartment to look for the keys. I hobbled in after him to get the keys first and hide them. Jerry had gone into the bedroom where Kori was, thinking she knew where the keys were. When he came out he saw that I had them and grabbed me. We started to wrestle for the car keys and with only one good leg I was struggling to keep my balance. Finally, he slammed me against a shelf and held me until I dropped the keys. Rod Fisher, who had a broken arm, was also powerless to stop Jerry. Billy Dykes had come downstairs and was standing by the door when Jerry rushed by, and though Billy's a big guy, he took one look at Jerry's eyes, and did nothing to stop him.

I turned to Rod: "Rod, look, you gotta do something. Go down there and try to stop him before he gets to the car. He's gonna do something stupid." Rod agreed and went to the car, but he wasn't quick enough and Jerry was soon on his way back, gun in hand. When he saw Rod he just flung him to the ground. Meanwhile, I went to the balcony and screamed up to Zarak on the third floor, "Jerry's coming up with a gun. Bolt your door, or go to another room because Jerry ain't the same!"

I had seen Jerry angry and wild, but never so out of control that I feared for my own life. Zarak was acting as if the whole thing were no big deal. "Hey, CT, I know Jerry," he said. "He ain't gonna shoot nobody. He's just putting on a big front. I ain't worried."

By this time Jerry was running up the stairs, yelling, "Where's that motherfucker now? He won't push me again." The twenty-two was cocked. I hopped upstairs, and when I got to Zarak's door Jerry was already inside screaming at Zarak: "C'mon, push me now, Zarak, you motherfucker." He inched closer to Zarak and was a gun barrel away from him. Zarak knocked the gun out of Jerry's hand, but he got crazier and dove for it on the floor. Another person in the room, Steve, a line-backer from California, tried to put his foot on the gun. Jerry got up from the floor, drove Steve into a wall, picked up the gun again, and started waving it, talking crazy like a wild man: "Push me now, push me now."

The door to the room was open and I screamed at Rod to shut it before somebody walking by got shot. The way Jerry was waving the cocked pistol anyone in sight was a target. Then things happened fast. Rod shut the door and at the same time I heard a shot and a scream, "Ah, motherfucker. . . ." Holy shit, I thought, Jerry shot him. People who were in the other room came in to see what had happened, and there was Jerry sitting on the floor muttering: "I told that motherfucker not to push me any goddamned more. I told . . ." Rod got really scared and ran downstairs the back way.

I didn't know what Jerry was going to do next. I thought I'd better get out of there, too, and started to hop off. Jerry got up and I tried to sneak to the other side of the room to hide. I was scared shitless. There were more bullets in the gun. He walked past me and saw me standing against the wall. He looked at me and I said, "Jerry, put that gun away before you do something stupid"; it wasn't registering that he'd already done something stupid. "Jerry, I'm your friend. Please put the gun away," I said, but he grabbed me and pushed me away, and headed out the door to our apartment downstairs.

I panicked. Kori was still in the room and Jerry and she did not get along. I got to the room and Kori was waiting for me: "Jerry came in," she said, "and tried to trap me. He's gone crazy." I got someone to take her out of the room and then tried to find Jerry. I didn't have to look long because he was soon back in the room kicking and throwing shit all over the place. I had just gotten my clothes out of the cleaners and he had kicked cokes and pizza all over them. The place was a mess and I was pissed off. "You dumb motherfucker," I screamed at him, "you need to cut this shit out. Go put that fucking gun somewhere before you make things worse than they are. You dumb piece of shit!" Jerry's back was turned so he wheeled around and pointed the gun at my head, snarling, "Get out of my way, motherfucker." I turned around and walked away, thinking that if he was going to shoot me, it might as well be in the back of the head.

When I got out to the street someone said: "I hope Zarak's okay." "What are you talking about?" I asked. "Man, don't you know? He shot him. Jerry shot him." It still hadn't dawned on me that Zarak had been shot. It was so weird; I was there, but I hadn't believed what my eyes had seen.

I went upstairs again. Zarak was lying in bed with blood pouring out of him, moaning: "Man, why did that nigger go crazy? Why did he do it? Why, why, why, did he go crazy? That boy ain't got no sense."

When I went back out, the police and an ambulance had arrived. When they got to Zarak's room, he wouldn't tell them who'd shot him. They went around the dorm checking the rooms. Jerry had gone to the room of a defensive back on the team. Reggie Finch, Lonnie's brother, was in the room with them when the police got there. The cops had their guns out and when the defensive back saw them he lost control and pissed all over himself. Jerry surrendered without a fight.

Zarak was rushed to the hospital and survived, the bullet lodged in a rib. Despite the amount of blood he had lost the doctors listed him in stable condition and decided not to remove the bullet. Jerry was taken to the Cleveland County Detention Center, where he pleaded no contest to the shooting charges and served eighty-two days in jail with two years probation. The media didn't know what to make of the shooting and decided that Jerry shot Zarak because the two had had an argument over a borrowed cassette. No, it was dumber than that; it was because of a haircut. Looking back, I'm very sorry that I allowed myself to get so angry at Zarak because he delayed cutting my hair, and making a big deal about it to Jerry, but I never expected Jerry to take a gun and shoot Zarak.

Jerry Parks

After the shooting we were told to get the guns out of the rooms because they were coming around to check. I know for a fact that at least seven players had rifles and pistols. There were guns everywhere. The coaches had to have known about them. One time we came through with three rifles in the middle of the day. Right in front of the dorms. We parked in the parking lot and came between the coaches' offices and the dorm and we didn't have covers for the rifles. One coach said something to the effect of "y'all need to have cases for those rifles."

I heard that Donnie Duncan told Coach Switzer not to talk to me. I think they got all this from the president, David Swank. Not to talk to me, not to say anything to me. They wouldn't do anything for me. Coach Jones called my mother when it happened, and she gave him my lawyer's name. He told me that this was a political thing and that I might have to go to jail.

Zarak wasn't even going to press charges. My lawyer kept telling me to plead no contest and I would get a short sentence. I was going to bring out that Zarak was acting weird. He never acted like that toward me before. After the shooting he told Billy Dykes he'd flushed some stuff down the toilet before the cops came in. I was going to tell everything, but my lawyer told me, "No, no, no, he ain't pressing charges, just keep quiet, say nothing. Don't give the university a bad image." And I said, "Fuck the university." Shit, they were talking about sending me to jail for ten years. This university

253

is going to be here until the day I die. It was the same thing with Charles. The federal attorney wanted him to go to jail.

What angered me after the shooting was the position of the school, especially that of acting president David Swank, who refused to acknowledge any responsibility for what had happened: "At the University of Oklahoma we go to great lengths to protect our students. Possession of a firearm on the OU campus is in violation of the student code. In enforcing the student code, the University of Oklahoma is more stringent on student athletes than any other students, with frequent room visitations by members of the coaching staff."

That was Swank's statement on behalf of the school, and it was a joke. If the school administration was leaving the policing of Bud Hall up to the coaches, they might just as well have left it up to the athletes. The coaches rarely came to the dorm, and they were as aware of the violations as I was. Bud Hall was a twenty-four hour revolving door of girls, students, and strangers. Nobody checked on us; in fact, none of the players thought it necessary to hide their guns. They hid their alcohol and drugs only because they didn't want them stolen.

One week after the Parks–Peters shooting, a more horrible incident took place in Bud Hall. There are different accounts of what happened, but the police report stated that a twenty-year-old woman claimed she was raped by five men. Like the shooting, the rape was one more disaster waiting to happen. Less than three weeks after David Swank's statement, weapons were found in the room of Nigel Clay, one of the accused and later convicted rapists. Dr. Swank refused to discuss both the shooting or rape incidents for this book.

There is no excuse for anyone to force a woman, or for that matter anyone else, against their will. What happened can only be understood within the context of life at Bud Hall. The day after the incident, most of the guys in the dorm knew something had happened. Coming from study hall, I bumped into Nigel Clay, a 290-pound lineman who was not noted for being a ladies' man. Earlier, I had been with some of the guys on the team who were saying that a girl had been gang raped in Nigel's room. It was one of those stories where the facts are wrong, but the core of it is right. I asked Nigel what everyone was talking about.

He began talking ninety miles a second and it was hard to follow him. "Oh, man," he stuttered, "I never did nothing. Fucking Bernard, well, man, he went and took some pussy last night. They might be in trouble, man. I was under the impression . . ."

"Nigel, man, slow down," I said. "What are you saying?"

"Yeah, yeah, man," he said. "I had nothing to do with it, but you know Bernard. She's trying to say we raped her, but you know Bernard."

It was still difficult to figure out what he was saying. My impression was that some girl had gone to Nigel's room and that both he and Bernard Hall had screwed her. At the time, I didn't think that was a big deal. It was not uncommon for women to come to the players' rooms, and after one had had sex with her his roomie might join him. Sometimes a woman would get upset, but it would blow over. I thought back to the time Jamelle and his friends had had a gang bang and the school had taken care of it.

Women in Oklahoma were no different than men when it came to Sooner football. Everything centered around the team, especially on campus. For good or bad, the players had top priority when it came to women. If a regular student and an athlete were going after the same girl, the athlete had a much better chance. To the players it was part of winning: when you win you reap all types of benefits, and women were one of the best. After a win we'd say, "Let's go home and get some VP (Victory Pussy)." For the few occasions OU lost there was another expression: "It ain't that bad, we'll go home and get some SP (Sympathy Pussy)."

The most attractive OU coeds were always in Bud Hall. Even after the rape they still came around. After the rape a curfew was established and women had to be out of the dorm by midnight, but that was more public relations than anything else. Waking up for breakfast, I'd see women leaving the dorm.

Musicians use the term "groupies"; at OU the expression was "freaks." There were plenty of women going out with several players at the same time. I know of a few who slept with seven different players within a two-week period. There were others who spent a night sleeping with five, six, seven guys. It was a common sight and you accepted it as normal. It was like rock music, with our stage the football field and the quarterback the lead singer. Our freaks were as attractive as any of Mick Jagger's groupies. We didn't have to force anyone to have sex with us, but like the gifts from the boosters, we expected it. None of this excuses what happened in Nigel Clay's room, but it does shed light on the mentality of the football team when it came to women.

It was common at OU for black players to be involved with white women. This wasn't only a matter of preference, but because most of the groupies who hung around the jocks were white (OU is an almost all-white school). The black girls who did hang out at the dorm usually had boyfriends. The coaches liked the players to think of the team as a family, but when it came to interracial dating, they thought differently. It was one thing if the woman was not attractive, but when a pretty white girl was seen in the company of a black player, the coaches let us know their displeasure. The white players felt the same as the coaches. When I started going out with Kori a few white

256

players went to her sorority sisters and told them to pressure her not to see me. Everyone on campus was for Charles Thompson on Saturday afternoon on the field, but not on Saturday night in his own bedroom.

Switzer was as bad as anyone else at OU when it came to race matters. He loved his black players scoring touchdowns and making tackles, but not scoring or making it with white women. Switzer went as far as to tell me, "Charles, stop fucking with my secretaries," when I flirted with them and had them type reports for me. The white secretaries in the athletic offices liked Jamelle and me, and we enjoyed receiving favors from them. One of them once stole Switzer's Rolodex with the names of all his boosters and big money people around the nation, and brought it to Jamelle and me at the apartment. Another secretary wanted to keep Switzer's quarterbacks happy and would visit us on weekends to clean our apartment. She would also cook dinner and after a few drinks hop into bed with us. Switzer knew about her, but was only bothered because she was white.

After the announcement of the gang rape, Switzer cited his daughter as the reason he would not tolerate such behavior by his team. What he didn't say was that his sweet little "Miss Muffin" also liked to hang around with the team. Switzer and his coaches carried on with women as much as their players. Coach Hill went to bed with several girls I introduced him to, and Coach Jones told me, when he met Kori: "What's she doing with somebody like you? I could go for some of that pussy." The issue was never sex with the coaches but race. At least it was at a dinner some of the players were invited to along with Coaches Jones, Gibb, and Hill. Some white ladies asked Hill for an introduction to a few of the black players. Scott looked at me and said, "Thompson, why don't you and your buddies go to one of those places where you can meet black women?"

Three of the players—Bernard Hall, Nigel Clay, and Glen Bell—were charged with first degree rape. I wasn't there that night, but I do have some impressions about those involved. Two women, one seventeen and the other twenty had come to the campus to see Nigel and go dancing. There were several players in the room when they arrived, and the seventeen-year-old left quickly to go to another player's room where, she later acknowledged, she had sex. The older woman left Nigel's room to buy liquor and returned. After a few drinks somebody grabbed her from behind, threw her to the floor, and her clothes were removed. The lights in the room were out and she couldn't see the men who raped her. At the trial, Jimmy Fennell, a former OU player who was in the room that night, testified that Clay, Hall, and Bell had raped her. After eleven hours of deliberation the jury convicted Clay and Hall. Bell, who did not testify in his own behalf, was acquitted.

Details came out at the trial that cast doubt on the testimony of the victim, but I believe that the essence of her story was true. The problem in this incident was that the players refused to stop when the victim asked them to. When Bernard Hall decided it was his turn, regardless of what had gone on before, she decided to put a stop to it. Bernard insisted, she refused, and that was what turned an ordinary orgy into a night of rape.

I never talked to Bernard Hall about what happened, but I don't doubt his involvement that night. To me it fit right in with his character. Bernard loved to boast that he was a ladies' man, that girls chased him all the time. Few of us believed him. Bernard was a very aggressive person, who liked to throw his strength around; if you wouldn't do what he wanted you to do he would try and make you do it. He was not a favorite among his teammates.

Once, and there were other incidents, Bernard had stolen
some money from another player. This player, who had left the
money in the ashtray of his car, had driven Bernard home and
after dropping him off had realized that the money was gone. It
was one more theft in which Bernard was the only suspect, and
Switzer was told about it. Switzer planned to call a meeting of
the players to decide if Bernard should remain on the team. We
thought it unfair for Switzer to place the burden on us, that it
was the coach's decision to make. But because Bernard was a
great athlete Switzer didn't have the balls to do whatever was
right.

Bernard remained outside the meeting room while Switzer
told us about the numerous reports of theft he had received. We
listened while he tried to explain that Bernard had psychological problems, an illness called kleptomania, and that he was at
the mercy of his disease. But, Switzer wanted us to know, he
had discussed this with Bernard and told him that the only way
he could help himself was to throw himself on the mercy of the
team. "Bernard is going to come in this room," Switzer said,
"and he is going to own up to what he has been doing, and I
want you guys to make the decision as to whether or not we
keep him on the team."

When Switzer left the room we all looked at one another.
Fuck, what could we do but forgive poor Bernard Hall, suffering
from a disease none of us could pronounce. Switzer returned to
the room with Bernard and asked him: "Are you sorry about
what you have stolen from your teammates?" Bernard looked at
Switzer as if he were from another planet, and said, "I never
stole anything, Coach." Switzer looked like he'd died, and we
eventually voted Bernard off the team. Of course, when we
needed a tight end, Bernard was quickly reinstated.

I didn't doubt Bernard Hall's role in the rape, since there was
little in his character to make me question the victim or Jimmy

Fennell. Nigel Clay who was from Fontana, California, had something in common with Bernard, who was from Detroit. Both of them looked down on Oklahomans. Both were slick talkers who thought Oklahomans had no common sense. Nigel's attitude toward everyone from the state leads me to believe he thought he could get away with anything. Glen Bell was the only one I believed, though I couldn't understand why a guy like him who had no trouble meeting girls would be involved in a rape. Glen was in Nigel's room when everything was happening, but it was not unusual for a woman to come to a player's room and wind up having sex with a group. There are aspects of Glen's personality I never liked, but I believe that when a woman decided that things were out of control he would not do anything against her will. In the aftermath of the rape the school's main concern was Barry Switzer's job; neither David Swank or Donnie Duncan showed any interest in the welfare of the victim. The issues were not the shooting and the rape, but can we save Barry Switzer?

Charles Thompson did not help matters. At the time the rape and arrests were announced, I was preparing to meet with Tiger Harris, John Green, and "Tony" to sell seventeen grams of cocaine. Within thirteen days the University of Oklahoma football team went on a felony rampage—shooting, rape, and cocaine dealing. It was a sad time in Norman, a time to come to grips with reality, but nobody knew how to deal with it and it became instead a public relations issue. Governor Henry Bellmon of Oklahoma saw no responsibility for what had happened in the school's permissiveness toward its football players; rather, he was "thoroughly disgusted" with the athletes, and underlined his confidence in the university and support of Barry Switzer "as long as he is on staff."

Switzer did not believe that he was responsible for the behavior of his players, although the student newspaper thought dif-

260

ferently—one of the few Oklahoma voices with another perspective—and called for his resignation. He let them know that he was not worried about losing his job: "Our regents and our president have told me they think Donnie Duncan and I are the people they want to get this thing under control. I think I am the most qualified person to get it done."

Switzer was at his best with the media when it came to the rape charges against Hall, Bell, and Clay. None of them had been tried, but Switzer was going to show how tough he could be: "I've made my decision. They won't play here again. And if they're found guilty in the courts, I want them behind bars. I want them caged." Of course, Switzer made no mention of the coverup of the incident involving more than a dozen of his players a few years earlier. Being tough is something Barry Switzer does as a matter of convenience. He didn't want Bernard Hall "caged" after he was caught stealing from other players. When the team was out of tight ends, Switzer quickly reinstated Hall; not, as he explained it to the media, because the players came to him and asked to have Bernard put back on the team, but because the coach knew we were in deep shit at that position.

Switzer continued to play to the press when it came to my arrest for drugs: "It destroyed me, it really destroyed me. I had a good relationship with Charles. I had talked to Charles about him being drug-free, him doing the right thing because he was a quarterback in the public eye. Now, I worry about Charles going the other way, going into that culture, those associations." Then Switzer wanted to explain why he warned me the FBI was investigating me:

"I've been accused of ruining an investigation by doing this. If I let it go on, after what's happened to me, how would that have looked? When it all came out, and people found out I had

261

known, how would that have looked? If we know that information, we have to protect ourselves."

I'm not blaming Barry Switzer for my drug use and dealing, but he deceived the public by portraying himself as the concerned, protective coach. He knew I had been involved with drugs six months earlier, but did little more than make me attend the rehabilitation clinic for less than two weeks. Yes, he talked to me about cleaning up my act in time for the football season, and it wasn't Barry Switzer who went to Dallas to score cocaine, but I. Still, what did my coach, teacher, and role model do about those "associations" he was so concerned about? Switzer was honest when he told the press: "We have to protect ourselves." That was his only reaction to the shooting, rape, and drug deal—protecting the program and himself.

Jamelle Holieway

Because I came from California they thought I was transporting drugs. That's what everyone said: Jamelle did it, Jamelle put Charles up to it. A good friend of mine, who was close to someone with the FBI in Oklahoma, told me "They're not watching you, but they're watching your house. Whatever Charles is doing back and forth, he needs to stop." I called Charles to let him know and he said okay and he stopped. It's strange because John and Tiger came out of nowhere and asked him to do this, but Charles is the only one who went to jail. Everyone else in that car is supposed to be in jail, too.

An incident that took place at OU in 1987 demonstrates what the overall problem was at the school. Joe Brett Reynolds, a wrestler at OU, had been caught having another student sit in for him to take one of his final exams. He was tossed out of

·

school, and according to law could not reapply for admission for two years. But Joe got a lawyer to appeal the suspension before the Board of Regents. The Board voted to reduce the suspension to eleven months. Faculty and students couldn't believe the decision; the faculty met and passed a resolution demanding that Reynolds suffer the original penalty and the student congress initiated a petition that censured the Board of Regents. There was an uproar over the matter, but in the end Joe Reynolds returned to school eleven months after his suspension. Rules may be rules, but to the OU Board of Regents Joe Brett Reynolds' 16–1–1 wrestling record came first. That is the overall problem at the University of Oklahoma.

I can't speak for Jerry Parks, Bernard Hall, Nigel Clay, and Joe Brett Reynolds; I speak only for myself and am responsible for my actions, but when people ask me why I would do what I did when I had everything in the world going for me, I can only try to explain by saying that student/athletes are unlike all other college students. Even before high school we are treated differently. We are special because we can run faster, throw faster, and hit a baseball farther than our classmates. We are pampered, and our behavior, never tolerated with other students, is excused.

In 1987 the NCAA surveyed college athletes about their experiences. This is from a *Wall Street Journal* article by Frederick C. Klein:

"They say that I am a student-athlete, but really I'm an athlete-student. They lied to me on a recruiting trip. Football is the No. 1 thing here."

"The pressure put on us to win at all times has resulted in physical violence, such as slapping and punching by coaches. Some days the coaches make you feel as though you are part of a large herd of animals. In other words, they treat you like a piece of meat."

263

"More often than not, college athletes go through college never experiencing collegiate life to the fullest."

"Somehow, and I don't know how, the game needs to be played for fun again, and not for the big bowl revenues or lucrative TV contracts."

I never want anyone to feel sorry for me, but I identify with what other student/athletes are saying. I never felt like other students because I was at the University of Oklahoma for the sole purpose of playing football, not for the reasons other students go to college. Nobody, including myself, was concerned about what I should study to prepare myself for the future. My future was immediate: play and win football games for OU. I could look forward to only two things after my eligibility—a career in the NFL or working for an OU booster. I lived in a world separate from the rest of the student body and had very little in common with them. If I gave my best on Owen Field, I was allowed to do my worst off it. I took advantage of the license given me, and when the FBI put the handcuffs on me in Robert Pendarvis's office, I realized for the first time I'd have to take responsibility for myself.

Jim Donnan

Well, the shocker was to see a young man we cared about get caught up with the wrong people. He can't blame anyone but himself. It was hard because we'd done a lot for Charles, as he did for the program. We gave him a lot of counseling, I think he can tell you that, spent a lot of time with him just being his friend and confidante.

I don't know if the boosters were or weren't taking care of Charles. That's something you have no control over. But I know we felt pretty good about him that summer we called him in and sent him to a rehab center. We tested him all fall, something like nineteen times, and he was clean.

He was a good player but that was the policy and we would have done it for anyone who wanted help. He was a very gifted athlete, just had everything ahead of him, but things were too easy, I guess. It's obvious what happened. We kept counseling and talking to him and it just seemed that no matter what, something would pop up.

AFTER THE FALL

Outside Robert Pendarvis's office the pack of media wolves was growing. The word had spread that the FBI had arrived to arrest me. Looking out the window I could see them jostling for position to get their pictures of Charles Thompson in handcuffs in time for the eleven o'clock news. One of the agents asked Pendarvis to get a towel so I could cover my face. After he returned with the towel, Pendarvis put on the front door lights to distract the media as we quickly ran out the back door. Before they realized that they had been fooled, I was in the backseat of the car headed toward FBI headquarters in Norman.

FBI agents Shockley and Hershley kept up a steady stream of conversation throughout the ride. At one point Shockley said, "Charles, we didn't mean it to end up this way"; meaning that if Switzer hadn't been warned about their interest in me, the investigation would have continued. They were unhappy with Switzer, and this was the first time I heard that he might be charged with obstruction of justice. Nothing came of that, but at the time the agents were pissed off. Shockley explained the arrest as though he were doing me a favor. He was concerned that once I knew about the FBI's interest in me, I would panic and try to run and get myself into even more hot water. I listened to him thinking, Yeah, right, what a big favor.

Actually, I think there was confusion and uncertainty at FBI headquarters about what to do with me. Normally, I later learned, the procedure after a suspect is indicted and arrested is to take him immediately to FBI headquarters in Oklahoma City. However, they'd learned that Switzer had tipped me off before there was an indictment charging me with a crime, so at the same time they were arresting me, an indictment was being written up. Until it was completed, the FBI was going to keep me in their Norman offices. I was so dazed by the arrest that I didn't think to ask to make a telephone call to get some help. I wanted someone other that Pendarvis to represent me, someone I could feel close to.

As I sat waiting for what would happen next, Hershley and Shockley said to me every few minutes, "We got some pretty good stuff on you, Charles. Maybe your friends Tiger Harris and John Green can help you out. If you can get them to cooperate, we may be able to do something for you." I was in such a fog that I didn't understand what they were talking about. There was a woman answering calls in the office, and I heard her repeat my name after she had picked up the phone. She looked up at one of the agents and then said to the caller, "No, nobody by that name is here." After we waited around for about forty-five minutes, Shockley said it was time to leave for Oklahoma City. I was told that the FBI in Oklahoma City had alerted him that a horde of newspaper and television reporters and cameramen was waiting for us outside the county jailhouse.

Throughout the ten-mile drive to Oklahoma City I tried to prepare for the scene awaiting me, but when we arrived it was worse than I had imagined. When we got out of the car, they began screaming: "There he is! Here he comes!" The cameramen were all over the place and lights were flashing in my face. We walked up to the courthouse and they followed us all the way to the elevator. One guy, walking backward, had his camera right in my face. He never saw the wall. He was walking fast because I was walking fast, and all of a sudden he slammed right into the wall and dropped his camera. It was the first time I had laughed that day.

I refused to comment to the reporters, and we took the elevator to the booking room, where I went through the regular booking procedure—answered questions to a deputy filling out a form, was fingerprinted, gave up my wallet, emptied my pockets and turned over my jewelry. I was sitting in a large room when Ken Brown and Jim Levine, a partner in Ken's law firm, came in. Although Ken was not my attorney, over the last year I had become good friends with the Brown family, and when he heard the news of my arrest he'd begun calling around to find out where I was being held. The FBI had given him a runaround; in fact, it was Ken on the telephone when the FBI secretary said that nobody by the name of Charles Thompson was there. It was now midnight, three hours after I'd been arrested.

I was so happy to see a friendly face that I threw my arms around Ken and told him everything that had happened since Switzer called me into his office that morning. I expressed my displeasure with Pendarvis, explaining to Ken that although the university had sent me to his office, I did not know whether or not Robert Pendarvis was a good lawyer, and that during the ten hours he had represented me, my situation had gone from bad to worse. Ken said he would take care of the paperwork necessary to represent me for the morning's bail hearing and that he would assist me in finding a new criminal attorney.

Because of my broken leg I was taken to one of the jail's hospital wards, where a television was on, and every five or ten minutes I heard: "Charles Thompson, star quarterback for the Sooners, was arrested today . . ." I didn't want to watch television; all I wanted to do was lie down and go to sleep hoping I'd wake up and it all would be a dream. One old geezer kept saying to me, "There you go, man, look at the TV. You keep popping up on the news bulletins." Between the inmate and the television I couldn't take it—I thought my head would explode as I lay there realizing that this was the fucking truth. This was for real. All night long they kept reporting it, until I was able to

269

doze off; but when I woke, the television was on again and they were still talking about my arrest.

The next day, I was scheduled to appear before Federal Magistrate Cauthron for a bail hearing. Driving to the courthouse, the marshals had warned me that large crowds were trying to get into the courtroom. In fact, officials were forced to move the hearing from the magistrate's regular courtroom to a larger one. This was one time I didn't need a crowd, and one reporter didn't make me feel any better when he described the scene: "Charles Thompson continues to draw large crowds. Today, however, he was not playing to seventy-five thousand Sooner fans at Owen Field, but in a packed courtroom before . . ."

Walking into the courtroom I felt like a common thug. They did not remove the handcuffs until I was in the room. I hated the way I looked. Whenever I put on my uniform to play football I wanted to look good and paid attention to every detail— socks, wristbands, even the way I folded the towel I kept in my waistband had to be just so. When I made a speech or was in front of a crowd, I had on nice clothes. I always looked sharp, wore gold. Now I was in front of these people and my hair wasn't even combed. I looked rough. I felt as if I had spent the night in jail, which I had. I felt as if misery were written all over my face. I felt confused, shamed, embarrassed. There I was in front of my mother, my girlfriend, my girlfriend's mother, the press. I felt miserable and ashamed.

I caught Kori's eyes and smiled at her. I wanted her to think that I was fine and that everything was under control. I wanted to leave an impression of strength and confidence with everyone in the courtroom. But inside my head a movie was playing, and amazing and frightening scenes rushed through my mind. When Blair Watson, Assistant United States Attorney, asked the court that I be held without bail, my mind snapped back to reality. This was no movie or dream, this was my life.

270

Watson argued that I was a poor risk for bail because I might run and was a threat to the community. I thought he was talking about a serial killer like Ted Bundy, not Charles Thompson. I stared at him, thinking, Who the fuck are you talking about? The magistrate was dubious about Watson's claim that I was some wild criminal, and asked the lawyers to return tomorrow with evidence demonstrating I was a poor risk for bail. While I was relieved that she didn't agree with the government, I was unhappy that I would be spending another night in jail.

When the magistrate banged her gavel, indicating that the hearing was over, the handcuffs were put back on and I was escorted back to the jail. As we rushed through the corridor to get out of the courthouse, Paul Sutherland, a *Daily Oklahoman* photographer, spotted us. He was at the right place at the right time and snapped the now famous picture that appeared on the cover of *Sports Illustrated.* We were leaving the building and getting into the car when one of the marshals joked about the pack of reporters and cameramen waiting to talk to or take a picture of me, and I cracked up. The next day a story ran in the newspapers with my smiling face next to it, and the editorial comment was that I was taking the drug charges very lightly.

When I returned to the jail hospital tank the television was still on, and sounded in the large room like an echo in a dungeon: "Today, at five, stay tuned for Charles Thompson's day in court." When someone switched the channel it seemed that nothing else was going on in the world: "Government asks judge for no bail in the Thompson case." I was so tired of it that I wanted to put my fist through the screen. Later, when the early evening news came on, I began to cry. A few days before I had spoken at a Norman elementary school about the dangers of drugs. The television station had the video of my talk and one of the children who was present there. As OU's quarterback I was frequently asked to speak at local schools and I never refused an

271

invitation. I did so because I believed in the dangers of drugs, whether or not I practiced what I preached. I never felt like a hypocrite because I didn't ask the kids to be like Charles Thompson. Telling them to "say no to drugs" was the truth.

The television station milked the situation. They asked the child to comment about me and he said: "I'm mad at Charles Thompson. He lied to me and let me down. My mother said I should never trust Charles." It may have been good television, but it broke my heart. They couldn't get enough of the story, and spoke to the child's mother, teachers, and principal. I meant what I'd said, yet I'd set myself up for what I was watching on television. I was sick with shame.

When they served dinner that evening, I couldn't touch the food and passed it on to another prisoner who couldn't believe his good fortune. I was miserable that night, thinking about all the hurt I had caused others. Everyone was suffering the consequences of my actions. Yet all that evening the jailhouse guards crowded around me to talk about Oklahoma football. It meant nothing to them why I was in there. Football was what mattered most.

The following morning I was taken to a holding pen to wait for my return to court. Several other prisoners were with me, and the topic of conversation was what they thought was going to happen to me. Everyone had an opinion and they argued about it. Some believed that because I was a football star the magistrate had to make a lesson of my case and would deny me bail. Others believed I was so important to the football program at OU that the judge would be forced to set me free without any bail. I never said a word while they discussed my future as if I wasn't even there.

Garvin Isaacs, a prominent Oklahoma City criminal attorney, had agreed to represent me, and met with the Assistant United States Attorney and the judge in chambers before I arrived in court. They had worked out an agreement to release me on a ten thousand dollar bond. When this was formally announced in the courtroom, Steve Bentley volunteered to put up the money. He got up and wrote out a check and handed it to the clerk. Bentley and other boosters had appeared in court that morning to testify on my behalf should a question be raised as to my reliability to appear at a later date. In addition to the boosters, coaches Ryker, Ahlschlager, Donnan, and Proctor were also present. Although Switzer wasn't there, the other friendly faces made me feel better about things. I was so happy to be getting out on bail that I almost forgot I was still facing a prison sentence.

When the hearing was completed I was allowed to wait in another room with several of my supporters, including Coach Ahlschlager. He was blunt with me about what was going on and angry that I had allowed myself to become involved with people like Otha Armstrong. He reminded me about some of the talks we'd had in the past about certain people, and that I was paying the price for not listening to him. Ahlschlager encouraged me to be optimistic about the future, but to prepare myself for some rough days ahead. "Charles, I know that it is hard to believe this now," he said, "but all this will one day come to an end. It's going to be difficult and don't listen to any of your so-called friends who tell you that this is no big deal. It is a big deal, but if you do right, everything will work out in your favor."

After I got dressed to leave the courthouse, I was told by Isaacs that my movements were limited to parts of Oklahoma. Because I was still a minor I would need a guardian in the state to take responsibility for me. Frank Vale, Sr., volunteered his services to the court. Frank also promised that he would help out with my legal and living expenses. I was off the football team, but some of the boosters—Steve Bentley, Marshall Brackin, and Frank Vale—were sticking by me. It made me feel better.

The depression I felt leaving the court stayed with me during the days, weeks, and months that followed. Many of the events are a blur and timeless. I lived the next seven months as a sleepwalker. A few days after my release we were able to review the government's evidence against me—recordings, videotapes, notes—and it was overwhelming. Viewing the video of my drug deal with Al I got sick, it was like watching "Miami Vice." We heard the recordings and read the notes made by Tony and my depression only deepened. Initially, Isaacs thought we might prove entrapment by the government, but the review of the evidence threw that defense out the window. I was guilty, and it would take a blind, deaf, and dumb jury to think otherwise. Isaacs was honest with me. He said he'd be willing to fight the government's case and perhaps would get lucky on cross-examination of witnesses, but the chances of success were very slim. It was time to consider other options.

As we went over the evidence in the attorney's office one afternoon, I realized that the government was interested in other parties than myself. The FBI files indicated that more than the sale of seventeen grams of cocaine was on the government's mind. There were references to "confidential informants" that led us to believe someone other than I was the target of the investigation. Isaacs told me that the government thought I could help them and asked me how I felt about it. I told him that it frightened me. I wasn't concerned about most of the people involved in the case—Otha Armstrong, John Green, Tiger Harris, and "Feets"—but I did worry about Snowman. "The man in Dallas" put the fear of God in me, and I was worried about the safety of Kori and my family. I would have to think about it.

Isaacs and I had long conversations about what the govern-

274

ment was really after. I was puzzled and wanted to know several things. How much did I really know that would make a difference in any government prosecution? What was really going on with John Green and Tiger Harris? I couldn't figure out why they were not arrested; unless they were cooperating with the FBI. John Green had been in trouble with the police since the previous summer, and it was no secret around Bud Hall that he was one of the players who could supply drugs. When Tony's frequent calls did not get me to go to Dallas to score cocaine from Snowman, I believed that John and Tiger were asked by the authorities to approach me to get rid of their cocaine. I wasn't sure what had happened, but the FBI must have fucked up their case against Tiger and John. Their voices on the tape that Tony recorded in his car were as loud and clear as mine, but something had gone wrong and I suspected my help was needed in nailing them.

There was more going on than the sale of seventeen grams of cocaine and John and Tiger. There was always Snowman, and that meant Moses and Flip. The FBI never brought their names up to me, but they were too close to Snowman not to be part of the larger picture. Although their names were not mentioned, they did acknowledge they were aware of the bribe offer made to Jamelle and me before the Nebraska game. If the government was interested in the bribe offer, others would be dragged in; namely, Jamelle and John Douglas, who was in the room when we were offered the bribe. I was confused and depressed about the whole thing. I didn't know what I wanted to do, but the worst thing was to do nothing.

As the weeks went by, strange things went on. Although Otha Armstrong had not contacted me, he called Jamelle constantly to reassure Jamelle that he was his friend, and that he had information that the FBI was looking to arrest him. He told Jamelle that other players on the team were talking to the FBI.

Jamelle wasn't involved in the selling of drugs, but because he had spent so much time with me, the FBI assumed the worst. I told Jamelle that it was impossible to know when Otha was telling the truth, if ever, and that the best thing he could do for himself was to keep away from him.

More strange things were going on. I learned that John Green had moved in with Jamelle. With John living there, Tiger Harris began to spend time there too. John kept reassuring Jamelle that if anyone had set me up it had to have been Otha. It was like rats on a sinking ship, and once more I warned Jamelle about keeping away from the three of them. My feeling was that somebody wanted to hand the FBI Jamelle's head on a platter. Why get one quarterback when you can get two of them?

I came to the conclusion that several people had something to hide, and that I'd better start looking after myself. To do that I had to get to the truth. I wanted to know who was talking to whom. I needed to talk to several people face to face, and I discussed it with Kori and my mother. We agreed that there was little to gain by talking to Tiger, John and Otha, but there were others who may have more to say to me in person. If the government was after more than a seventeen gram cocaine sale, and if I was to get caught up in whatever it may be, I wanted to protect myself.

I decided to fly to Los Angeles and talk to Jamelle about the bribe offer. Later, I planned to visit Lawton and talk to Moses and Flip about the thirty thousand dollar offer to dump the Nebraska game. Maybe I thought, Jamelle knew more about the bribe offer than he had told me. We met in a hotel room and talked for several hours; drinking beer and reminiscing about better times. Jamelle spoke openly about everything he knew about the bribe offer, and, to Jamelle's credit, urged me to be truthful to the FBI when questioned about it. Jamelle felt that we had done nothing wrong by turning down the money to throw the game. When it was time to leave I felt sad. Things between Jamelle and me would never be the same again. Jamelle embraced me when I left.

I went to Lawton to see Moses and Flip. Flip knew that the FBI was interested in the bribe offer, but believed the government had nothing on him and his partner. He acknowledged that the two of them had offered money to Jamelle and me to dump the Nebraska game, but reasoned that because we had refused it, no crime was committed. I did not bring up the word "conspiracy." I was annoyed with their attitude. They acted cocky about the whole thing, and didn't seem to care about the possibility of the FBI talking to Jamelle and me. They didn't seem to care about what was going to happen to me. I didn't want to spend any more time than necessary with them, and once I realized they had nothing more to tell me I left them to return home. As of this writing I have no idea whether or not the government will seek indictments against them.

Time was closing in on me, and after several postponments I showed up for sentencing in August. I had done all I could do, and I could only pray that the judge would spare me a prison term. I was hoping he would find some alternative to incarceration; perhaps, working with youthful offenders. Emotionally, I was beaten and remorseful. I didn't know how time in prison could punish me more. Although Isaacs had warned me not to expect too much, in the back of my mind was the hope that I would get probation. Judge Ralph Thompson (no relative), thought otherwise, and sentenced me to two years. I was given three weeks to get my affairs in order before reporting to the federal prison camp in Big Springs, Texas.

I was disappointed, but relieved that the ordeal was over. Since my arrest I had been living in a world of uncertainty.

Weeks before the sentencing many people began to drift from my life. Some, like Marshall Brackin and his father, remained loyal, but other OU coaches and boosters had disappeared. While there had been hope in February that I would be able to walk away from the drug charges, by late spring most of them knew that I wouldn't be OU's starting quarterback for the 1989 season.

What happened to me was an important learning experience. People like my high-school coaches Ryker and Ahlschlager, former OU coach Jim Donnan, teammates like Jerry Parks, Jamelle Holieway, and others, and my family and Kori taught me that I didn't have to be a quarterback for them to care about me. I would be a liar to say that I was happy to arrive at the prison in Big Springs, but I knew that I could live with my punishment and begin a new life after it.

Coach Carl Ryker

I think Charles and I have hashed most of it out over the phone. My wife is a social worker and she has a lot of training with kids who are messed up. I'd learned from her that when we do things that are wrong, that we know are wrong, we beat ourselves up far more than anyone else could ever do. I really feel that Charles has conscience enough—he was and is a real decent kid—that anything I can say to berate him wouldn't be any more than he has said to himself.

I teach kids for a living and I don't know how many times you get on to them and they turn around and do the same thing again. It's almost as if they can't help it. I don't think it's a matter of having a criminal mind. We get caught up in so much peer pressure, for lack of a better term. I suspect in Charles's case a lot of the problem stemmed from a lack of security. I've seen him open up and be nice, really a sweetheart and not a fake, and he's generally a good kid and would worry about his future.

I can say this: Charles is a good kid, but I don't think he had enough character, or strong enough confidence in himself, to push away from the sort of things that got him into trouble. It was easier for him to do the things people expected him to do. Once my wife and I were in a mall together and saw Charles at the sunglass counter, flirting with some girls. He was with Jamelle and Lonnie Finch. He was happy to see me, and introduced us to Lonnie and Jamelle, but I had the feeling that he was embarrassed, as if he was aware that I knew he was getting caught up with a crowd that didn't quite fit into the scenario he had created for himself.

The federal prison camp in Big Springs is a minimum security institution. Most of the inmates are on their way out of the prison system, and do not want any trouble to postpone their discharges. The prison personnel are another matter; they've treated me specially but it was not the treatment I wanted. For most of them it was time to teach this little nigger a lesson. They were going to let me know that I was not a superstar to them.

I promised myself before I entered prison that I would behave like a gentleman, and give the authorities no reason to single me out for either special treatment or punishment. At times I've found it difficult to keep that promise. I don't understand why people choose to work in prisons, but I do know that many of them have a great deal of resentment in their lives. It has been very important for some to go out of their way to let me know that they're better than I and that they control my life. There have been several incidents, but the cruelest of them had to do with my father, who in early 1990 was diagnosed as suffering from terminal cancer. There was a strong possibility that he would die soon or fall into a coma. Emergency furloughs are not uncommon for inmates in minimum security camps and I made an application to visit him. It was approved by the Bureau of Prison's Regional Office in Dallas, and my caseworker in Big Springs told me to work out travel plans. I called Ken Brown, and he took care of the airline tickets to Lawton. A few hours before my departure, the warden called up my father's doctor. The doctor confirmed the seriousness of my father's condition, but was asked by the warden if he could make a determination about exactly when my father would die. The doctor explained that it was impossible to do so, but that the man was either going to die or lapse into a coma very soon. It wasn't good enough for the warden, and he pushed the doctor, asking "Is Charles Thompson's father going to die within the next twenty-four hours?" My father's doctor reiterated that it was impossible to make such a prediction. The warden pushed and pushed for an exact hour of death, and when the physician said that he could not give one, my emergency furlough to visit my father was cancelled. Later, I was able to see my father, but when he died in June, the prison authorities refused to allow me to attend his funeral.

No purpose would be served to describe all the head games prison employees play with prisoners. I have seen grown men and women whose one shining moment of their day is to boast about how they kept some hotshot nigger quarterback in his place. When they learned that I was writing this book many tried to convince me that it wouldn't be in my best interest. If they could have kept my co-writer out of the prison they would have done so, but he works for a national magazine and they were forced to allow him to visit and talk to me.

Regardless of what has gone on here, I am not asking for anyone's pity. I am obliged to serve a period of my life in Big

Springs, and I choose to do it with a minimum of complaining.
I want to walk out of here with my head high. I deserved to be
humbled after what I'd done, but I wonder why that cannot be
accomplished without humiliation.

THE POINT AFTER

I am sorry that Barry Switzer was forced to resign after the 1988 season. The university had been embarrassed before the nation by its football team, and the easy way out was to demand Switzer's resignation. If the rapes, shooting, and cocaine dealing had been confined to a local level, the state of Oklahoma would have supported Switzer. Once these became national issues, it was a matter of the chickens coming home to roost. Things that had happened in the past—shady business dealings, marital infidelities, the less-than-satisfying Marcus Dupree—returned to haunt Switzer. The same university officials and politicians who had tolerated his behavior for years now used him as a scapegoat.

Jim Donnan
What people don't understand is that Barry was so good to everyone because he cared about those kids. But he didn't have any control over the boosters. I hate to see Switzer blamed; ultimately, all of us take responsibility for anything that happens to the program. He was a player's coach if there's ever been one.

Jerry Parks, Bernard Hall, Nigel Clay, and myself are responsible for what we did, but it did not happen in a vacuum. Even after my arrest, I thought that I'd be taken care of by the University of Oklahoma. They would see to it that nothing happened. I assumed that they would tolerate my worst behavior. I had developed a twisted sense of self-importance because of my athletic ability. I liked doing what I wanted to do.

283

I enjoyed the company of millionaire businessmen who flew me on their private planes and would give me whatever I asked for. I enjoyed the attention I received from attractive women on and off campus. I enjoyed knowing that millions of people knew my name because they had seen me play football on national television. I didn't worry that there would be a day I'd have to pay a price for all of it. Nobody ever asked me to.

I can't blame anyone but myself for selling drugs, but the fact remains that there was a system at the University of Oklahoma that was not in the best interests of its student football players. We were not brought to the school to be taught but to be tolerated and protected. If they wanted us to play, they had to keep us out of trouble. I even had my traffic tickets taken care of by the school.

Teenage athletes must be aware that once they sign that letter of intent to play ball at a university, they are on their own. They must learn to trust themselves when it comes time to make major decisions, not because there are people at the university looking to hurt them, but because those people have a different agenda than theirs. Athletes have to face the fact that when they go to a school like the University of Oklahoma, it is because of what they can contribute to a multi-million-dollar sports industry, nothing more. It will be up to them to take advantage of the education offered. Barry Switzer did not go out looking to recruit rocket scientists. He needed teenagers who could throw, run, block, and sacrifice their bodies.

If student athletes know that, they can avoid some of the pitfalls waiting for them in college. From the vantage point of hindsight, there are many things I would do differently and others I would do the same. I would not refuse the money and gifts made available to me by the university boosters, but I would like every college athlete to accept those gifts in public,

284

and force the NCAA to accept the reality of college sports. It is time to stop making athletes act like criminals because of the booster system. If NCAA and school officials can eat, drink, and live off the billions of dollars generated by college athletes, isn't it time for the players to share in the windfall? But I doubt that the NCAA and universities are going to change anything. There is even less hope in having some of football's most influential coaches lead the battle for reform. For example, I know that Barry Switzer is preparing a book about his life as a coach, but, because he was a winner under the present system, I am certain that he will be an apologist for what is wrong in college sports. If anything, he will condemn players like myself for anything that is bad in college football.

What is sad is the attitude of the NCAA and the University of Oklahoma when contacted to discuss the abuses cited in this book. President Van Horn refused to return telephone calls; former acting President Swank, citing his previous experiences with writers, chose not to comment; and a spokesman for Donnie Duncan and the athletic department summed up their views: "Charles Thompson and what happened in 1989 is old history. There is nothing more to talk about."

The NCAA had a stranger reaction to continued abuse at OU when asked to comment. David Berst replied that I'd had an opportunity to tell the NCAA about rule violations at OU when one of his representatives contacted me in jail, and that I'd refused to discuss them at the time. Unfortunately, according to Berst, it was too late in the game to have that discussion now. When the NCAA official visited me in prison I had good reasons not to talk to him: I was without legal representation, my status as a prisoner was uncertain, and I wanted a little time to consider what my cooperation might mean. I never said that I wouldn't talk to them, only that I needed time. That has come to mean to the NCAA that because Charles Thompson wasn't ready when they were, he can rot in prison. If my refusal to talk to them then is justification for the NCAA to drop its investigation of OU, it only proves their lack of sincerity and determination in ridding the system of abuse. And as long as the NCAA is content to slap offenders on the wrist, schools like OU will always be willing to take the gamble and risk the death penalty to win football and basketball games.

Contrary to what David Berst and Donnie Duncan believe, there is plenty to talk about and do. Why, in the face of the death penalty, does the University of Oklahoma continue to blatantly defy the rules and regulations governing college athletics? Sitting here in a Texas federal prison I know of several OU players on the 1990 team who are receiving illegal payments and gifts from one of the same boosters who took care of me. The coaches and athletic department are aware of such payments, but, as when I was playing, it's easier to ignore it and think of it as the price of getting to the bowls.

I agree with coaches like Barry Switzer, screaming their lungs out that the rules are unrealistic, but they are the rules. Until the NCAA is prepared to greet the twenty-first century, all colleges are obliged to follow the present rules. Sadly, in the state of Oklahoma there appears to be a far greater obligation, and that is to produce the greatest football teams in the nation. There is enormous pressure on everyone involved with OU's football team to meet a production quota of perfect seasons and national championships. The pressure comes from the public, media, alumni, and boosters with the big bucks. This pressure reaches the ridiculous when, after what would have been a decent season at other schools, with Barry Switzer's team losing three games, newspapers wrote editorials demanding that he be fired. People living outside Oklahoma do not understand the football madness in the state, the hysteria of OU fans.

THE LIFE AND CRIMES OF OKLAHOMA FOOTBALL

Coach Ryker

It's the nearest thing you've got to professional sports, Oklahoma football. I love football, I'm not going to deny it and I don't think that we're a bunch of yokels who don't know there are things that have to be changed. But the average Joe doesn't know, and if he did know I don't think he would put up with it. Everybody wants a clean program, but they also want to win. And somewhere in between there, is winning at all costs and somewhere in there is a line.

For the boosters it's a way to be popular. It's a way to be part of something. I think a lot of those people's viewpoint is sick. They do some of the things they do because they want to be part of something that is revered in the state. I'm sure there are hundreds of people who will tell other people they did something for a player they didn't really do just to have people think they are in the inside. I guess you have to live here to know how important football really is.

As a child growing up in Oklahoma, I believed that every year there would be Christmas on December twenty-fifth and on New Year's Day the University of Oklahoma would be playing in a major bowl game. It's the way things were, and I would have been shocked if they weren't. What I didn't understand as a child was what it takes to put OU in those bowls. I had no idea that it was much more than putting a few dozen great athletes on the field to do their thing, that it was instead a total commitment by a greater number of people in the state to do whatever it takes, fair and foul, to make OU a winner.

My concern now is not the NCAA, the University of Oklahoma, or other football factories, but rather the thousands of teenagers who pray every night, as I once did, to play ball for the Barry Switzers of the world. I want them to know what

287

happened to me. I want them to know about the environment they will be entering. I hope that after four years at some university they will have more going for them than a faint hope of going to the NFL, or time in a federal prison because they allowed their lives to get out of control.